SHADOW NEGOTIATORS

Emerging Frontiers in the Global Economy

SERIES TITLES

Jobless Growth in the Dominican Republic:
Disorganization, Precarity, and Livelihoods
Christian Krohn-Hansen, 2022

Precarious Asia: Global Capitalism and Work in
Japan, South Korea, and Indonesia
Arne L. Kalleberg, Kevin Hewison, and Kwang-Yeong Shin, 2022

Unwitting Architect: German Primacy and the Origins of Neoliberalism
Julian Germann, 2021

Revolutionizing World Trade: How Disruptive
Technologies Open Opportunities for All
Kati Suominen, 2019

Globalization under and after Socialism: The Evolution of
Transnational Capital in Central and Eastern Europe
Besnik Pula, 2018

Discreet Power: How the World Economic Forum Shapes Market Agendas
Christina Garsten and Adrienne Sörbom, 2018

Making Money: How Taiwanese Industrialists Embraced the Global Economy
Gary G. Hamilton and Cheng-shu Kao, 2017

Sweet Talk: Paternalism and Collective Action in North-South Trade Relations
J.P. Singh, 2016

Breaking the WTO: How Emerging Powers Disrupted the Neoliberal Project
Kristen Hopewell, 2016

Intra-industry Trade: Cooperation and Conflict in the Global Political Economy
Cameron G. Thies and Timothy M. Peterson, 2015

Shadow Negotiators

HOW UN ORGANIZATIONS SHAPE THE RULES OF WORLD TRADE FOR FOOD SECURITY

Matias E. Margulis

STANFORD UNIVERSITY PRESS
Stanford, California

Stanford University Press
Stanford, California

Printed in the United States of America on acid-free, archival-quality paper
ISBN 9781503633520 (cloth)
ISBN 9781503634503 (electronic)

Library of Congress Control Number: 2022011763

Library of Congress Cataloging-in-Publication Data available upon request.

Cover design: Rob Ehle
Cover art: iStock | rvimages
Typeset by Elliott Beard in Galliard 10/14

Contents

Figures and Tables

Figures

Tables

Abbreviations

AoA	Agreement on Agriculture
CAP	Common Agricultural Policy
CBD	Convention on Biological Diversity
CESCR	Committee on Economic, Social, and Cultural Rights
CFF	Compensatory Financing Facility
CFS	Committee on World Food Security
CGIAR	Consultative Group on International Agricultural Research
CHR	Commission on Human Rights
EU	European Union
FAC	Food Aid Convention
FAO	Food and Agriculture Organization
FIAN	Food First Action Network
GATT	General Agreement on Tariffs and Trade
GEF	Global Environmental Facility
G7	Group of Seven
G33	Group of Thirty-Three
G20	Group of Twenty
HRC	Human Rights Council
IATP	Institute for Agriculture and Trade Policy
ICESCR	International Covenant on Economic, Social, and Cultural Rights

ICTSD	International Centre for Trade and Sustainable Development
IFAD	International Fund for Agricultural Development
IFPRI	International Food Policy Research Institute
IGC	International Grains Council
IMF	International Monetary Fund
IOs	international organizations
IPCC	Intergovernmental Panel on Climate Change
IPPC	International Plant Protection Convention
LDCs	least developed countries
NFIDCs	net food-importing developing countries
NGOs	nongovernmental organizations
OECD	Organisation for Economic Co-operation and Development
OHCHR	Office of the High Commissioner for Human Rights
SDGs	Sustainable Development Goals
SDT	special and differential treatment
SRRTF	United Nations Special Rapporteur on the Right to Food
SSM	Special Safeguard Mechanism
TRIPS	Agreement on Trade-Related Intellectual Property Rights
UDHR	Universal Declaration on Human Rights
UN	United Nations
UNCTAD	United Nations Conference on Trade and Development
UNDP	United Nations Development Programme
UNEP	United Nations Environment Programme
UNFCCC	United Nations Framework Convention on Climate Change
UNGA	United Nations General Assembly
UNHCR	United Nations High Commissioner for Refugees
UNICEF	United Nations Children's Fund
VGRTF	Voluntary Guidelines to Support the Progressive Realization of the Right to Adequate Food in the Context of National Food Security
WFP	World Food Programme
WTO	World Trade Organization

Acknowledgments

I HAVE BEEN FORTUNATE to work professionally at the intersection of international trade and food security for two decades, first as a Canadian representative to the WTO and more recently in my capacity as a scholar. This book project turned out much differently than originally intended. When I started the research for this project, my plan was to do a deep dive into the interstate politics of negotiating food security at the WTO. Yet as I undertook the research I kept being drawn to the actions by international organizations, such as the World Food Programme and the Office of the High Commissioner for Human Rights, and what appeared to be their sincere efforts to protect food security at the WTO agriculture negotiations. I found their actions surprising and puzzling, since their efforts did not accord with the prevailing view among trade negotiators that UN organizations "didn't matter" to trade rulemaking (a view I unquestioningly accepted during my time as a representative to the WTO) or with the consensus in the international relations canon that also essentially claimed that UN organizations played little role in the global governance of trade. This book is my attempt to challenge the conventional wisdom and to help us better understand the role of UN agencies in shaping global trade rulemaking.

I am deeply grateful to the many people who have offered their time, wisdom, and encouragement during the research and writing of this book.

Many thanks are due to Graeme Auld, Sean Bevan, Sebastian Bödeker, Jun Borras, Gerard Breeman, Josh Brem-Wilson, Robin Broad, André Broome, Jennifer Clapp, Will Coleman, Thomas Cottier, Daniel Drache, Matthew Eagleton-Pierce, Benjamin Faude, Thomas Gehring, Christophe Gollay, Laura Gómez-Mera, James Gow, Eric Helleiner, Angela Heucher, Anna Holzscheiter, Kristen Hopewell, Tana Johnson, Michelle Jurkovich, Juliet Kaarbo, Matthias Kranke, Sarah Martin, Philip McMichael, Kerstin Mertens, Andreea Mihalache-O'Keef, Jean-Frederic Morin, Sophia Murphy, Scott Nelson, Simon Nicholson, Robert O'Brien, Amandine Orsini, Tony Porter, Sigrid Quack, Steven Ratner, Lena Rethel, Andrea Schapper, James Scott, Leonard Seabrooke, Joel Shelton, Adam Sneyd, Hannes Stephan, Patrick Theiner, Diana Tussie, Heidi Tworek, Catherine Weaver, and Hannah Wittman for helping me take a collection of muddled thoughts and transform them into (hopefully) coherent arguments.

I thank the organizers of the Warwick Manuscript Development Sessions hosted by the University of Warwick for the opportunity to present and receive feedback on an early version of the book. I also thank the two anonymous reviewers of the book manuscript for their constructive comments, as well as J. P. Singh, editor of the Emerging Frontiers in the Global Economy series, and Steve Catalano at Stanford University Press for their enthusiastic support for the project. Finally, a huge debt of gratitude goes to the many national and international officials who graciously agreed to be interviewed for this project and were generous not only with their time but in offering their candid insights on politically sensitive topics.

SHADOW NEGOTIATORS

INTRODUCTION

THE WORLD TRADE ORGANIZATION (WTO) has become a central flash point for global political battles over the governance of agriculture and food security. Agriculture is among the most contentious areas of global trade politics—so contentious, in fact, that it was excluded from the international trade regime for nearly fifty years. The controversy surrounding agricultural trade stems in part from the fact that food is not just a widget or commodity like any other: agriculture plays a critical role in food security and economic development and is essential for human survival. Agriculture, trade, and food security are deeply intertwined, especially in the global South, where over 2.5 billion people—nearly a third of the world's population—depend directly on agriculture for their livelihoods (IFAD and UNEP 2013). Food insecurity, which exists when individuals lack access to sufficient food, remains a pressing global problem, with two billion food-insecure people worldwide and that number rising (FAO 2020). Access to food is recognized as a human right in international law, and there is a concern that trade liberalization and global trade rules may risk infringing on the right to food (Fakhri 2015; Ferguson 2018).

The creation, in 1995, of the WTO and its Agreement on Agriculture (AoA) was a transformative event that brought agriculture and food under the authority of the trade regime for the first time. However, the issue of how food security should be treated under WTO law remains bitterly contested. At the core of this political contest are conflicting views of whether agricultural trade liberalization bolsters or undermines food security. The principal goal of the WTO is to liberalize trade along market-based lines, but agricultural trade liberalization can have both positive and negative effects on food security that are highly context specific (Brooks and Matthews 2015; Mary 2019). Moreover, states now make agriculture and food policy—including policy related to food security—under the shadow of global trade rules. WTO rules constrain the policy space available for states to intervene in food and agriculture markets (including through tariffs and other trade barriers, subsidies, and public procurement and distribution) and may therefore have significant implications for world food security.

What is more, WTO rules governing agriculture and food are the product of interstate negotiations, which are shaped by economic interests and power asymmetries. Global trade rulemaking is dominated by powerful states, many of which—such as the US and EU—are agricultural exporters and not food insecure, and as a result multilateral trade negotiations have typically prioritized opening markets rather than ensuring food security or protecting vulnerable groups (Clapp 2015; Margulis 2017). Political conflict over how to treat food security at the WTO is considerable, and multiple Southern governments have threatened to exit multilateral trade negotiations out of stated concerns that global trade rules risked increasing hunger within their own borders.[1] Conflict over trade and food security has also galvanized global civil society actors seeking to stop the WTO's drive toward deeper agricultural trade liberalization, most notably La Via Campesina, the world's largest transnational social movement, whose goal is to "get the WTO out of agriculture."

The expansion of the WTO's authority has led to potential conflicts between its goal of liberalizing trade and the goals of other international organizations (IOs) involved in the global governance of food security. In this book, I argue that other IOs have not been passive in the face of this shift but have responded by seeking to influence global trade rulemaking. Thus not only states, private sector actors, and civil society are contesting global trade rules at the WTO, but also other IOs. Drawing on four cases—the Food and Agriculture Organization (FAO), World Food Programme (WFP), Office of the High Commissioner for Human

Rights (OHCHR), and the Special Rapporteur on the Right to Food (SRRTF)—I show that multiple UN actors have intervened in the trade regime in an effort to steer global trade rulemaking toward outcomes that protect world food security. These IOs inserted themselves into the politics of multilateral trade negotiations in order to contest specific trade rules being created by states. UN actors were motivated to intervene because they anticipated that certain proposed trade rules would worsen food insecurity—an outcome that they perceived as running counter to their own missions and social purpose to fight hunger. Moreover, I show that these actions had meaningful effects on the trade regime: UN actors have had a discernable influence on the discourse, agendas, and outcomes of global trade rulemaking.

At a conceptual level, this book contributes to our understanding of IOs by identifying an important yet previously unrecognized type of political behavior by IOs that I term *intervention. Intervention* refers to independent action taken by one IO intended to alter a decision of another organization that it perceives as undermining its ability to achieve its own goals or those of the international community it has been charged to uphold. When successful, IO intervention may help to bring greater coherence to global governance by reducing conflicts among the principles, goals, and rules of different governance regimes. In the cases analyzed in this book, for instance, UN actors successfully inserted food security concerns into global trade rulemaking, thereby reducing conflicts between the trade regime and the agriculture and food, humanitarian assistance, and human rights regimes.

Contributions of the Book

This book contributes to multiple bodies of scholarship: global trade politics, including contestation over global trade rules and the relationship between the multilateral trade system and other areas of global governance; the UN's role in global economic governance; and theories of IOs and regime complexes.

The Politics of "Trade-and" Conflicts

This book offers important insights into how UN actors are shaping the politics of global trade rulemaking. The WTO is one of the most powerful institutions in global governance: it makes "hard law" that is binding on states and backed by a strong enforcement mechanism (K. Abbott and Snidal 2000; Goldstein and Martin 2000; Goldstein et al. 2001). In contrast to its predecessor, the General Agreement on Tariffs and Trade (GATT), the creation of the WTO represented a dramatic expansion in the scope and depth of global trade rules into new areas such as agriculture, services, investment, intellectual property rights, and government procurement (Koremenos, Lipson, and Snidal 2001; Barton et al. 2008). In addition, rather than simply governing trade measures "at the border" (such as tariffs), the WTO's reach is much wider, as it extends "beyond the border" to govern domestic policies that affect trade (Wade 2003; Rodrik 2018). WTO rules seek to address nontariff barriers and to harmonize domestic policies, standards, and regulations—in areas including state aid (i.e., subsidies), antidumping measures, customs procedures, cross-border mobility, health and safety requirements, sanitary and phytosanitary measures, and technical barriers to trade—in order to promote deep economic integration.

The WTO's authority goes far beyond the governance of international trade, as its rules have implications for a wide range of different issue areas, making it a "linkage machine" (Alvarez 2002). Indeed, the broad reach of WTO rules has given rise to a number of so-called "trade-and" conflicts, in which the goals of trade liberalization potentially conflict with the goals of other global governance regimes, such as those for the environment, public health, development, labor, and human rights (Eckersley 2004; Joseph 2011; S. Bernstein and Hannah 2012; Friel, Hattersley, and Townsend 2015; Langille 2020). While existing scholarship on the politics of "trade-and" issues has concentrated on the interface of conflict between WTO rules and efforts to protect the environment (Conca 2000; Zelli, Gupta, and van Asselt 2013; Jinnah 2014) and public health (Sell 2001; Shadlen 2004; Chorev 2012b; Scott and Harman 2013), this book demonstrates that food security is a key "trade-and" issue, with the nexus between trade and food security becoming a highly contested issue in multilateral trade negotiations.

Addressing "trade-and" conflicts has become one of the most vexing issues in global trade governance, and a major preoccupation for scholars of international trade (Cottier and Delimatsis 2011; Blanchard 2015; Pauwelyn 2016; Kanade 2017; Krämer-Hoppe 2020; Krisch, Corradini, and Reimers 2020). The expansion in the scope of the WTO's authority and the binding nature of its rules mean that WTO agreements can potentially come into conflict with, and threaten to undermine, the goals of other global governance institutions. Drawing on analysis of IOs active in the field of food security, I show that other IOs are not passive amid the threat that WTO rules may undermine other important international goals; instead, these IOs have sought to respond to potential "trade-and" conflicts by intervening directly in the WTO's rulemaking process.

It would be a mistake, however, to view intervention by UN actors as part of the antiglobalization movement in opposition to the WTO. The WTO is seen as a key institution in the project of neoliberal globalization, which has prompted a countermovement, involving labor, environmental, and social justice groups, seeking to push back against its agenda of trade liberalization (McMichael 1996; Chorev 2005; Woods 2006; A. Lang 2011). Civil society opposition to the WTO has been strikingly visible in dramatic mass protests at several WTO meetings (R. O'Brien et al. 2000; J. Smith 2001; Gill 2003; Hopewell 2017). Global battles over trade liberalization are often framed as a clash between states and the market, with the WTO seen as driving the marketization and corporatization of the world economy (McMichael 2014). In the case of agriculture and food, the view that the WTO is a threat to farmers and food security has fueled the rise of the food sovereignty movement. The food sovereignty movement has gained considerable prominence in global food politics, campaigning to abolish the WTO with the aim of reversing agricultural trade liberalization, relocalizing food production, and enabling greater state support to agriculture (Desmarais 2007; H. Bernstein 2014; Andrée et al. 2014; Claeys 2015; Dekeyser, Korsten, and Fioramonti 2018). This has generated a fierce debate within global civil society about whether the goal should be to reject or reform the WTO (Burnett and Murphy 2014; Edelman et al. 2014; Hopewell 2015b; Soper 2020).

As this book will show, UN actors have *not* intervened out of blanket opposition to the WTO and its agenda of trade liberalization in fact, some, like the FAO, are strong advocates of agricultural trade liberalization. Instead, interventions by UN actors have been narrowly targeted at altering specific proposed trade rules in order to cushion the potential ill effects of agricultural trade liberalization on food security and vulnerable populations. The behavior of UN actors is therefore in line with reformist efforts to improve global trade rules and not a rejection of the trade regime itself. To the extent it is successful, IO intervention may serve to reduce and ameliorate "trade-and" conflicts in the multilateral trade system.

Who Makes the Global Rules of Trade?

This book also advances our understanding of who makes the rules of global trade. Given the salience of global trade rules to regulation of the global economy and to states' power and wealth, who gets to make those rules is a central question for scholars of international political economy, international law, and international negotiations (Steinberg 2002; Shaffer 2009; Quark 2013; Block-Lieb and Halliday 2017). Traditionally, scholars have primarily focused on the competing interests and asymmetric capabilities of states to explain the dynamics and outcomes of global trade rulemaking. A state-centric approach is appropriate considering that the WTO is a "member-driven" organization where only states have the formal right to enter into multilateral trade negotiations and undertake binding commitments. Yet scholarship has shown that states are not the sole players shaping international trade law. It is well established that private sector actors, which have direct economic stakes in the outcomes of multilateral trade negotiations, engage in extensive lobbying and seek to exert influence over global trade rules in accordance with their commercial interests (Sell 2003; Woll 2008; Curran and Eckhardt 2017; Ryu and Stone 2018; Milsom et al. 2020). Global civil society organizations are also players in global trade politics, pressuring states to reform global trade rules to address a myriad of social justice, development, and environmental issues (H. Murphy 2010; Steffek 2012; Hanegraaff et al. 2015; Hannah 2015; Hopewell 2017).

While scholars have paid increasing attention to the role of nonstate actors in multilateral trade negotiations, they have largely overlooked the role of IOs in shaping global trade rules. Although the existing literature acknowledges that IOs offer important services to support the trade negotiation process, such as providing information and demand-driven technical assistance (Deere Birkbeck and Marchant 2011; VanGrasstek 2013), IOs are generally not regarded as being consequential to bargaining outcomes, since they are not direct participants in negotiations.[2] In this book, I challenge this view by demonstrating that IOs are playing a more active and important role in global trade rulemaking than existing scholarship suggests. I show that the FAO, WFP, OHCHR, and SRRTF, despite lacking a seat at the bargaining table, nonetheless inserted themselves directly into the politics of multilateral trade negotiations on agriculture at the GATT/WTO. While the WTO agriculture negotiations have generated large volumes of scholarship (e.g., Clapp 2006; Daugbjerg and Swinbank 2009; Eagleton-Pierce 2013; Singh and Gupta 2016; Scott 2017), this role of UN actors has been largely overlooked. By demonstrating the active role of UN organizations as influential actors in multilateral trade negotiations, this book contributes to advancing a multiactor approach to the study of global trade rulemaking, in which IOs are important players alongside states, private actors, and global civil society.

The UN in Global Economic Governance

The conventional wisdom suggests that UN organizations are peripheral players when it comes to governing the global economy (Ruggie 2003; Toye and Toye 2004). In creating the postwar international order, states charged the UN with maintaining peace and security, while delegating the management of international economic problems to institutions outside the UN system, including the International Monetary Fund (IMF), the World Bank, and the GATT. Powerful states subsequently resisted efforts to expand the UN's authority in global economic governance; Northern governments, for example, refused to allow the UN system to play a role in regulating transnational corporations in the context of the global South's push for a New International Economic Order and severely curtailed the mandate of the UN Conference on Trade and Development (UNCTAD) (Krasner 1976; C. Murphy 1983; Taylor and Smith 2007). Powerful states have also kept the UN from playing a greater role in global economic governance by turning to club organizations, such as the Organisation for Economic Co-operation and Development (OECD) or the Group of Seven (G7) and Group of Twenty (G20), to retain control over the international economic agenda, including on trade (Woodward 2009; Kirton, Daniels, and Freytag 2019). While trade has been frequently debated within various UN bodies, the prevailing view is that such "deliberations have not been particularly influential and have certainly not resulted in binding legal instruments" (Finlayson and Zacher 1981, 562).

Since UN organizations lack powers comparable to those of the international economic institutions, scholars have instead focused on the

UN's production of ideas as its key contribution to global economic governance (Emmerij, Jolly, and Weiss 2001). UN organizations have generated and disseminated many important economic ideas, including the terms of trade thesis and the concept of "human development" (Toye and Toye 2004; McNeill 2007). By putting ideas out into the world, UN organizations have contributed to changing how actors understand the workings of the global economy and have influenced economic policy debates (Ruggie 2003; Toye and Toye 2004; Thérien and Pouliot 2006; Sagafi-Nejad and Dunning 2008; Ocampo 2018). Yet existing accounts that focus narrowly on the role of UN organizations as wellsprings of ideas elide the issue of their political agency. Emphasizing that UN organizations generate and disseminate ideas but are unable to translate those ideas into rules governing the global economy can be argued to confirm, rather than dispel, the prevailing view of UN organizations as marginal players in global economic governance.

This book challenges the conventional wisdom that UN organizations are not significant actors in global economic governance. I show that UN actors are playing a far more consequential role in global economic governance than typically recognized—not, however, in the traditional manner of being delegated authority by states to make or enforce trade rules, but by intervening to alter the trajectory and results of rulemaking at the GATT/WTO. Despite having no power to make international trade law themselves, I demonstrate that the FAO, WFP, OHCHR, and SRRTF have used their expert, legal, and moral authority (Barnett and Finnemore 2004; Avant, Finnemore, and Sell 2010) to influence global trade rulemaking at the GATT/WTO. As a result, the UN's contributions to the fight against hunger are not limited to raising global awareness about the state of world food insecurity or delivering food to starving people: UN actors have also taken decisive action to shape the rules governing global trade.

IOs Navigating Complex Global Governance

This book also sheds light on how IOs are responding to increasing complexity in global governance. A striking feature of contemporary global governance is the proliferation of international institutions, now counting in the thousands, that co-govern a plethora of cross-border problems (F. Biermann et al. 2009; K. Abbott, Green, and Keohane 2016; Clarke

2019). As a result, many areas of global governance feature "crazy-quilt" arrangements where authority is diffused among multiple, overlapping international institutions, rather than vested in a single, stand-alone institution or fully integrated regime (Rosenau 2004, 149). These governance arrangements are commonly referred to by scholars as "regime complexes," a concept originally developed by Kal Raustiala and David Victor (2004) that has provided a leading framework for understanding the changing institutional contours of global governance and its resulting political effects (Alter and Raustiala 2018; Orsini et al. 2019; Kreuder-Sonnen and Zürn 2020).

The system-like properties of regime complexes create new international political dynamics whereby decisions taken in one institution in a regime complex may affect other institutions that have overlapping authority in the relevant issue area. In particular, regime complexes increase the chance of spillover effects because "changes within one institution could reverberate across parallel institutions" (Alter and Meunier 2009, 20). Spillovers in a regime complex may be positive or negative in their effects. Positive spillovers are associated with improvements in IO performance, reduced uncertainty, and more flexible approaches to problem-solving, whereas negative spillovers result in policy incoherence, reduced incentives for cooperation, and/or conflicts across the norms and rules of overlapping institutions (Helfer 2009; T. Johnson and Urpelainen 2012; Gómez-Mera 2016; Henning 2017). Unlike integrated regimes, which by design have mechanisms to resolve conflicts among constituent institutions, regime complexes are notable for their absence of a centralized authority to address problems arising from negative spillovers.

This book contributes to understanding how IOs navigate these dynamics. While the existing literature has focused on the behavior and political strategies of states in regime complexes, the question of how IOs themselves behave in the regime complexes in which they are embedded has received scant scholarly attention. The extant scholarship has primarily viewed IOs as part of the architecture of regime complexes—and specifically as sites where states pursue cross-institutional political strategies—rather than as actors in regime complexes with their own goals and capabilities for political action. This is puzzling in light of a well-established body of scholarship on IOs as independent actors in world politics, which has shown that IOs have their own organizational goals and preferences and may utilize their material, ideational, and symbolic capabilities to change the behavior of states and influence global policy (Barnett and Finnemore 2004; Hawkins et al. 2006; Weaver 2008; Chwieroth 2009; Chorev 2012b; Oestreich 2012; Weinlich 2014; Bauer, Knill, and Eckhard 2017).

This book builds on theories of IOs as actors and extends them to explain the political behavior of IOs in regime complexes. Drawing on analysis of the regime complex for food security, in which the authority of the FAO, WFP, OHCHR, and SRRTF overlaps with that of the WTO, I show that IOs are not indifferent to decisions taken by states at other institutions in a regime complex that they anticipate will result in negative consequences for their goals and interests or those of the international community. This book contributes to our understanding of how IOs are navigating the politics of regime complexes by demonstrating novel forms of externally oriented, self-directed political action by IOs with the purpose of altering decision-making by states, not within their own institutions, but at other, overlapping institutions outside their control. Whereas previous scholarship on IOs as actors has focused on how they influence decision-making within their institutions, this book examines how IOs influence decision-making *outside* their own institutional boundaries and in areas where they have not been delegated formal authority. By identifying and theorizing this previously unrecognized type of IO behavior, this study advances our understanding of how IOs are navigating and responding to institutional proliferation and rising complexity in global governance.

The Argument: Intervention by IOs

This book is the first to identify a new and distinct type of political behavior by IOs in regime complexes: intervention. Intervention occurs when the secretariat of one IO takes action with the intention of altering the trajectory of decision-making at another organization. My overarching argument is that an IO may choose to intervene when it expects that an anticipated decision at another organization will have negative consequences for the goals it has been charged by the international community to uphold. I demonstrate the existence of intervention by IOs through four detailed case studies of actions taken by the FAO, WFP, OHCHR, and SRRTF to influence global trade rulemaking at the GATT/WTO.

The case studies will show that these UN actors chose to intervene in multilateral trade negotiations in an effort to alter proposed trade rules that they expected would have negative implications for world food security and vulnerable populations.

Intervention is conceptualized in this book as self-initiated and unsolicited political behavior by an IO—meaning that it is undertaken independently by an IO, rather than at the behest of states. While states create IOs to manage collective problems, and IOs fulfill the mandates and tasks assigned to them by states, IOs are not just the servants of states: they may also act of their own volition (Barnett and Finnemore 2004; Oestreich 2012). However, by choosing to intervene, IOs may find themselves confronting states and challenging their interests, which may result in backlash against their organizations. This book shows that the FAO, WFP, OHCHR, and SRRTF did not intervene on the formal or informal orders of their member states but chose of their own accord to insert themselves into the politics of global trade rulemaking at the GATT/WTO. In each case, I will demonstrate that it was UN officials who conceived, initiated, and executed these interventions. Moreover, intervention by UN actors in the trade regime drew objections from powerful states that did not welcome what they perceived as uninvited forays by IOs into the exclusive domain of interstate bargaining over global trade rules. Indeed, UN actors, most notably the WFP and SRRTF, experienced significant backlash from powerful states that viewed these interventions as undermining their economic interests.

Why do IOs choose to intervene in decision-making at other organizations, thus risking potentially costly backlash? I argue that intervention is driven primarily by an IO's sense of social purpose. Each IO has a distinct social purpose—most simply understood as its goals for improving the world—which is determined by an organization's mandate, its history, and the normative orientation of its staff (Ruggie 1982; Barnett and Finnemore 2004; Zürn 2018). In the case of the four UN actors analyzed here, the FAO's social purpose is to reduce world hunger; the WFP's mission is to prevent starvation among vulnerable populations; and the OHCHR and SRRTF work to promote and protect the human right to food, which is intrinsically linked to the goal of fighting hunger. I demonstrate that these UN actors were motivated to intervene at the GATT/WTO because they feared that proposed global trade rules would worsen food insecurity, an outcome that they perceived as running counter to their social purpose and the international goal of creating a world free from hunger. In each case, the decision to intervene was driven by the values and principled beliefs of the organization, rather than instrumental motives. Their sense of social purpose led these IOs to determine that intervention was the appropriate course of action. Although these interventions by UN actors at the GATT/WTO dissatisfied many states, their behavior was not an instance of "mission creep" where IOs move away from their mandates (Hall 2016; Littoz-Monnet 2017a). Instead, as the analysis will show, UN officials believed that their interventions were consistent with the mandates delegated to them by states.

Intervention is a distinct type of political behavior that differs from both cooperation and competition among IOs. Intervention is distinct from cooperation, as it does not involve collaboration among two IOs in order to achieve a shared objective, nor is the goal of the intervening IO to aid in the work of the other organization. And unlike competition, intervention does not involve a struggle between IOs, where, for example, one organization sees the other as a threat to its mandate and resources. Instead, intervention is targeted action by one IO directed at influencing a *specific* decision taken at an overlapping organization over which it has no formal control. The following analysis will demonstrate that the actions by UN organizations were not taken to assist the GATT/WTO secretariat in carrying out its duties, nor were they attempts to supplant the GATT/WTO as a forum for multilateral trade negotiations and dispute settlement or undermine its authority. As I will show, UN organizations intervened at the GATT/WTO in an effort to alter specific proposed global trade rules that they feared would have adverse consequences for food-insecure populations.

Drawing on these cases, I identify four distinct intervention strategies utilized by IOs to influence decision-making by states at other, partially overlapping institutions in a regime complex: mobilizing states, public shaming, invoking alternative legal frameworks, and taking sides. IOs can *mobilize states* at the target organization to affect change. IOs can use *public shaming* to pressure states at the other organization to change a prospective decision. They can *invoke alternative legal frameworks* to present a prospective decision at another organization as inconsistent with international law. And last, an IO can *take sides* with one group of states at the target organization to tilt the political balance in its favor. These intervention strategies involve IOs employing a combination of moral, expert, and legal authority to exercise influence.

IOs develop these intervention strategies because they have no formal authority or control over other institutions in a regime complex. The FAO, WFP, OHCHR, and SRRTF have no direct control over the WTO, for example, and they cannot simply render null and void the global trade rules that they disagree with. They lack a seat at the bargaining table at the WTO, which is exclusive to states. Only WTO member states have the power to decide global trade rules, meaning that in order to shape global trade rules, UN actors must shape the behavior of states. However, UN actors cannot rely on the typical strategies of influence that they utilize within their own institutions when seeking to alter the trajectory of decision-making at another institution over which they have no formal authority. The most common internally oriented strategies of influence used by IOs, such as manipulating procedural rules and controlling privileged information (Bauer, Knill, and Eckhard 2017; Ege, Bauer, and Wagner 2019), are likely to have limited impact beyond their own institutional boundaries. UN organizations cannot manipulate the procedural rules of multilateral trade negotiations, for instance, because they are not delegated a role in coordinating or managing the bargaining process at the WTO. And since global trade rulemaking is not dependent on information produced by UN organizations, the FAO, WFP, OHCHR, and SRRTF cannot expect to alter negotiating outcomes by withholding or manipulating privileged information provided to WTO members. The inadequacy of their internally oriented strategies for exercising influence spurred UN actors to develop innovative externally oriented strategies—mobilizing states, public shaming, invoking alternative legal frameworks, and taking sides—to gain influence in global trade rulemaking.

This book shows not only that IOs intervene but that their interventions can have important consequences for decision-making at the target IO. To demonstrate the influence of UN organizations on global trade rulemaking, I analyze whether their interventions are successful in altering the discourse, agenda setting, or outcomes of multilateral trade negotiations. These are standard criteria employed by scholars to assess any actor's influence in global governance, including in multilateral trade negotiations at the GATT/WTO (Steinberg 2002; Sell and Prakash

2004; Odell 2009; Jones, Deere-Birkbeck, and Woods 2010; Strange 2013). Influence on *discourse* occurs when an intervening IO introduces new, or alters existing, understandings of a policy issue at the target IO. In the analysis that follows, I show that UN organizations have had an impact on discourse at the GATT/WTO by introducing new framings of trade issues that have changed the terms of debate in trade negotiations. *Agenda setting* is a process that defines the scope of issues under consideration, thereby delimiting the range of possible future outcomes. At the GATT/WTO, agenda setting is a pivotal stage of bargaining among states in multilateral trade negotiations. As I will show, interventions by UN organizations have influenced the agenda at the GATT/WTO by inserting, blocking, or removing issues from the negotiations. Influence on *outcomes* is the ability to shape the terms of an official agreement. In multilateral trade negotiations, influence over negotiating outcomes is equated with an actor exerting a substantial effect on the terms of the final deal. As the analysis will demonstrate, UN actors have exercised influence over the substantive content of global trade rules and commitments taken by states.

The case studies analyzed in this book show that interventions by UN organizations have had a meaningful impact on the discourse, agenda, and outcomes of multilateral trade negotiations at the GATT/WTO. The FAO was instrumental in putting food security concerns on the agenda of the agriculture negotiations and in securing a designated WTO agreement designed to protect food-insecure developing countries from higher food prices. Actions by the WFP blocked agreement on proposed WTO trade rules that would have drastically reduced the supply of international food aid to feed the world's hungriest people. The OHCHR's efforts were instrumental in bringing human rights concerns into the WTO agriculture negotiations and led to the incorporation of new food security safeguards for vulnerable groups. The SRRTF intervened to propose a legal waiver to end uncertainty about the legality of public food stockholding for food security; this was taken up by states and became part of new global trade rules. Taken collectively, these cases show that, through their interventions, UN actors introduced food security concerns into multilateral trade negotiations.

The analysis presented in this book demonstrates that intervention is not limited to a specific type of IO but is undertaken by a diverse range of

IOs. While all the IOs examined in this study are part of the UN system, the FAO, WFP, OHCHR, and SRRTF differ from each other in important ways, including in their mandates, functions, membership, and resources. These UN agencies also come from different areas of global governance— agriculture and food policy (FAO), humanitarian assistance (WFP), and human rights (OHCHR, SRRTF). Another important difference is that these IOs intervened with respect to different food security–related issues at the GATT/WTO, including higher food prices (FAO), international food aid (WFP), protections for food-insecure groups (OHCHR), and public food stockholding (SRRTF). In addition, these IOs intervened at different times and during distinct junctures in multilateral trade negotiations on agriculture, including the GATT Uruguay Round (1986–94), the WTO Doha Round (2001–11), and the post-Doha period.[3] Interventions by the FAO, WFP, OHCHR, and SRRTF in the trade regime have thus targeted different trade issues and have occurred at different points in time over a more than thirty-year period. Their actions were taken independently from one another and were unrelated, indicating that their interventions were not part of some larger coordinated "grand strategy" among various UN organizations directed at the WTO.

In their interventions seeking to alter the trajectory and results of multilateral trade negotiations, I argue that UN actors are effectively acting as "shadow negotiators" in the trade regime. First, authority to decide global trade rules rests solely with states. UN actors are not formal participants in the negotiation of international trade agreements, and they lack a seat at the bargaining table. They thus operate in the shadow of states: altering the trajectory of decision-making at the GATT/WTO requires altering the behavior of states. Since states are the decision makers at the GATT/WTO, UN actors must work with or through states in order to shape global trade rules. Second, UN actors have operated "in the shadows" in the sense that while most attention has focused on bargaining among states in multilateral trade negotiations, the role of UN actors in GATT/WTO negotiations has gone largely unnoticed by scholars. Third, although UN actors have no official negotiating role at the GATT/WTO, as the following cases will show, they sometimes behave very much like negotiators—including drafting bargaining proposals and putting forward specific measures to be incorporated into trade agreements, steering the negotiating agenda, devising negotiating strategy, blocking proposals that they object to, and mobilizing coalitions of like-minded states to support and advance initiatives. While not formal or official negotiators, UN actors may nonetheless at times assume the role of shadow negotiators in GATT/WTO negotiations.

Research Design and Methods

The purpose of this book is to demonstrate the existence of intervention as a form of political behavior by IOs in regime complexes. To do so, I draw on analysis of multiple, in-depth illustrative cases of intervention: intervention by the FAO during the GATT Uruguay Round (which established the WTO and its rules) and the WTO Doha Round, by the WFP and OHCHR in the WTO Doha Round, and by the SRRTF during the Doha Round and post-Doha Round negotiations. Multiple cases of intervention provide a significantly higher threshold of evidence than a single case and demonstrate that this phenomenon is not merely a one-off occurrence or an aberration but happens with enough frequency to warrant greater attention. These four cases are not meant to be exhaustive of all instances of intervention by IOs at the GATT/WTO but were selected to highlight four distinct intervention strategies: mobilizing states by the FAO, public shaming by the WFP, invoking alternative legal frameworks by the OHCHR, and taking sides by the SRRTF. Moreover, the fact that these IOs intervened at the GATT/WTO is all the more surprising given that—unlike UNCTAD, for example—they are not trade institutions and have no trade mandate.

The analysis presented in this book draws on in-depth field research conducted at the WTO, FAO, WFP, OHCHR, and UN Human Rights Council (HRC; this is the institutional home of the SRRTF) in Geneva and Rome between 2008 and 2019. I collected, analyzed, and triangulated between multiple sources of evidence to carefully trace and reconstruct events; understand the context, motivations, and processes by which UN actors intervened; and assess their influence on global trade rulemaking. Data analyzed in this study included over three hundred official documents—such as reports, speeches, formal decisions, minutes of meetings, summaries of bargaining sessions, and internal memoranda—produced by the secretariats and member states of the GATT/WTO, FAO, WFP, OHCHR, and SRRTF/HRC. Additional archival research was undertaken at the FAO headquarters for the analysis of the FAO's interventions during the GATT Uruguay Round (1986–94).

The documentary and archival analysis was supplemented with eighty-five in-depth elite interviews. Selected through purposive sampling, interview respondents included current and former executive heads and senior international civil servants of the FAO, WFP, OHCHR, SRRTF/HRC, and GATT/WTO who directly participated in, or were knowledgeable about, the events analyzed in the study. Additional interviews were conducted with current and former member-state representatives at these IOs, including ambassadors, heads of mission, chairpersons of negotiation committees, and other delegates, as well as staff of other IOs with observer status at the GATT/WTO, such as the World Bank, UNCTAD, OECD, and International Labor Organization. Interviews were also conducted with representatives from nongovernmental organizations (NGOs) working on the WTO agricultural trade negotiations, including Oxfam International, the International Centre for Trade and Sustainable Development (ICTSD), and the Institute for Agriculture and Trade Policy (IATP). Interviews were semistructured, with questions tailored to the specific knowledge and experience of each respondent. Interviews were one to two hours in length. The vast majority of interviews were conducted in person, either in the interview respondent's office or at a neutral venue. The remaining interviews were conducted by telephone or video conference (i.e., Skype). To address the potential for respondent bias to skew the data, I triangulated and cross-checked between multiple interview respondents and other information sources to verify statements and ensure an accurate account of events. Representative quotations drawn from the interview data are presented in the analysis to provide evidence of, and context to situate, interventions by UN actors. Additional data were obtained from direct observation of several public and closed official meetings at the WTO, FAO, HRC, UNCTAD, and Committee for World Food Security, as well as specialized events and workshops organized by IOs, NGOs, and think tanks on the WTO negotiations on agriculture.

Plan of the Book

The concept of intervention is further theorized in chapter 1, where I specify the conditions for intervention by IOs, explain the four intervention strategies, and define how the impacts of intervention can be evaluated. The chapter sets out the book's contributions to contemporary scholarship on the agency of IOs in global governance and the political dynamics of regime complexes. Chapter 2 traces the evolution of global food security governance from an international regime to a regime complex. The chapter provides context for understanding how institutional proliferation and diverging goals among the institutions active in the global governance of food security have given rise to intervention by UN actors at the GATT/WTO.

Chapters 3, 4, 5, and 6 are the main empirical chapters of the book. Each chapter analyzes the intervention strategies pursued by UN actors and assesses their influence on the discourse, agenda, and outcomes of multilateral trade negotiations at the GATT/WTO. Chapter 3 examines intervention by the FAO in two multilateral trade negotiations: the GATT Uruguay Round and the WTO Doha Round. I show that FAO officials sought to insert themselves into the politics of the agriculture negotiations in both rounds and did so by mobilizing GATT/WTO member states. In the Uruguay Round, the FAO director-general and senior officials chose to intervene out of concern that proposed global trade rules would make food less affordable and less accessible for the world's poorest people. To avoid backlash from powerful states dissatisfied with the FAO's attempts to play an active role in the GATT agriculture negotiations, FAO officials took to working quietly behind the scenes by organizing and steering a bargaining coalition of GATT member states. The FAO worked with and through this bargaining coalition to reframe food security as a trade issue and put food security onto the agenda of the agriculture negotiations. The FAO exerted influence over the outcome of the Uruguay Round as the chief architect of the AoA's Decision on Measures Concerning the Possible Negative Effects of the Reform Programme on Least-Developed and Net Food-Importing Developing Countries, a WTO agreement under which states committed to safeguard food security in the event that agricultural trade liberalization led to higher food prices. In addition, the FAO later mobilized WTO member states during the Doha Round negotiations to drive forward the agenda on establishing a WTO-based food financing facility intended to address the difficulties of food import–dependent countries in financing adequate levels of commercial food imports.

Chapter 4 showcases the WFP's public shaming of WTO members in order to block proposed trade rules intended to discipline international food aid transactions. International food aid has been a source of perennial conflict in the trade regime because of its potential to be used as a form of agricultural export subsidy. Political conflict over international food aid reached fever pitch during the WTO Doha Round, when states sought to establish new rules that would ban certain types of food aid. WFP officials were alarmed by the proposed WTO rules, which they predicted would cause a precipitous decline in the supply of international food aid and would thereby increase the number of hunger-related deaths. However, WFP officials were unable to persuade trade negotiators to change the proposed rules through face-to-face dialogue. As a result, the WFP took the dramatic step of publicly shaming WTO members by launching a media campaign that depicted trade negotiators as recklessly endangering the lives of starving people. The WFP's self-initiated political actions were controversial and elicited significant backlash from states. Yet its intervention at the WTO proved successful in pressuring trade negotiators to change course and drop the proposed food aid ban. Moreover, when WTO members finally reached a new agreement on agricultural export subsidies in the 2015 Ministerial Decision on Export Competition, which included new global trade rules on international food aid, this agreement incorporated the demands made by the WFP to WTO members.

Chapter 5 examines how the OHCHR invoked international human rights law in an effort to alter global trade rulemaking in the WTO Doha Round. OHCHR officials were concerned that WTO rules were inadequate to protect the human rights of vulnerable populations from the potential adverse effects of agricultural trade liberalization. Although WTO members signaled their preference to keep discussions of human rights out of the agriculture negotiations, the OHCHR, led by the High Commissioner for Human Rights, sought to steer global trade rules toward greater alignment with international human rights standards. In doing so, the OHCHR took extraordinary and unconventional political action, including making unsolicited proposals directly to trade ministers and creating uncertainty about the consistency of WTO rules with international human rights law. Intervention by the OHCHR contributed to new safeguards to protect food security in the draft Doha agriculture agreement that justified exemptions from tariff reductions for crops produced by poor farmers and other marginalized groups.

The final case, presented in chapter 6, examines intervention by the SRRTF in the context of the Doha and post–Doha Round agriculture negotiations. The SRRTF took sides in the negotiations by endorsing the bargaining position of WTO members demanding greater flexibility in global trade rules to pursue domestic food security goals. The SRRTF chose to intervene in the WTO agriculture negotiations out of a conviction that major reform of global trade rules was necessary in order to combat rising food insecurity. Despite starting as an outsider to the world of global trade rulemaking, the SRRTF became an influential player at the WTO by leveraging moral authority as a UN voice for food-insecure people. While the SRRTF's interventions prompted political backlash by many powerful states, they were nevertheless influential in shaping the agenda and outcomes of the agriculture negotiations. Most notably, the SRRTF's advocacy for a legal waiver to protect developing countries' public food-stockholding programs from legal challenge—even when such programs violated existing WTO rules—provided the blueprint for a new WTO agreement, the Ministerial Decision on Public Stockholding for Security Purposes, agreed upon by WTO members at the 2013 Bali Ministerial Conference. Chapters 5 and 6 also show how human rights have become increasingly central to contests over trade and food security, by bringing attention to how trade affects the most vulnerable groups in society and as an instrument to challenge the harmful effects of global trade rules on food-insecure populations.

The last chapter presents the conclusion of this study. It summarizes the findings of the empirical chapters and assesses the influence of UN actors on global trade rulemaking at the GATT/WTO. The case studies provide the basis for developing more generalizable insights about this previously unknown type of political behavior by IOs in the context of complex global governance. The situation that UN organizations find themselves in, where they have a direct stake in, and seek to affect change of, decisions taken by states at another international institution, is not, I argue, unique to the regime complex for food security but is reflective of wider transformations occurring in the institutional structures of global governance.

This book offers compelling evidence to show that IOs have chosen to intervene at other organizations in a regime complex when they expect that a prospective decision will undermine their goals or those of the international community they have been charged to uphold. In the four case studies, UN actors intervened to alter the trajectory and results of decision-making at the GATT/WTO in an effort to steer global trade rulemaking toward outcomes that protect world food security. Intervention may therefore serve to address "trade-and" conflicts by introducing other important international objectives, such as food security and human rights, into the trade regime. This book contributes to our understanding of who makes the rules governing global trade by revealing the previously unrecognized role of UN organizations in the politics of the WTO. To the extent that intervention is successful it may help to reduce incoherence between overlapping institutions in global governance. The book expands our understanding of IOs as actors in global politics by showing how they are exercising influence over decision-making beyond the boundaries of their own institutions and at other overlapping institutions over which they have no formal control.

CHAPTER 1

Intervention by International Organizations

RISING INSTITUTIONAL COMPLEXITY and overlapping authority among international institutions are changing the behavior of IOs. Overlapping authority among IOs can lead to situations where a decision taken by states at one organization may be viewed by another organization as undermining its core goals or the interests and values of the international community it is tasked to uphold. This chapter makes the case that regime complexity is engendering a new form of independent behavior by IOs that I term "intervention," in which IOs utilize their material and ideational capabilities to influence decision-making not within their own institutions but at other, overlapping organizations in a regime complex over which they have no direct control. Intervention is a previously unrecognized and distinct type of behavior by IOs that differs both from bureaucratic competition for mandates, resources, and members, and from cooperation to achieve joint goals.

In this chapter, I develop the concept of intervention by IOs and present the theoretical argument made in the book. The first section of the chapter sets out one of the core assumptions guiding the analysis in this study—that IOs can be self-directed actors. The second section situates the theoretical contribution of the concept of intervention to the extant scholarship on regime complexes, IO interaction, and IO influence. The third section specifies the concept of intervention and the necessary conditions for this type of independent political action by IOs to occur. The fourth section identifies four distinct intervention strategies—mobilization, public shaming, invoking alternative legal frameworks, and taking sides—that IOs utilize to influence decisions at other IOs over which they have no formal control. The final section proposes a framework to assess the impacts of intervention by an IO on the decision-making process of an overlapping organization.

IOs as Self-Directed Actors

The analytical starting point for this study is that IOs can be self-directed actors. In other words, IOs have "the ability to act on their own, in ways not dictated or perhaps even foreseen by the states that create them" (Oestreich 2012, 2). To be self-directed actors, IOs must express their own preferences and have the capabilities to undertake actions independently of their member states (Reinalda and Verbeek 1998; Barnett and Finnemore 2004; Hawkins et al. 2006; F. Biermann and Siebenhüner 2009; Oestreich 2012; T. Johnson 2014; Bauer, Knill, and Eckhard 2017). The study of IOs as actors is a well-established research program within in the field of international relations. Theoretical work on the agency of IOs emerged in the 1990s as a challenge to neorealist and neoliberal institutionalist scholarship that viewed IOs as "mere arenas or mechanisms" through which states pursue their interests and therefore did not treat the agency of IOs as consequential to the study of world politics (Barnett and Finnemore 1999, 707; see also Martin and Simmons 1998; Weaver 2007).

Two approaches—constructivism and principal-agent theory—have primarily shaped scholarship on IOs as actors. Constructivism focuses on the role of ideas and bureaucratic culture to explain the behavior of IOs in world politics. Michael Barnett and Martha Finnemore (2004), whose work has been especially influential in establishing a constructivist approach to the study of IOs as actors, argue that the agency of IOs lies in their ability to obtain deference from other actors because they are perceived to promote socially valuable goals in rational, technocratic, impartial, and nonviolent ways. Constructivist scholarship emphasizes the importance of norms, values, and beliefs, which provide international bureaucracies with their social purpose and shape how they interpret and exercise their mandates (Barnett and Finnemore 1999; Oestreich 2007;

Weaver 2008; Chorev 2012b; Chwieroth 2009; Nielson, Tierney, and Weaver 2006). In contrast, principal-agent approaches to IOs as actors focus on the strategic behavior of international bureaucrats. States (the "principals") conditionally delegate authority to IOs (the "agents") to perform specialized tasks on their behalf (Nielson and Tierney 2003). This in turn provides IOs with discretion to independently determine how to fulfill their mandates and exercise their powers (Hawkins et al. 2006, 7). Principal-agent approaches predict that international bureaucrats will act strategically in order to expand their mandates, members, and resources, even if this is not what their member states want (Pollack 1997; Nielson and Tierney 2003; Hawkins et al. 2006; Elsig 2011).

While starting from different ontological positions and differences in how they conceptualize the independence of IOs, constructivist and principal-agent approaches share important assumptions about IOs as actors, namely that IOs can develop their own preferences and that such preferences may diverge from those of their member states (Nielson, Tierney, and Weaver 2006; Weaver 2007; Oestreich 2012). In addition, both approaches expect that IOs will utilize their delegated, expert, and/ or moral authority to take independent actions to change the behavior of states to achieve their organizational goals (Barnett and Finnemore 2004, 19, 27–29; Hawkins et al. 2006, 24–25; Avant, Finnemore, and Sell 2010, 11–14). IOs may exercise their authority to pursue their own agendas that are neither solicited nor desired by their member states (Nielson and Tierney 2003; Johns 2007; Mathiason 2007; Graham 2014). Furthermore, constructivist and principal-agent approaches both recognize that IOs vary in their functions, institutional design, leadership styles, and organizational cultures and in the material and ideational capabilities at their disposal, all of which combine in different ways to shape how and when IOs will act in seeking to influence world politics (Barnett and Finnemore 2004; F. Biermann and Siebenhüner 2009; Oestreich 2012; Hall and Woods 2018). Of course, the ability of IOs to take independent action is always subject to constraints, with both constructivist and principal-agent approaches recognizing that an IO's scope for action may be limited by its internal rules, as well as its staff's awareness that certain actions may undermine the organization's relationship with its member states and/or other audiences and thus risk its security (Knill et al. 2018; Cortell and Peterson 2021).

Numerous detailed studies drawing on constructivism or principal-agent theory, or a combination of the two (see Nielson, Tierney, and Weaver 2006), have convincingly shown that IOs, including the FAO, World Bank, International Monetary Fund (IMF), World Health Organization (WHO), and United Nations Environment Programme (UNEP), have pursued independent agendas and policy goals that have diverged from those preferred by their member states (Oestreich 2007; Weaver 2008; F. Biermann and Siebenhüner 2009; Oestreich 2012; Chorev 2012b; Jinnah 2014; T. Johnson 2014; Weinlich 2014; Hall 2016; Xu and Weller 2018). As self-directed actors with their own preferences and capabilities to take independent action, IOs are thus an important group of actors in global governance, which, alongside states, exercise power and influence over international policy and decision-making (Avant, Finnemore, and Sell 2010; Xu and Weller 2018; Knill et al. 2018).

Theoretical Contributions to IO Scholarship
Partially Overlapping Authority in Global Governance
Scholars now recognize that IOs do not operate in splendid isolation from one another. As a result of institutional proliferation, IOs are increasingly embedded in "regime complexes," in which their authority partially overlaps with that of other IOs in the governance of an issue area (Raustiala and Victor 2004; Alter and Meunier 2009; Alter and Raustiala 2018). A regime complex is defined as "an array of partially overlapping and nonhierarchical institutions that includes more than one international agreement or authority" (Alter and Raustiala 2018, 333). Institutional proliferation makes global governance more complex and can lead to conflicting rules and policy incoherence. The lack of formal hierarchy among institutions in a regime complex means that there is no definitive arrangement or meta-authority to which actors can appeal to settle jurisdictional ambiguity or treaty conflicts (Alter and Meunier 2009; Keohane and Victor 2011; Pratt 2018; Kreuder-Sonnen and Zürn 2020). Regime complexes is a leading concept used by international relations scholars to examine the causes and consequences of overlapping authority across a diverse set of policy fields, ranging from security to international finance to climate change (Alter and Raustiala 2018; Brosig 2013; Colgan, Keohane, and Van de Graaf 2012; Davis 2009; Keohane and Victor 2011; K. Abbott 2012; Mallard 2014; Rabitz 2014; Henning 2017; Murray-Evans 2020).

A substantial body of scholarship has convincingly shown how states pursue their interests in regime complexes through novel cross-institutional political strategies (Alter and Meunier 2009, 16), such as "strategic inconsistency" (Raustiala and Victor 2004), "regime-shifting" (Helfer 2009), "institutional deference" (Pratt 2018), and "hostage-taking" (Hofmann 2019), which range from states playing overlapping international institutions off one another to promoting harmonization among international institutions. While this literature has significantly advanced our understanding of the political behavior of states in regime complexes, it has largely overlooked the role and behavior of IOs themselves.[1] The likely reason is that regime complexes have been chiefly theorized by scholars working from functionalist paradigms that view IOs as *mechanisms* created by states to lower transaction costs and solve coordination problems (K. Abbott and Snidal 1998). Most research on regime complexes thus focuses on whether partially overlapping authority increases or decreases the incentives for states to cooperate (Raustiala and Victor 2004; Oberthür and Gehring 2006; Alter and Meunier 2009; Keohane and Victor 2011; T. Johnson and Urpelainen 2012; Orsini, Morin, and Young 2013; Gehring and Faude 2014; Pratt 2018; Hofmann 2019). While this is undoubtedly important research, it has come at the cost of neglecting the agency of IOs in regime complexes.

While scholars of regime complexes have taken steps to model in the behavior of private actors (Green and Auld 2017; Zelli, Möller, and Asselt 2017) and NGOs (Orsini 2013; Gómez-Mera 2016; Schapper 2020), theorizing and research on IOs as actors in regime complexes has lagged behind. The regime complex literature tends to treat IOs merely as the arenas in which states and other actors play out their cross-institutional political strategies, rather than as actors capable of pursuing their own interests and political objectives. This omission is surprising given that nearly all regime complexes identified to date are populated by two or more IOs that have the responsibility for implementing and upholding the overlapping rules and policies that scholars have identified as the key drivers of the politics of regime complexes. The question of how IOs navigate the political dynamics of the regime complexes in which they are embedded has received inadequate scholarly attention. IOs are too important a set of actors, I contend, to be relegated to the margins of analysis of how the political dynamics of global governance are being reconfigured by the emergence of partially overlapping authority among international institutions.

Just as we can expect the behavior of states to be shaped by the knowledge that a decision taken at one institution can unsettle, weaken, and/or nullify the goals of another institution in a regime complex (Alter and Meunier 2009; Gehring and Faude 2014; Alter and Raustiala 2018), it is reasonable to expect that the behavior of IOs may be shaped by similar dynamics. The literature on IOs as actors has demonstrated that IOs are not passive to decisions taken by their member states that they believe to be against their organization's interests or those of the international community. Building on these insights, I posit that IOs are unlikely to be indifferent to decisions taken at other institutions in the regime complex that they expect will have negative, undesirable effects and that this may prompt them to undertake independent political action directed at altering those decisions.

IO Interaction: Beyond Cooperation and Competition

Existing theories of IO interaction expect that relationships between IOs that govern similar issue areas and whose authority overlaps will be either cooperative or competitive (R. Biermann and Koops 2017; Lipson 2017). Cooperation among IOs can involve organizations working together toward joint policy or regulatory goals by coordinating their policies and operational activities, pooling their resources, and/or engaging in joint decision-making (Gest and Grigorescu 2010; Gehring and Faude 2014). Zhao (2020), for example, demonstrates that the secretariats of the WTO and the Cartagena Protocol on Biosafety to the Convention on Biological Diversity share information and pool expertise to prevent noncompliance by states. Another form of cooperation, known as orchestration, involves an IO enlisting and supporting intermediaries to enhance states' consent to and compliance with its rules and policies (K. Abbott et al. 2015a, 2015b). Intermediaries for orchestration may include other IOs, as well as private actors, NGOs, or national institutions, that possess information and capabilities that the orchestrating IO lacks. For example, the Global Environmental Facility (GEF) enlists the support of the United Nations Environmental Program (UNEP) and the World Bank by channeling climate financing through those intermediaries in order to improve states' take-up of adaptation policies (Graham and Thompson 2015).

Conversely, competition among IO secretariats is typically characterized by rivalry for mandates (Gehring and Faude 2014; Betts 2013; Hall 2015, 2016), members and resources (Frey 2008; R. Biermann and Harsch 2017; Hofmann 2009), and focality (Momani and Hibben 2015; Gómez-Mera 2016; Holzscheiter 2017; Littoz-Monnet 2017a; Heldt and Schmidtke 2019; Pantzerhielm, Holzscheiter, and Bahr 2019) but can also manifest in open conflicts over global policy influence (Morse and Keohane 2014; Hannah, Ryan, and Scott 2017). Betts (2013, 76) argues that institutional proliferation encourages competition among IOs because it provides states with more choices "in terms of which institutions they could use to address a given problem." IO secretariats have been shown to respond to competitive pressures by pursuing boundary maintenance to protect their focality (Holzscheiter 2017; Kranke 2020), forum shifting to regain focality "lost" to other IOs (Betts 2013; Gómez-Mera 2016; Hall 2016), and/or working with like-minded states to supplant rival organizations by creating a new challenger institution (Morse and Keohane 2014).

Intervention by IOs, however, differs from both cooperation and competition among IOs. Unlike cooperation, intervention does not involve multiple IO secretariats pooling their resources, coordinating their activities, or working toward a joint policy or regulatory goal, but rather one IO seeking to insert itself into the politics of decision-making at an overlapping organization in order to influence a particular outcome there. In contrast to competition, intervention is not characterized by two secretariats engaging in a zero-sum game, struggling over turf, members, resources, or policy influence. Instead, intervention is a political action by one IO secretariat directed at altering a specific decision at an overlapping organization. As demonstrated in the empirical chapters that follow, the interventions taken by the FAO, WFP, OHCHR, and SRRTF were never intended to weaken the GATT/WTO or to obtain mandates or resources at its expense. In all cases, these intervening IOs affirmed their support of the WTO's mandate to establish a rules-based global trading order but intervened in an effort to alter specific trade rules that they anticipated would have negative consequences for food security.

IOs' Influence outside Their Organizational Boundaries

The concept of intervention pushes forward our theorizing of IOs as actors. The existing literature on IOs as actors has focused on the capabilities of IOs to influence decisions taken *within* their organizational boundaries. However, in regime complexes, IOs may be concerned not only by the activities of their own members but by decisions taken at overlapping organizations. The absence of hierarchy among IOs means that there is no meta-authority to which an IO can appeal to prevent or reverse objectionable decisions taken in other parts of the regime complex. The absence of hierarchy also means that one IO cannot simply legislate against or overrule a decision taken at an overlapping IO. While some scholars expect that inconsistent rules, norms, and policies among overlapping IOs should drive states to bring order to a regime complex (see Gehring and Faude 2014; Pratt 2018), it is just as likely that regime complexes will persist in a state of incoherence for extended periods of time, even possibly indefinitely (F. Biermann et al. 2009; T. Johnson and Urpelainen 2012; Morin and Orsini 2014). Even if states do take actions to bring greater order to a regime complex, there is also no guarantee that this will result in an outcome preferred by the IO, given that its interests may not align with those of states. Under these conditions, an IO may find choosing to take matters into its own hands a reasonable option.

The question then is *how* IOs seek to influence decision-making at overlapping organizations in a regime complex. The conditions faced by IOs in regime complexes differ from those under which existing constructivist and principal-agent approaches have theorized the agency of IOs. Focusing on situations in which an IO has exclusive authority to govern an issue area, these approaches have analyzed how an IO wields influence over the behavior of its member states by utilizing political strategies unique to the delegation relationship, including withholding privileged information in order to bias decision-making toward its preferred ends (Martin 2006; Jinnah 2014; Eckhard and Ege 2016); manipulating its organization's procedural rules and decision-making processes to prevent or delay states from voting on objectionable decisions (Cortell and Peterson 2006; F. Biermann and Siebenhüner 2009; Dijkstra 2017); or leveraging its claims to exclusive competence in an issue area to engage in policy learning/socialization of its members (Barnett and Finnemore 2004; Chwieroth 2009; Broome and Seabrooke 2012; Ban, Seabrooke, and Freitas 2016; Littoz-Monnet 2017b; Busch and Liese 2017; Hannah, Ryan, and Scott 2017; Well et al. 2020). However, this repertoire of strategies that an IO utilizes to exercise influence internally will not apply when the IO seeks to exercise influence externally at an overlapping organization, where, for example, it does not have control over the other organization's procedures or rules and cannot claim exclusive competence. IOs, I argue, respond creatively to the conditions they face in regime complexes by devising distinct strategies—such as mobilizing states, public shaming, invoking alternative frameworks, and taking sides—to influence decision-making at overlapping organizations. The study of IO intervention makes an important contribution to scholarship on IOs as actors by demonstrating how IOs are able to directly influence decision-making *outside* their organizational boundaries.

Conceptualizing Intervention

In this section, I further specify the concept of intervention by IOs. Intervention occurs when the secretariat of an IO—its executive head, bureaucracy, and/or other officials delegated authority by states—acts with the intention of altering an anticipated decision at an overlapping organization in a regime complex. As the existing literature on IOs as actors has shown, the secretariat of an IO can hold preferences that are independent of those of its member states and can take self-directed actions on behalf of the organization (Cox 1969; Kille and Scully 2003; Barnett and Finnemore 2004; Xu and Weller 2008; Schroeder 2014; Hall and Woods 2018). Secretariats carry out the day-to-day work of the IO according to bureaucratic procedures and routines, and they embody and reproduce the organization's values and culture. The target of intervention is the decision-making body of the partially overlapping organization (typically its member states).[2] A decision is defined here as a choice, judgment, or course of action that is reached through a formal process involving preestablished procedures and rules. Decisions result in manifold outcomes, including international agreements, regulations, policies, resolutions, financial commitments, political declarations, new tasks for IOs, and so forth.

Intervention is depicted in figure 1, with the intervention by the secretariat of IO[1] targeting the decision-making body of IO[2] represented by a transversal arrow. Clarifying the units of analysis and who is "doing the doing" is especially important in the study of IOs, which are complex and multilayered organizations (Reinalda and Verbeek 2004; Weaver 2008). This also helps to more clearly delineate the concept of intervention from existing work on regime complexes, much of which analyzes conflicts between overlapping international treaties (see Alter and Raustiala 2018; Kreuder-Sonnen and Zürn 2020), as well as from concepts such as cooperation and competition that are based on interaction between secretariats (Frey 2008; Lipson 2017).

FIGURE 1. IO intervention

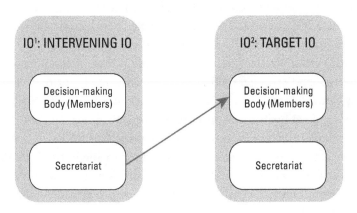

Importantly, intervention is a self-directed action by an IO secretariat, meaning that it is (1) unsolicited (i.e., not in response to a request from the target IO or its member states) and (2) not driven by its own member states. IOs are routinely asked to assist and support the work of other IOs, including by being granted observer status and called in as expert advisers (P. Haas 1989; F. Biermann and Siebenhüner 2009). In addition, IOs may be periodically asked by a subset of another IO's member states to provide analysis and advice based on their expertise; UNCTAD, for instance, frequently receives requests for technical assistance from developing countries at the WTO (Hannah, Ryan, and Scott 2017). In contrast, however, intervention involves an IO undertaking actions that are unsolicited by states—and that may indeed be unwanted and perceived as unwelcome interference or meddling in the business of states—at the target IO. As the following cases will show, the interventions of the FAO, WFP, OHCHR, and SRRTF were self-initiated and not solicited by either GATT/WTO members or the GATT/WTO secretariat.

An alternative explanation for an IO secretariat taking action to influence a decision at another IO in a regime complex is simply that it is acting on the directions of its own member states, either collectively or a subset. Member states of the intervening IO could be dissatisfied by a decision at the overlapping organization and issue formal instructions—such as through a resolution or tabled motion—or informal guidance to the secretariat to interfere in the decision-making of the target IO. However, as the analysis that follows will show, the FAO, WFP, OHCHR, and SRRTF all initiated their interventions independently and were not directed—formally or informally—to do so by their member states. Indeed, in some cases, these IOs faced backlash once their members became aware of their activities to influence decision-making at the GATT/WTO.

What then motivates intervention? While IOs are predominantly seen as strategic and self-interested actors (Hawkins et al. 2006; T. Johnson 2014; Littoz-Monnet 2017a), it is also recognized that the behavior of an IO is guided by its social purpose and organizational culture (Barnett and Finnemore 2004; Weaver 2008; Chwieroth 2009; Baker 2012). An IO's social purpose and organizational culture are interrelated. The social purpose of an IO can be understood as its mission and goals for improving the world. Each IO has a social purpose, which provides its staff with a collective identity and concrete goals to work toward (Xu and Weller 2018; Murdoch et al. 2018; Ege 2020). An IO's social purpose is shaped by the formal mandate bestowed by states, which sets out an IO's long-term mission and its core functions, objectives, and powers, as well as how the IO's leadership and staff interpret what are typically broad and vague mandates into actionable goals and bureaucratic practices (F. Biermann and Siebenhüner 2009; Hall 2016; Sinclair 2017; Murdoch et al. 2018). Each IO also develops its own organizational culture, which refers to "the shared ideologies, norms, and routines" that shape the secretariat's expectations about how its mandate is to be operationalized, its professional identities and values, and what behavior will be rewarded or punished (Nielson, Tierney, and Weaver 2006: 109; Chwieroth 2013; Weaver and Nelson 2016). An IO's social purpose and organizational culture are not static but may transform over time in response to new tasks and problems, changing international political conditions, and self-directed efforts by secretariats to transform their mandates (Park 2005; Hall 2016; Cortell and Peterson 2021). Social purpose and organizational culture inform how a secretariat understands the causes and solutions to international policy problems and how it responds to changes in its external environment (Sarfaty 2009; Oestreich 2012; Kentikelenis and Seabrooke 2017). As the cases that follow will demonstrate, the FAO, WFP, OHCHR, and SRRTF chose to intervene because they anticipated that a specific decision taken by GATT/WTO members would harm world food security—an outcome that the intervening IO viewed as contrary to its own social purpose to promote food security (in the cases of the FAO and WFP) or the human right to food (in the cases of the OHCHR and SRRTF). Their interventions were primarily driven by principled beliefs, that is, "shared values" and "ideas about what is wrong and right" (Sikkink 1993, 412), even if intervening meant challenging the interests of powerful states and risked exposing their organization to backlash.

Scholarship has shown that IO behavior may be guided by both instrumental *and* principled considerations (Oestreich 2007; F. Biermann and Siebenhüner 2009; Vetterlein 2012; Bauer, Knill, and Eckhard 2017). In the cases analyzed in this book, I argue that intervention cannot simply be explained as strategic or self-interested behavior on the part of IOs to increase their organization's standing or to obtain more resources. These instances of intervention were not, as I will show, intended to result in new mandates, funding, staff, or members for the intervening IO, nor did they. In other words, there was little direct benefit to UN actors from intervening at the GATT/WTO. Instead, on the contrary, as the cases analyzed in the book will demonstrate, intervention carries potentially significant risks to an intervening IO. Intervention may bring reputational costs: the behavior of IOs is "closely scrutinized" by states, making secretariats careful to avoid taking actions that could diminish their organization's reputation and credibility (Broome 2008; Daugirdas 2019). A particular concern for secretariats is the risk that intervention may provoke a backlash from (powerful) states. By intervening, a secretariat is seeking to alter a prospective decision arrived at by states through a formal process of interstate bargaining and political compromise; states could view such an action as inappropriate political interference by the intervening secretariat. In choosing to intervene, the IO secretariat knowingly runs a risk of provoking a backlash from states, which could make the organization vulnerable to cuts to its budget, curtailment of its mandate, exit by dissatisfied members, and/or other punitive measures. Indeed, in several cases analyzed in the book, intervening IOs experienced backlash from states that were dissatisfied with their efforts to influence decision-making at the GATT/WTO. A narrowly instrumental view of IO behavior would thus suggest that the interventions by UN actors were irrational because their actions offered little or no direct benefits to the intervening IO while carrying significant potential risks. Why then intervene if the risks vastly exceed any potential reward to the intervening IO? In these cases, as I will show, IOs were motivated to intervene not by anticipated benefits to their organization but by concern that anticipated decisions at the GATT/WTO would have harmful consequences for food security and human rights. That the IOs analyzed in this book will be shown to have intervened for principled reasons does not, of course, exclude the possibility that IOs may also be motivated to intervene for more instrumental or self-interested reasons.

The cases analyzed in this study demonstrate that intervention is undertaken by a wide range of different types of IOs. The FAO, WFP, OHCHR, and SRRTF differ from each other in important ways, including in their mandates, functions, institutional design, and elemental regimes (see table 1). These four intervening IOs stem from three distinct elemental regimes: agriculture and food (FAO), humanitarian assistance (WFP), and human rights (OHCHR, SRRTF). They vary considerably in their functions and mandates (K. Abbott and Snidal 1998): the FAO's core function is to collect and disseminate information and provide technical assistance; the WFP's primary function is to deliver international food aid; the OHCHR's function is to elaborate human rights norms and support treaty implementation; and the SRRTF's function is to promote the human right to food. They also vary in the nature of their membership (i.e., whether universal or exclusive) (Koremenos, Lipson, and Snidal 2001): the FAO, for example, has universal membership with 194 member states, whereas the WFP Executive Board is composed of 36 rotating members that include both food aid donors and recipients. These IOs also vary in terms of their size and resources (Haftel and Thompson 2006; Bauer and Ege 2016; Heldt and Schmidtke 2017), how they are financed (Bayram and Graham 2017), their maturity (Eilstrup-Sangiovanni 2020), and whether they hold observer status at the target IO (Orsini 2013). As these cases show, intervention can be undertaken by IOs with both very large (WFP) and very small (SRRTF) budgets, IOs with large (WFP) and small (OHCHR) numbers of staff, and IOs that are comparatively older (FAO) and newer (OHCHR). These cases therefore suggest that intervention behavior is not limited to a specific type of IO but is undertaken by a diverse range of IOs.

Authority and Legitimacy across Organizational Boundaries

Critical to an IO secretariat's ability to alter the trajectory of decision-making at a partially overlapping institution is that its authority be recognized as legitimate by (at least some of) the members of the target IO. Otherwise, an intervening IO is less likely to be seen as credible and to

TABLE 1. Institutional design features of the FAO, WFP, OHCHR, and SRRTF

IO	Mandate	Function(s)	Number of staff	Annual budget ($US, 2020)	Observer status to WTO	Maturity (year created)
FAO	Reduce hunger and improve agricultural production	Produce, collect, and disseminate information; provide technical assistance	4,000	$2.9 billion	Yes	1945
WFP	Provide emergency food relief	Coordinate and deliver international food aid	17,000	$8.4 billion	Yes	1961
OHCHR	Promote and protect human rights	Elaborate norms; set standards; implement treaties	1,200	$340 million	No	1993
SRRTF	Promote the human right to food	Monitor and report on compliance with human rights treaties	<5	<$50,000	No	2000

have its demands taken seriously. Unlike the authority of states, which is premised on the collective acceptance of their right to rule (Hurd 1999; Lake 2010), the authority of IOs is based on other actors recognizing them as competent and deferring to their judgment (Steffek 2003; Zürn 2018; Tallberg and Zürn 2019; Kustermans and Horemans 2021). IOs enjoy multiple sources of authority that enable them to tell others "what is the right thing to do" and to seek deference (Barnett and Finnemore 2004, 20), the most prominent sources being their *delegated authority*, which comes from the authority "on loan" from states that put them in charge to solve particular problems; their *moral (or principled) authority* in being able to claim to uphold widely accepted principles and values and/or present themselves as acting on behalf of the interests of the international community; and their *expert authority*, based on their specialized knowledge and competences in a given issue area (Barnett and Finnemore 2004, 20–25; see also Joachim, Reinalda, and Verbeek 2007; F. Biermann and Siebenhüner 2009; Avant, Finnemore, and Sell 2010).

Since an intervening IO is not "in authority" at the target IO, it must engage in practices of *legitimation*, that is, communicating and justifying its actions to others (Zaum 2013; Ecker-Ehrhardt 2018; von Billerbeck 2019). First, an intervening IO must legitimate its choice to enter the politics of decision-making at the target IO, since in most cases it will lack a formal say in decision-making within that institution. Second, an intervening IO must justify its particular position regarding the prospective decision at the target IO; it must explain to states why the prospective decision is incorrect and/or why an alternative choice would be more appropriate. When seeking to legitimize its actions, the intervening secretariat is likely to draw on one or more sources of authority. An intervening secretariat may, for example, claim the right to be heard at the target IO by referring to its delegated authority when it views itself as having some responsibility for the issue under decision. Or a secretariat may justify its intervention on the basis of its expert authority by claiming it is more knowledgeable about the issue at hand and therefore better able to identify the full consequences of the prospective decision at the target IO than the decision-making states themselves.

In addition to justifying its right to intervene, legitimation by the intervening IO can serve another purpose: to guard against, preempt, or lessen potential backlash from states. States have heterogenous interests, and by intervening an IO is likely to challenge the interests of certain states, which will come to be dissatisfied by its actions. We would expect that states whose interests are directly threatened should be more likely to express dissatisfaction with, and engage in efforts to delegitimize, an intervening IO (Zürn, Binder, and Ecker-Ehrhardt 2012; Dingwerth and Witt 2019; Yang 2021). Dissatisfied states may respond to the intervening IO's efforts to influence decision-making by questioning the appropriateness of its actions and its credibility to speak on the issue or by accusing it of mission creep to diminish its legitimacy. Its own legitimation efforts may thus help to insulate an intervening IO from such criticism or to minimize the severity of backlash from states. The intervening secretariat, however, need not successfully legitimate its action in the eyes of *all* member states at the target IO. It may need only to justify its actions to some, or a particular group of, states in order to generate sufficient support and ensure that the balance of opinion is in its favor (Symons 2011). IOs may also seek to legitimate their actions to other audiences beyond their member states and/or those of the target IO to further shore up their credibility and insulate themselves from backlash, including NGOs, expert communities, other IOs, the media, and the public (Halliday, Block-Lieb, and Carruthers 2010; Bexell 2014; Ecker-Ehrhardt 2018).

Conditions for Intervention by IOs

The existence of a regime complex characterized by partially overlapping authority among IOs is a necessary precondition for intervention. I propose four additional, cumulative requirements for intervention to occur. These requirements are:

1. The IO secretariat has capabilities for undertaking independent political action;

2. The IO secretariat has access to information about anticipated decision-making at the partially overlapping organization;

3. The IO secretariat expects that a decision taken at the partially overlapping organization will have negative consequences; and

4. The IO secretariat makes an independent choice—that is, not one ordered by its member states—to undertake political action to alter the course of decision-making at the partially overlapping organization.

I discuss each of these criteria in turn.

First, the capacity for independent action by an IO is essential for intervention. This means that an IO secretariat not only expresses its own preferences but also has the capabilities and will to undertake independent action in pursuit of its preferences. States delegate authority to IOs to carry out specialized tasks on their behalf and empower them to achieve their mandates and missions, such as by granting secretariats the power to enforce international agreements or discretion to allocate moneys. Secretariats may draw on various forms of material and ideational capabilities to pursue their own agendas and influence policy outcomes. IO secretariats vary considerably in their scope for independent action and the material and ideational capabilities at their disposal (Haftel and Thompson 2006; Heldt and Schmidtke 2017; Ege, Bauer, and Wagner 2019). The intervening IO secretariat must have a sufficient degree of independence in order to have the capacity to intervene.

Second, an IO secretariat will be unable to intervene if it is unaware of relevant decisions taken in other parts of the regime complex. Intervention occurs *prior* to a decision being made at the target IO, when there is still a window of opportunity for a secretariat to influence the decision trajectory. A secretariat must therefore have information about the anticipated decision in order to intervene. Secretariats routinely monitor developments at other IOs that operate in similar or overlapping policy domains (R. Biermann and Koops 2017; Zhao 2020), which can alert them to relevant anticipated decisions. A secretariat can also learn about anticipated decisions through formal informational exchanges, as is the case when secretariats enjoy reciprocal observer status with the overlapping organization, or through other channels such as epistemic communities and professional networks (P. Haas 1989; Jinnah 2014; Littoz-Monnet 2017a; Hannah, Ryan, and Scott 2017). IOs can also invest resources to scan their environments and detect relevant information about overlapping organizations (Martin 2006; Dijkstra 2015).

A third criterion for intervention is that an IO secretariat expects that an anticipated decision at a partially overlapping organization will have negative consequences. How a secretariat evaluates an anticipated decision and whether it interprets the consequences as positive or negative are partially subjective and filtered through the lens of its social purpose and organizational culture. A secretariat must evaluate a prospective decision and judge it as harmful to consider intervening; this would include decisions that it views as undermining its core goals and/or as against the interests and values of the international community it is tasked to uphold. We would not expect a secretariat to seek to alter a decision that it views as positive or beneficial, or to intervene in a decision that it sees as neutral or inconsequential, or negative but only mild or moderate in its effects.

Fourth, the secretariat must independently choose to initiate an intervention, which requires deliberation by the executive head and/or senior officials to evaluate the expected harm caused by the anticipated decision, the costs of intervention, and the likelihood of success. Intervention inevitably comes at a cost for secretariats because it requires expending scarce financial and human resources and will therefore at the very least always entail an opportunity cost. Intervention also carries the risk of potential reputational and legitimacy costs and/or punitive measures (e.g., budget cuts, dismissals, mandate shrinkage, membership exits) from dissatisfied states. The secretariat must weigh the potential costs of intervention against the potential benefits, while also attempting to assess the likelihood of success. Since intervention is costly for IOs, a secretariat must be convinced that the anticipated decision will cause sufficient harm to warrant intervention and that it has a realistic chance of successfully altering the decision. It is reasonable to assume that if the secretariat determines that there is little or no chance of success, or that the costs of intervention exceed the benefits, it will not intervene.

In sum, a secretariat takes numerous factors into account in choosing whether to intervene at another IO in a regime complex. Any choice to intervene will involve careful deliberation. Given these conditions, and the potential costs and risks to secretariats from intervening, it is reasonable to expect that intervention will be an episodic rather than constant occurrence in regime complexes.

Intervention Strategies

Drawing on analysis of the regime complex for food security, I identify four distinct intervention strategies that can be utilized by IOs: (1) mobilizing states; (2) public shaming; (3) invoking alternative legal frameworks, and (4) taking sides. Each intervention strategy encapsulates different forms of deliberate and purposeful action by an IO secretariat and requires it to draw on multiple sources of authority and expend some combination of material, ideational, and/or symbolic resources. A secretariat will choose the intervention strategy that it believes has the greatest chance of success, best corresponds with its existing capabilities, and/or minimizes political backlash. These intervention strategies are not mutually exclusive, as a secretariat could feasibly utilize two or more strategies simultaneously, or sequentially, depending on the situation and constraints it faces. Nor is this necessarily an exhaustive list of intervention strategies; rather, it is intended as a starting point for understanding the political behavior of IOs in regime complexes.

Mobilizing states occurs when the intervening secretariat enrolls member states of the target IO and steers them toward actions intended to alter the outcome of decision-making. Working with and through member states in the target IO—who have the right to debate and vote on decisions there—provides the intervening secretariat with a means to influence the decision-making process in an organization over which it has no direct control. Mobilizing states involves the intervening secretariat taking an unsolicited and de facto leadership role in coordinating states to enhance their bargaining effectiveness, engaging in problem definition and proposing policy solutions, and devising political strategy to advance their shared objectives. Mobilizing states at the target IO is possible because behind most decisions is a heterogeneity of state preferences and varying power capabilities (Nielson and Tierney 2003; Hawkins et al. 2006; Haftel and Thompson 2006). The intervening secretariat can enlist dissatisfied states at the target IO by offering strategies to alter the anticipated decision, specialized information, and resources (such as staff time, capacity, and expertise) to help achieve their mutual goals. Such leadership will be especially attractive for less well resourced or weaker states at the target IO. It is reasonable to expect that states will agree to defer to, and be steered by, the intervening secretariat if they believe that doing so will enhance their political effectiveness and ability to influence the decision-making process. Mobilizing member states of the target IO to obtain a channel to influence decision-making is distinct from situations when IOs build coalitions with actors such as NGOs to raise issue awareness (Gómez-Mera 2016). Mobilizing states is also different from orchestration by IOs (K. Abbott and Snidal 2010), since the intervening secretariat enrolls states rather than nonstate actors, and its goal is to alter a decision at a partially overlapping organization rather than to collaborate with other organizations to achieve joint goals.

Public shaming involves the intervening secretariat exerting its moral authority to present the prospective decision at the target IO as a violation of appropriate behavior, with the intervening secretariat positioning itself as the defender of the values of the international community. Public shaming has similarities to the practice of "naming and shaming" by the UN and NGOs to bring attention to a state's violation of international norms and urge reform (Lebovic and Voeten 2006; Hafner-Burton 2008; Sharman 2009; Adler-Nissen 2014). But in the context of intervention, public shaming involves the intervening secretariat presenting a *collective decision* by the member states of the target IO as unethical and wrong, rather than singling out a particular state. The purpose of public shaming is to generate international opprobrium against the anticipated decision at the target IO in order to pressure its member states to change course. To carry out this intervention strategy, the intervening secretariat must articulate and communicate to international audiences why the decision is at odds with a widely held value or values of the international community. Public shaming is predicated on the assumption that most states care about their reputations and international standing (Zarakol 2014; Terman and Voeten 2018; Squatrito, Lundgren, and Sommerer 2019) and may thus be potentially responsive to such criticism.

Invoking alternative legal frameworks occurs when the intervening secretariat claims that the anticipated decision at the target IO is likely inconsistent with, or in violation of, existing international law. Invoking an alternative legal framework is distinct from an intervening secretariat taking formal juridical action, such as bringing a case to an adjudicating body. Instead, an intervening secretariat invokes an alternative legal framework when its purpose is to create the *perception* of potential rule inconsistency and thereby to put the question of the legal implications of the anticipated decision up for political debate at the target IO. Creating a perception of potential rule inconsistency may lead to uncertainty among the members of the target IO about whether the decision will result in a violation of their existing commitments under the invoked international agreement or produce a treaty conflict. Given that states favor being in compliance with their international legal obligations (Simmons 2000) and that resolving treaty conflicts is "notoriously difficult" (Raustiala and Victor 2004, 300), the uncertainty created by invoking an alternative legal framework may prompt states to revisit the correctness of the decision. This intervention strategy makes most sense when all or the majority of the members of the target IO are parties to and bound by legal commitments under the invoked agreement.

Taking sides involves the intervening secretariat publicly endorsing the position of a state or group of states concerning an anticipated decision at the target IO. The goal of taking sides is for the intervening IO to tilt the balance in favor of the outcome advocated by one side over the other. The mandates of most IOs require secretariats to remain impartial when it comes to the interstate politics of decision-making (K. Abbott and Snidal 1998; Thompson 2006). While IO secretariats do sometimes break with impartiality (Hurd 2002; Rhoads 2016), they usually strive to be seen as impartial because their authority rests on "their ability to present themselves as impersonal and neutral—as not exercising power but instead serving others" (Barnett and Finnemore 2004, 22). The perception that IOs are impartial actors serving the common good means that their actions carry significant symbolic weight when they decide to intervene in favor of one side or outcome over another. Such actions serve to present that outcome as better for the international community and thus the appropriate way forward, while discrediting others. In practice, taking sides can involve an intervening secretariat expressing its solidarity with, or formally endorsing, the position taken by one group of states at the target IO. An intervening IO secretariat can also take sides by expressing its disagreement with a position taken by a group of states, even if it does not take steps to formally endorse the opposing group's position. An intervening secretariat can draw on its delegated, expert, and/or moral authority to make claims about why the position of one set of states at the target IO is more appropriate and consistent with the values and preferences of the international community.

The Impacts of Intervention by IOs

Intervention has an impact on the decision-making process of the target IO when it influences discourse, agenda setting, and/or outcomes, which are standard measures of influence in global governance institutions (Keck and Sikkink 1998; Barnett and Duvall 2005; Ege, Bauer, and Wagner 2019).

Influencing *discourse* refers to the ability of an intervening IO to introduce new, or alter existing, framings and understandings of a prospective decision at the target IO. Discourse encompasses both the substantive content of ideas and the interactive processes by which ideas are produced and communicated within a given institutional context (Schmidt 2008, 305–7). One of the key roles of IOs is to make the world legible to states by utilizing their expert authority to define and frame global policy problems (Barnett and Finnemore 2004; Oestreich 2007). Discourse and ideas matter because how states understand a global policy problem shapes what kinds of solutions they are likely to view as appropriate and desirable (E. Haas 1990; Risse 2000; Joachim 2003). An intervening IO has an impact on discourse at the target IO when it alters the terms of the debate by influencing the framing of issues and how problems are defined. Discourse is central to global trade rulemaking at the GATT/WTO, where collectively shared understandings of economic and legal ideas drive problem definition and issue framing and shape debate (A. Lang 2011; Strange 2013; Cho 2014; Dingwerth and Weinhardt 2019). Trade scholars have long observed that the material capabilities of states alone do not fully explain global trade rulemaking and that ideas play an important role (Goldstein 1988; Wolfe 1998; Daugbjerg and Swinbank 2009; Siles-Brügge 2014). Influencing discourse at the GATT/WTO may involve an intervening IO challenging existing conceptions of a problem/decision; reframing how prospective trade rules and their consequences are understood by trade negotiators by introducing alternative understandings that are taken up by states; and defining a new and previously unrecognized problem that states come to recognize as in their interests to address.

Influence over *agenda setting* is defined as the ability of an intervening IO to successfully insert, block, or remove issues from the decision-making process at the target IO. *Agenda setting* refers to the process of delimiting the range of issues under consideration by the member states of an IO (Keck and Sikkink 1998; H. Murphy and Kellow 2013). Agenda setting is a common feature in most IOs that design and implement international policies and rules. It is an especially important part of the decision-making process of the GATT/WTO, because through agenda setting states determine what trade issues will be included or excluded from formal bargaining. In this way, agenda setting sets the stakes at play in multilateral trade negotiations and directly shapes the range of possible negotiating outcomes (Steinberg 2002; Albin and Young 2012). In practice it is difficult even for states to get an issue on the negotiating agenda, because securing agreement on the agenda requires consensus among all of the WTO's 164 member states. The agenda-setting stage of the negotiation process is therefore often dominated by powerful states and large single-issue bargaining coalitions (Narlikar 2003; Hawthorne 2013; Singh and Gupta 2016). An IO influences the trajectory of global trade rulemaking at the GATT/WTO if its intervention has the effect of adding or barring issues from the negotiating agenda.

The *outcome* of decision-making by states is typically some type of formal agreement, such as an international treaty or binding commitments. An intervening IO influences the outcome of decision-making when it shapes the substantive content of the official agreement negotiated among states at the target IO. In other words, despite lacking a formal seat at the bargaining table, the intervening IO manages to have a hand in influencing the "output" of bargaining among states. Not all interstate bargaining processes are identical, and therefore what constitutes an outcome, and how to assess the influence of IO intervention on that outcome, will vary. One approach to assess an intervening IO's impact on outcomes at the target IO is to determine whether the resulting agreement incorporates the preferences or goals advocated by the intervening IO and/or to demonstrate that states altered the substantive content of the agreement in response to action taken by an intervening IO. In the case of the GATT/WTO, the purpose of multilateral trade negotiations is for states to conclude an international trade agreement that sets out new global trade rules. Therefore, in the context of global trade rulemaking at the GATT/WTO, an intervening IO can be said to influence the negotiation outcomes if its self-initiated action shapes the substantive content of a GATT/WTO trade agreement. An IO influences the outcome of trade negotiations when its intervention steers states to either construct new trade rules or modify or abandon proposed trade rules. Notably, outcomes at the WTO—in the form of new multilateral trade rules and agreements—have been relatively limited over the past twenty years. Amid intense interstate conflict over the substance of global trade rules, WTO negotiations have been beset by repeated stalemate, evident most strikingly in the collapse of the Doha Round (Schwab 2011; Hopewell 2020). WTO negotiations have continued, however, primarily focused on narrower, more targeted agreements, and do periodically result in the creation of new trade rules (R. Wilkinson, Hannah, and Scott 2016).

The success of intervention and its effects on decision-making at the target IO will of course vary. This book will demonstrate that intervention by UN actors has had meaningful impacts on the global trade rulemaking process at the GATT/WTO. The interventions undertaken by the FAO, WFP, OHCHR, and SRRTF altered the trajectory of decision-making at the GATT/WTO by influencing the discourse, agenda setting, and/or outcomes of trade negotiations.

Conclusion

This chapter has developed the concept of intervention to capture a new type of behavior by IOs in contexts of overlapping authority in global governance. Drawing on the scholarship on IOs as actors, I argue that IOs are not just part of the architecture of regime complexes but important actors in their own right. Overlapping authority in global governance is creating situations where decisions made at one IO can have negative spillover effects for other IOs in a regime complex. An IO may respond to these situations by seeking to intervene in decision-making at an overlapping IO. Intervention differs from traditional conceptualizations of IO interaction such as cooperation and competition because it involves an IO seeking to insert itself into the politics of decision-making by states at another IO in order to influence a specific outcome there. An IO may be prompted to intervene at an overlapping institution when it expects that a decision by states will have negative consequences for the international community. The decision to intervene is thus driven by the social purpose and organizational culture of the intervening IO, which informs how it interprets the potential consequences of a prospective decision at the target IO.

Importantly, intervention is self-initiated by an IO secretariat, rather than taken at the behest of states. It is thus potentially costly to an IO because it may be viewed by states as unwanted political interference and may provoke backlash. Intervention is therefore not likely to be undertaken lightly by an IO but only after careful consideration of the costs, benefits, and likelihood of success. Since the intervening IO does not have control over, or direct involvement in, decision-making at the target IO, it must develop distinct strategies—such as mobilizing states, public shaming, invoking alternative legal frameworks, and taking sides—to exert influence at the target IO. To assess the effects of intervention, it is necessary to show that the strategies employed by the intervening IO resulted in a meaningful change in the discourse, agenda, or outcomes of decision-making at the target IO. The next chapter analyzes the emergence of the regime complex for food security, which has created the conditions for interventions by UN organizations seeking to alter the trajectory of global trade rulemaking at the GATT/WTO. In subsequent chapters, I analyze the intervention strategies undertaken taken by the FAO, WFP, OHCHR, and SRRTF in an effort to influence agricultural trade negotiations and assess their impacts on discourse, agenda setting, and outcomes at the GATT/WTO.

CHAPTER 2

The Regime Complex for Food Security

A KEY TRANSFORMATION IN the global governance of food security has been the transition from a postwar international regime for food security, characterized by a set of IOs with a shared goal to end hunger, to a regime complex for food security composed of overlapping IOs with divergent goals and different understandings of food security as a global policy problem. The WTO, with its expanded authority over agriculture and food policy, is a powerful institution in the regime complex for food security. The central goal of the WTO is to liberalize international agricultural trade. Although its binding rules can have significant implications for world food security, achieving food security is not a stated goal or priority of the WTO. Concerns that WTO rules can result in significant negative consequences for food security have been the key drivers leading UN actors to seek to influence the trajectory and outcomes of global trade rulemaking. This chapter analyzes how the transition from an international regime to a regime complex for food security has created the conditions for interventions by the FAO, WFP, OHCHR, and SRRTF at the GATT/WTO.

The International Regime for Food Security

The fight against hunger has been a long-standing area of international cooperation and institution building since the Second World War. The war decimated food production in European and Asian countries. Famine accounted for over eighteen million deaths during the war, and the specter of future famines was a pressing social and political concern (Jachertz and Nützenadel 2011). The Allied nations recognized that ensuring adequate food supplies was essential not just to winning the war but also to maintaining the peace (Wilson 1980). A major focus of postwar efforts was thus the reorganization of international food production and trade to improve nutrition levels and facilitate European and Asian economic reconstruction (Staples 2006).

It was in this context that US president Franklin D. Roosevelt convinced the Allied nations in 1945 to establish the FAO, the first agency of what was to become the UN system, to coordinate the world's food supplies and eliminate hunger. The creation of the FAO ushered in an international regime for food security to govern how food was produced and distributed at the world scale. International regimes are defined as "sets of implicit or explicit principles, norms, rules, and decision-making procedures around which actors' expectations converge in a given area of international relations" (Krasner 1982, 186). John Ruggie (1982, 382) famously argued that the utility of international regimes as a concept is that it forces scholars not only to think about the forms that international institutions take but also to examine the ways in which they represent "a fusion of power with legitimate social purpose." A fusion of power and social purpose was evident in the international regime for food security. The regime was led and underwritten by the US, which emerged after the Second World War as the world's greatest power as well as the largest food producer and exporter (Parotte 1983; Friedmann and McMichael 1989; McMichael 1994). The regime's social purpose was to end hunger. Policy makers and experts at the time believed such a goal was imminently attainable because of advances in the science of nutrition and their sense that the successful experiments by the Allied nations in wartime food planning could be feasibly expanded to operate at the world scale (Staples 2003; L. Phillips and Ilcan 2003; Jachertz and Nützenadel 2011).

The international regime for food security had distinguishable principles, norms, and rules that shaped and guided the behavior of actors and international policy making. The principles were reflected in a shared understanding among policy makers that the central food security problem facing the world was inadequate food production and that fighting hunger was both a political and moral imperative (Grigg 1997; J. O'Brien 2000). The guiding norm of the international regime for food security was that states had an obligation to avoid the starvation of their populations and those of other nations (Hopkins and Puchala 1978). States were also expected to intervene in national and international food markets to stabilize production and prices (Friedmann and McMichael 1989; Coleman 1998). The rules for prescriptive action were enshrined in two key practices: the redistribution of food from surplus to deficit countries and the transfer of agricultural knowledge and technology by the West to developing countries (Perkins 1997; Cullather 2004).

The international regime for food security had three major international policy objectives: food affordability, price stability, and abundant supply. First, affordable food was intended to raise world food consumption and nutrition levels. Ensuring cheap food in developing countries was also intended to free up other national resources for industrialization and development (Byerlee 1987). Second, price stability was seen by policy makers as central to preventing a return to the "starve thy neighbor" food policies of the interwar period when states had frequently turned to food export bans that resulted in acute food shortages for other food-importing nations. Stable food prices were seen as essential to ensuring orderly international markets and providing farmers with economic incentives to invest in future production (Jachertz and Nützenadel 2011, 108–9). Last, abundant food supplies on the international market were intended to provide a physical food security guarantee to food-deficit countries such as Japan and other client states of the West (Kodras 1993). Abundant food supplies could also be used to smooth variations in world food demand and supply, as well as to make international food aid readily available for famine relief (Uvin 1992).

Over time, states created a number of IOs to help achieve these international policy goals. First and foremost was the FAO, which was the focal institution in the international regime for food security and served several key functions—ranging from offering a forum for intergovernmental policy making, to providing developing countries with technical assistance, to producing information on world food production and consumption (Staples 2006; Shaw 2007). Alongside the FAO, the WFP was created in 1961 to coordinate the delivery of international food aid from food-surplus to food-deficit nations (Ross 2011; Clapp 2012). The international regime for food security was not, however, limited to the FAO and WFP—the so-called Rome-based UN food agencies—but was also populated by other IOs actively working in the field of food security. This included, for instance, the International Grains Council (IGC), created in 1949 to stabilize the price of wheat—a key food staple in many countries—by coordinating international production levels and prices and by overseeing government-to-government wheat sales (Cohn 1979), and the Consultative Group on International Agricultural Research (CGIAR), which was established in 1971 to direct a network of international crop research centers and to coordinate the transfer of high-yield seed varieties to developing countries (Cullather 2007).[1] While the international regime for food security was constituted by multiple, functionally differentiated institutions, these IOs nonetheless shared the same overarching social purpose: to fight hunger. Despite their different institutional affiliations, the staff of these organizations shared a common professional and scientific understanding of hunger as an international policy problem and of the appropriate set of policies to improve world food consumption and nutrition levels (L. Phillips and Ilcan 2003; Staples 2003).

Shared norms, principles, and policy goals did not mean, however, that the international regime for food security operated without political discord. While the international community was in agreement that ending hunger and ensuring food affordability, price stability, and abundant supply were priority objectives, just as in other fields of global governance, states frequently disagreed over the design of specific policy instruments and who would be responsible for paying for them (Talbot and Wayne Moyer 1987; Uvin 1994). A prime reason for this was that states varied widely in their vulnerabilities to food insecurity, depending to a large degree on whether they were net exporters or importers of food, and likewise differed in their expectations of the scope and depth of international cooperation necessary to achieve world food security. The international regime for food security was also shaped by changes in the external environment, in particular the North-South politics of the Cold War era and efforts by developing countries to establish a New International Economic Order, which led to the politicization of food policy (Weiss and Jordan 1976; Talbot 1982). International political discord served to constrain IOs such as the FAO, WFP, and CGIAR, whose staff had to navigate interstate disagreements over the direction of international food policy, as well as over how much authority should be delegated to IOs (Shaw 2007).

The Regime Complex for Food Security

Starting in the 1990s, the international regime for food security was supplanted by a regime complex for food security. Regime complexes are composed of overlapping international institutions with authority in a particular issue area. Unlike international regimes, which are characterized by shared norms and goals, regime complexes may be constituted by a set of international institutions with divergent, even contradictory, norms and goals (Alter and Raustiala 2018; Kreuder-Sonnen and Zürn 2020). In contrast to the international regime for food security, the regime complex for food security is composed of overlapping institutions with a wide range of different norms and goals.

The proliferation of international institutions with authority related to world food security led to the emergence of the regime complex for food security (Margulis 2013). An important driver behind this shift was the increased authority for food security both in the trade regime, with new global trade rules governing food security established at the WTO, and in the human rights regime, where the development of new international human rights standards—such as the 1999 General Comment No. 12 on the Right to Adequate Food and the 2004 Voluntary Guidelines to Support the Progressive Realization of the Right to Food—made human rights an increasingly important legal framework for food security policy making and advocacy.

Several features distinguish the regime complex for food security from the previous international regime for food security. First, the current regime complex for food security is very dense and constituted by a far larger number of IOs than the international regime for food security. This institutional proliferation has included both established IOs whose mandates have been expanded to include aspects of food security policy, such as the WTO, and the creation of new institutions with authority in this area, such as the SRRTF (Shaw 2007; Fukuda-Parr and Orr 2014). Second, the regime complex for food security is constituted by a more diverse range of IOs. Whereas the international regime for food security largely consisted of IOs from the agriculture and food regime and the development regime, the regime complex for food security also includes IOs from the trade regime (i.e., the WTO), the human rights regime (e.g., the OHCHR), and the climate change regime (e.g., the UNEP), among others (Margulis 2013; Orsini and Godet 2018; Breitmeier et al. 2020).

Third, institutional proliferation has produced a regime complex composed of IOs with different goals and orientations toward food security. Whereas ending hunger is the primary goal of IOs such as the FAO, WFP, and CGIAR, this is not the case for many other IOs now part of the regime complex for food security. The primary goal of the OHCHR, for instance, is to promote the protection of human rights. Ensuring that states do not violate their citizens' right to food is just one among a plethora of civil, political, economic, cultural, and social rights that the OHCHR is responsible for monitoring and advocating. Food security has also been recently integrated into the work of IOs from the climate change regime, such as the UNEP and the Intergovernmental Panel on Climate Change (IPCC) (Newell, Taylor, and Touni 2018). This is due in large part to new knowledge about climate change as a threat to the stability of global food production (IPCC 2019). Yet food security is just one of a myriad of pressing environmental concerns that compete for attention, resources, and collective action in global environmental politics (Clapp and Scott 2018). For many of the IOs in the regime complex for food security, including the WTO, ending hunger is not therefore necessarily their primary goal.

An illustration of the regime complex for food security is presented in figure 2. Selected IOs with partially overlapping authority spanning their home elemental regimes and the regime complex for food security are depicted. While the figure displays only formal and informal IOs, such as the G7 and G20, many nonstate actors are also active in the regime complex for food security but not depicted here. NGOs and business actors are, for example, formally involved in the policy-making process at the UN Committee on World Food Security (CFS) (Duncan 2015); they also assist the WFP with logistical planning and the delivery of international food aid in emergency situations.

FIGURE 2. The regime complex for food security (selected IOs)

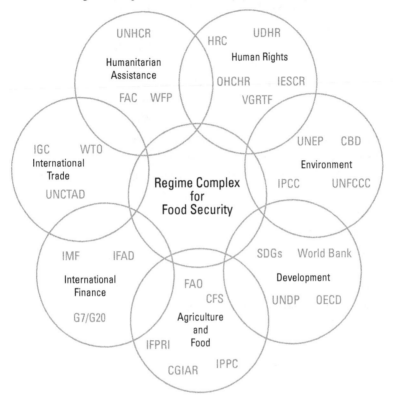

Diverse Goals and Policy Incoherence

That the regime complex for food security is constituted by overlapping IOs with diverse goals is crucial for understanding the political dynamics that drive intervention behavior by IOs in this issue area. Recall that regime complexes generate their own system-like dynamics and that decisions taken in one IO can result in positive or negative effects for other overlapping IOs (Alter and Meunier 2009). In general, IOs with similar goals are more likely to converge around shared norms, rules, and values. While IOs with similar goals may in some cases disagree on the particular details of policy (Lütz, Hilgers, and Schneider 2019), there is a tendency for them "to minimize uncertainty by promoting similarity and coherence" (Heldt and Schmidtke 2019, 1164). However, regime complexes populated by multiple IOs with distinct goals are less likely to produce coherent outcomes (Keohane and Victor 2011; Morin and Orsini 2014).

While the international regime for food security also featured multiple IOs, these had a shared social purpose and broadly congruent norms, principles, and understandings of world food security as an international policy problem. In sharp contrast, there are now no overarching norms, principles, and understandings to bind together the many overlapping IOs constituting the regime complex for food security. Indeed, the regime complex for food security features IOs with highly differentiated, and sometimes contradictory, understandings of food security as an international policy problem (Maxwell 1990). The FAO and World Bank are a notable example of IOs with contradictory understandings of food security: FAO staff understand the source of food insecurity to be poverty and inequality, whereas, in sharp contrast, World Bank officials view food insecurity as a problem caused by insufficient agricultural production and market liberalization (T. Lang and Barling 2012).

Research on the global governance of food security has shown that diverging goals among overlapping IOs can produce negative outcomes on the ground. Scholars have argued that the existence of overlapping IOs with divergent goals and understandings of food security is a significant source of uncertainty about which IOs are responsible for leading international food policy making, which has contributed to inadequate action to end hunger (Maxwell 1996; Shaw and Clay 1998). Diverging goals among IOs with responsibility for food security also produces global policy incoherence and situations where the policies of one IO undermine the efforts of other IOs to fight hunger (Clapp 2009b; Brooks 2014). Legal scholars argue that overlapping IOs with different goals in the field of food security can give rise to rule ambiguity and treaty conflicts (Joseph 2011; Ferguson 2018; H. Johnson 2018). While states have experimented with various approaches to improve functional coherence and coordination among overlapping IOs, including issuing memorandums of understanding and creating new institutional structures, such as the UN High-Level Task Force for Global Food and Nutrition Security, the regime complex for food security nonetheless lacks a centralizing meta-authority to arbitrate between overlapping IOs with distinct goals or to settle resulting policy incoherence or potential treaty conflicts. What this book demonstrates is that diverging goals among IOs in a regime complex can also lead to the phenomenon of intervention. Intervention behavior by IOs targeting the GATT/WTO has been a striking feature of the regime complex for food security.

The WTO in the Regime Complex for Food Security

Prior to the creation of the WTO in 1995, the multilateral trading system was not part of the international regime for food security. For most of the history of the multilateral trading system, agriculture was effectively excluded from global trade rules because of resistance by the US and EU to the idea of reducing farm protection.[2] The situation changed with the launch of the GATT Uruguay Round of multilateral trade negotiations in 1986, after the US and EU decided to end their decade-long "farm war" of competitive subsidization and to establish more liberal agricultural trade (Wolfe 1998). This dramatic reversal in the US and EU's position on agricultural trade liberalization was driven by both material and ideational factors. The farm war was a significant fiscal drain on US and EU coffers (Thies 2001). US spending on agricultural subsidies increased fivefold between 1980 and 1986 to reach $26 billion (Paarlberg 1997, 419). The EU doubled its farm spending in the early 1980s to compete with the US, which plunged it into a severe budgetary crisis (Daugbjerg and Swinbank 2009).

While agricultural subsidies had been previously seen as being in the national interest, by the 1980s policy makers took a very different view of the issue (Lake 1989; Goldstein 1993). The ascent of neoliberalism as a policy paradigm, with its emphasis on fiscal conservatism and limited government intervention in the economy, was well under way (Winders 2004). By the 1980s, policy makers overwhelmingly came to see agricultural subsidies as distorting self-regulating markets and as an irresponsible use of scarce national resources (Coleman 1998; Skogstad 2008; Daugbjerg and Swinbank 2009). This was reflected in the drive to establish the WTO, with the goal of liberalizing international trade along market-oriented principles, by limiting state intervention and regulatory practices that were perceived to act as barriers to free trade (Krueger 1998; Chorev 2005).

While its predecessor, the GATT, had focused on liberalizing trade in industrial goods, the creation of the WTO marked a dramatic expansion in the scope and depth of global trade rules to cover many other economic sectors—such as agriculture, investment, intellectual property rights, and services—as well as to govern trade beyond the border and to regulate domestic policies (Sell 2003; Woll 2008). In creating the WTO, states made it one of the most powerful institutions in global governance, with its legally binding rules backed by a dispute settlement mechanism that acts effectively as a world trade court (Goldstein and Martin 2000; Srinivasan 2007; Shaffer, Elsig, and Puig 2017). Its wide economic coverage and powerful rules mean that decisions taken by states at the WTO have significant distributional consequences, creating economic winners and losers (Steinberg 2002; Wade 2003). Many believe, for example, that developing countries' weaker bargaining position in the Uruguay Round resulted in an unbalanced agreement skewed against their interests (Finger and Nogués 2001; Ostry 2002; Bukovansky 2010).

The WTO introduced extensive rules governing international agricultural trade and food security policy. Under the Uruguay Round AoA, states agreed to convert all nontariff agricultural barriers into tariffs. Developed countries were required to reduce their overall agricultural tariffs by 36 percent, while developing countries had a lower reduction commitment of 24 percent. Moreover, the AoA went far beyond tariff reductions. It also phased out and prohibited many types of long-used domestic and export agricultural subsidies, forcing states to cut their overall level of trade-distorting support and to shift their farm spending to less trade- and production-distorting programs. In addition, the rules of the AoA regulate many international food security policies, such as the provision of food aid, as well as domestic food security policies, including programs that provide free or subsidized food to food-insecure populations (e.g., the US food stamps program), support for small and resource-poor farmers in developing countries, and public food stockholding, which is often used to minimize countries' vulnerability to global price and supply shocks (Margulis 2017; Nakuja 2018; Ito 2020). States intended the AoA to be the first step in a larger process of agricultural trade liberalization. Article 20 ("Continuation of the Reform Process") of the AoA required WTO members to return to the bargaining table in 1999 in order to negotiate further reductions in agricultural tariffs and subsidies.

Agriculture and food security are two sides of the same coin for most developing countries, where the agricultural sector accounts for a significant portion of employment, food supply, and foreign exchange (A.

Sneyd 2011; Diaz-Bonilla 2014; Graeub et al. 2016). Trade liberalization can have positive or negative consequences for food security, depending on the context. Agricultural trade can, for example, lead to a more secure and reliable food supply, thus enhancing world food security (Gillson and Fouad 2014). Yet trade liberalization may also undermine food security, as when agricultural dumping displaces local food production and rural livelihoods (Watkins and Von Braun 2003; Rosset 2006). While the causal relationship between agricultural trade liberalization and food security has long been debated by economists, policy makers, and global civil society, there is widespread consensus that the AoA restructured patterns of global food production, prices, and trade—all of which directly affect economic and physical access to food by households (McMichael 1993; Guha-Khasnobis, Acharya, and Davis 2007; Clapp 2017). Many studies have demonstrated that WTO rules can impose significant barriers and costs on countries seeking to implement pro–food security policies (Gonzalez 2002; Watkins and Von Braun 2003; Desta 2001; Paasch 2007).

IOs Contesting Global Trade Rules

Although the WTO, because of its binding hard law and enforcement mechanism, may be considered a powerful IO in the regime complex for food security, ending hunger is not a priority for the organization. The overriding goal of the WTO is "to help trade flow smoothly, freely and predictably" (WTO 2021). In the area of agriculture, the main objectives for the WTO are set out in the AoA, which are "to establish a fair and market-oriented agricultural trading system" and "provide for substantial progressive reductions in agricultural support and protection sustained over an agreed period of time, resulting in correcting and preventing restrictions and distortions in world agricultural markets" (GATT 1994a, 1). The WTO's focus is thus on liberalizing agricultural trade, which has historically been one of the most protected sectors. Global trade rules recognize that there may be potential conflict between the goals of liberalizing agricultural trade and achieving world food security. The preamble to the AoA recognizes that food security is a "non-trade concern" and envisages situations where WTO rules intended to curb state intervention in food markets may come into tension with policies to promote food security.[3] Yet beyond recognizing that such potential situations may arise, the AoA is vague on what rights states have to deviate from global trade rules in order to address other societal goals such as achieving food security (F. Smith 2000). Despite the power of its rules and their potentially significant consequences for food security, achieving world food security is not written into the WTO's mission or mandate or officially identified as an objective of the institution. It is concerns about the potential of WTO rules to result in significant harm for food security that, I contend, have spurred the FAO, WFP, OHCHR, and SRRTF to seek to intervene in multilateral trade negotiations.

In addition to the power of WTO rules and their potential negative consequences for food security, a related factor that contributes to intervention by UN actors at the GATT/WTO is unequal bargaining power in multilateral trade negotiations. Because of power asymmetries among states, global trade rules are most likely to reflect the interests and preferences of powerful states. Historically, the US, the EU, and other advanced-industrialized states, with their mature, diverse economies and large consumer markets, enjoyed greater bargaining and rule-setting power in multilateral trade negotiations (Kapoor 2004; Conti 2009; Woolcock 2011). Developing countries, which have much smaller economies and markets and which often lack adequate representation in Geneva and technical expertise, have often been marginalized in trade negotiations and far less successful in safeguarding their interests (Finger and Nogués 2001; Hoekman and Kostecki 2001).

Such power asymmetries between developed and developing countries are found in bargaining over trade-related aspects of food security at the GATT/WTO. Food insecurity is a pressing concern for many developing countries, which have a much greater prevalence of hunger and malnutrition among their populations than rich countries and are often dependent on food imports to meet their domestic consumption needs (Baer-Nawrocka and Sadowski 2019). In contrast, many of the most powerful states at the GATT/WTO—such the US, the EU, Canada, and Australia—are also major agricultural producers and exporters, for whom food insecurity is not a priority in negotiating trade agreements. These major agricultural exporters have long dominated multilateral trade negotiations on agriculture and used their bargaining leverage over weaker, developing countries to create trade rules that expanded their access to foreign markets while maintaining high levels of protectionism at home (Watkins 1991; Josling, Tangermann, and Warley 1996). While this pattern has somewhat shifted recently with the rise of emerging powers, such as China and India, that are using their newfound power to protect their food security interests, the potential negative effects of WTO rules for food security remain a major source of disagreement between developed and developing countries at the WTO (A. Sneyd 2015; Singh and Gupta 2016; Scott 2017; Hopewell 2019). The weak bargaining power of food-insecure developing countries at the GATT/WTO can give IO secretariats further impetus to insert themselves into the politics of global trade rulemaking when they expect that such countries will be unable to adequately defend their food security interests in trade negotiations. This may spur IOs to intervene to strengthen the bargaining power of food-insecure states in an effort to steer multilateral trade negotiations toward more pro–food security outcomes.

There are, however, complex fault lines in multilateral agricultural trade negotiations that go beyond a simple North-South divide (Margulis 2014; Hopewell 2019). While developed-country net food exporters like the US, the EU, Canada, and Australia are among the principal demandeurs of agricultural trade liberalization at the GATT/WTO, some developed countries, including Japan, Switzerland, Israel, South Korea, and Norway, are food import dependent and seek greater policy space to protect their food security in the agricultural trade negotiations. Similarly, even though most developing countries are net food importers demanding lesser liberalization commitments in order to pursue domestic food security goals, some developing countries—including Argentina, Brazil, and Thailand—are major agricultural exporters, whose negotiating demands for greater agricultural trade liberalization frequently correspond with those of developed-country exporters. When UN organizations choose to intervene at the GATT/WTO, they must therefore navigate these highly politicized negotiating dynamics, which include divides among both developed *and* developing countries.

Conclusion

This chapter has provided the wider context for understanding why UN actors have chosen to intervene in global trade rulemaking at the GATT/WTO. A major transformation in the global governance of food security has been the emergence of a regime complex for food security beginning in the 1990s that superseded the postwar international regime for food security. While the international regime for food security included institutions that shared an overarching goal to end hunger, the regime complex for food security is composed of overlapping IOs with divergent, and sometimes contradictory, goals. The WTO is a powerful institution in this regime complex and has authority over key areas of international and domestic food security policy. Yet achieving food security is not a priority goal or indeed part of the WTO's mandate. As the following chapters show, the WTO's expanded authority over agriculture and food, and concerns arising from the potential of its rules to have negative effects for world food security, catalyzed the decisions by UN actors to insert themselves directly in the politics of multilateral trade negotiations.

CHAPTER 3

The FAO

Mobilizing States to Protect Food Security

THE FAO HAS REPEATEDLY inserted itself into the politics of global trade rulemaking at the GATT/WTO—in spite of resistance from powerful states—because of concerns that proposed trade rules would worsen food insecurity in food import–dependent developing countries. This chapter analyzes two significant instances of intervention by the FAO secretariat in an effort to shape global trade rules. The first occurred during the GATT Uruguay Round (1986–94) of trade negotiations, which created the WTO and the AoA. The second occurred during the WTO Doha Round negotiations launched in 2001. Both instances involved the FAO secretariat pursuing the intervention strategy of mobilizing states: in the Uruguay Round, the FAO mobilized and led a group of GATT members to insert new trade rules intended to protect food security into the negotiating agenda; in the Doha Round, it mobilized a group of WTO members to push for the creation of a new WTO-based food-financing facility.

These interventions by the FAO secretariat were self-initiated actions and not undertaken at the behest of states. Not only did FAO officials instigate their interventions independently, but they undertook them despite clear pushback from powerful states that sought to prevent the

FAO from interfering in interstate bargaining at the GATT/WTO. The FAO's decision to intervene in multilateral trade negotiations was driven by its social purpose—to end hunger worldwide—and its activist organizational culture. Interventions by the FAO were neither acts of cooperation nor acts of competition with the GATT/WTO. Its interventions targeted global trade rulemaking by states, not the work of the GATT/WTO secretariat. The FAO's actions were not intended to obtain mandates or resources at the expense of the WTO—in fact, just the opposite, the FAO's interventions sought to expand the WTO's role and authority in the global governance of food security.

The FAO's interventions had a meaningful impact on global trade rulemaking. Its intervention in the Uruguay Round was influential in reframing food insecurity as a trade policy issue and putting the issue on the negotiating agenda. Moreover, the FAO's intervention directly shaped the outcome of the agriculture negotiations: FAO officials were the architects of the 1994 WTO Decision on Measures Concerning the Possible Negative Effects of the Reform Programme on Least-Developed and Net Food-Importing Developing Countries—a WTO agreement to safeguard the food security of food import–dependent developing countries. Similarly, the FAO's intervention in the Doha Round was influential in steering WTO members to pursue the creation of a WTO-based multilateral food-financing facility to address the food import bills of developing countries. The FAO also took on a leading role in the design of the facility at the WTO. Although the Doha Round negotiations ultimately collapsed without a final outcome, the FAO's proposal for a WTO-based multilateral food-financing facility continues to shape ongoing deliberations by WTO members about the effects of agricultural trade liberalization on food security.

The chapter is organized as follows. The first section situates the role of the FAO in the global governance of food security and contextualizes its activist organizational culture and views on agricultural trade liberalization. The second section analyzes intervention by the FAO secretariat during the Uruguay Round agriculture negotiations. The next section analyzes intervention by the FAO secretariat in the Doha Round. The final section concludes by assessing the impact of the FAO's interventions to protect food security in multilateral trade negotiations.

The FAO and the Global Governance of Food Security

The FAO is a specialized agency of the UN established in 1945 with the mission of ending world hunger (Wilson 1980; UN Conference on Food and Agriculture 1943). The FAO's mandate is to enhance world nutrition and diets, expand agricultural production, and improve rural living conditions (FAO 1945). As a specialized agency, the FAO is legally independent from the UN and has its own rules, decision-making procedures, membership, and budget.

The FAO's social purpose to end world hunger has shaped the professional identity and actions of its leadership and staff. The FAO's architects and its early directors-general all had professional backgrounds in food policy and believed that advances in nutrition and agricultural science made ending world hunger possible for the first time in human history (Staples 2003, 2006). They were also ardent progressive internationalists who infused the values of international cooperation and scientific management into the FAO's organizational culture (J. O'Brien 2000; L. Phillips and Ilcan 2003; Pernet and Ribi Forclaz 2019). The FAO secretariat has pursued its mission to end hunger with what has been described as a "crusading zeal" (Staples 2006, 106; Jachertz and Nützenadel 2011). Its mission to end hunger continues to strongly shape the FAO's organizational culture, especially the identity and professional values of its staff (Christoffersen et al. 2008, 251–52).

In its first decades, the FAO served as "a global department of agriculture" (Staples 2006, 100). The organization focused its efforts on technical assistance projects in developing countries, such as providing agricultural extension training, mitigating pest and disease outbreaks, supporting plant-breeding research, and diffusing food-processing techniques. In the 1960s, the FAO redefined its role to become a vocal advocate for the world's hungry people (Staples 2006; Shaw 2007). The impetus for this change in the FAO's role came not from its member states but from its then director-general, R. B. Sen (1956–67), who in 1963 launched the Freedom from Hunger Campaign, intended to bring global public attention to the scale of the world hunger problem and put pressure on states to make greater efforts to tackle the problem (Jurkovich 2020).

The FAO has had several other highly activist directors-general who have transformed the organization's role and priorities. These include

Edouard Saouma, who was the director-general between 1976 and 1993, during the period of the FAO's intervention in the Uruguay Round. Saouma, an agricultural engineer by training, began his career in the Lebanese civil service and later gradually worked his way up the FAO's bureaucracy before running for the organization's top position. Saouma was among the longest-serving directors-general in FAO history, and, as such, he had a major influence over the FAO's mission and culture. Among Saouma's main achievements were establishing a network of local FAO offices in over sixty developing countries to increase the organization's presence in the field, prioritizing funding for technical assistance projects to improve agricultural production, and putting environmental issues, such as the overexploitation of fish stocks, onto the FAO's agenda (Davies 2013). Saouma was also well known for his activist and confrontational leadership style. As a vocal supporter of Third Worldism and the New International Economic Order, Saouma enjoyed the backing of most developing-country UN members, but his politics regularly put him at odds with developed countries, the FAO's main donors (Shaw 2007, 235–36). Saouma also launched major policy initiatives without prior consultation or the full consent of the FAO membership (Davies 2013). In his third and final term (1988–93), Saouma openly clashed with key donors such as the US, Canada, and Australia, which had become increasingly dissatisfied with his leadership and, as a result, withheld their membership dues, putting the organization under severe budgetary stress.

The FAO's intervention in the Doha Round occurred during the leadership of Jacques Diouf (1994–2011). Diouf, a Senegalese national and agronomist by training, held various governmental and international diplomatic posts prior to being elected as FAO director-general. Diouf held the position for eighteen years and was successful in bringing greater attention to the scale of the global food insecurity problem, including by organizing a series of high-profile summits. For example, Diouf's 1996 World Food Summit, which was attended by over one hundred world leaders, was instrumental in achieving a consensus definition of food security and resulted in a commitment by FAO members to halve world hunger by 2015, which subsequently led to the establishment of the UN Millennium Development Goals (Christoffersen et al. 2008). As director-general, Diouf also brought a greater focus on gender and South-South technical cooperation to the FAO's work. Diouf also took several positions, such as supporting genetically modified crops and calling for greater cooperation with the private sector, that resulted in heavy criticism by NGOs.

The FAO as a Demandeur of Agricultural Trade Liberalization

While the analysis that follows shows that the FAO secretariat intervened in multilateral trade negotiations because of concerns that proposed trade rules could worsen food security, it would be incorrect to assume that the FAO as an organization is a critic or an opponent of agricultural trade liberalization, or that it sought to challenge neoliberalism like IOs such as UNCTAD (Hannah, Ryan, and Scott 2017) and the WHO (Chorev 2012a). On the contrary, the FAO secretariat was one of the first IOs to urge states to pursue agricultural trade liberalization. In particular, the FAO has called on developed countries to remove their agricultural trade barriers and other forms of protectionism since the late 1960s, well before GATT member states finally agreed to begin addressing agricultural trade protectionism in the Uruguay Round in the 1980s.

The FAO has played an important role in informing global debates about the relationship between agricultural trade and food security. As a knowledge-producing organization that collects and disseminates information on international agricultural trade, the FAO secretariat was the first to identify the trend in the 1970s and 1980s that a large number of developing countries were transitioning from net food exporters to net food importers (Manitra, Iafrate, and Paschali 2011). This was a significant transition because it meant that for an increasing number of developing countries, their food security was now determined less by their own domestic food production than by their ability to pay for imports of staple foods, such as wheat and rice, with foreign exchange earned through the export of cash crops, including coffee, cocoa, sugar, and tropical fruits (FAO 1978). Since 1970, the share of GDP spent on food imports by developing countries had tripled from about 1 percent to 3 percent, meaning that the growth of gross food import bills outstripped overall economic growth in these countries, placing increasing strain on their economic resources (FAO 2004, 17). The FAO also released several landmark studies in the early 1980s that brought international attention to the sharp rise in agricultural trade barriers and farm subsidy spending by developed countries (FAO 1980, 53–57; 1983, 20–25; 1985c, 5–6; 1987g). The FAO's reports provided evidence to show that agricultural trade protectionism by developed countries had resulted in a fall in the export income of developing countries, thus weakening the latter's capacity to pay for food imports critical for food security (FAO 1987g). Through the dissemination of its research, the FAO played an important role in shaping policy makers' understanding of how agricultural trade protectionism in the global North contributed to food insecurity in the global South and in making the case of the potential positive effects that liberalizing trade in agriculture, especially by reducing Northern trade barriers, could have for world food security (Cépède 1984; Shaw 2007).

The FAO was not content only to disseminate information about rising agricultural trade protectionism. The FAO director-general, Edouard Saouma, took a highly public stand against agricultural trade protectionism, calling it "one of the most pernicious developments in the conduct of world trade" (FAO 1983, 2). In particular, he singled out the policies of the US and EU and accused them of willfully disregarding the norms of international trade by putting up trade barriers against developing countries, stating: "Whichever way you look at it, they [developing countries] are the losers. No regulatory mechanism protects them. . . . International trade rules are increasingly flouted and poor countries too often find themselves barred from the markets in developed countries by a panoply of restrictive measures" (FAO 1981, vi). Saouma's message to the world was that agricultural trade protectionism by developed countries weakened developing countries' economies and threatened their food security, and thus violated the values and interests of the international community (FAO 1986a). Saouma's actions broke with the convention that FAO directors-general should remain neutral and not directly criticize the policies of FAO member states. Many developed-country governments, including the US, the EU, Canada, and Australia, took issue with the public criticism of their policies by the FAO director-general (Davies 2013; Jachertz 2014; Schindler 2014). These events deepened developed countries' dissatisfaction with the FAO's activist leadership and prompted them to try to force Saouma out of his position and use the tactic of "reducing, delaying, and withholding [financial] contributions and sporadically issuing exit threats from 1980 onward" to punish the organization (Lall 2017, 270). However, while developed countries paid the lion's share of the FAO's budget, their tightening of the purse strings did not have the desired effect of silencing Saouma or the FAO's critique of agricultural trade protectionism (Talbot and Wayne Moyer 1987; Schindler 2014).

The FAO's Relationship with the GATT/WTO

The FAO secretariat has had a long-standing cooperative relationship with the GATT/WTO secretariat that dates back to the 1950s (R. Phillips 1981, 183; FAO 1989). Historically, the FAO has cooperated with the GATT by providing specialized information on a demand-driven basis to inform deliberations by states on international agricultural trade policy issues. The launch of the Uruguay Round and subsequent creation of the WTO led to a widening and deepening of cooperation among the FAO and WTO secretariats (WTO 1998c). In addition to providing and exchanging information and analysis on agricultural trade policy issues, the FAO supports the WTO secretariat to carry out its core function of monitoring states' compliance with WTO rules, especially in standard setting for the protection of human, animal, and plant health, as well as in protection of intellectual property rights for plant genetic resources (FAO 1997; R. Andersen 2003; WTO 2007c, 2–3). Cooperation among the FAO and WTO secretariats is deepest in the area of food safety and technical barriers to trade, where officials work closely together to organize training workshops for policy makers and co-publish technical reports.

The FAO Intervenes in the GATT Uruguay Round

This section analyzes the intervention by the FAO secretariat in the Uruguay Round of multilateral trade negotiations to safeguard the food security of food import–dependent developing countries. Launched in 1986, the Uruguay Round was intended to remake agricultural trade along market principles and called for the "urgent need to bring more discipline and predictability to world agricultural trade" (GATT 1986, 6). The Uruguay Round was propelled by the momentous decision by the US and EU to put an end to their "farm war" (Josling, Tangermann, and Warley 1996; Paarlberg 1997; Wolfe 1998). By the mid-1980s, the US and EU had put in place massive farm subsidy programs that were intended to artificially boost the competitiveness of their farm sectors but that were widely criticized for destabilizing agricultural trade and prices and were the source of considerable trade tensions with the other major agricultural-exporting countries (Friedmann 1982; Coleman and Tangermann 1999). As a long-standing advocate of agricultural trade liberalization, the FAO secretariat welcomed the prospect of developed countries committing to negotiations to reduce agricultural protectionism (FAO 1985c, vi; 1987g, vi; 1988, v–vi). FAO director-general Saouma, for example, warmly praised the decision by GATT members to launch the Uruguay Round, stating that "GATT talks have given us a slender ray of hope. For the first time ever, [GATT member states] agreed to review some basic problems regarding raw materials, and in particular to discuss the restrictions and distortions affecting agricultural commodities. I welcome this move and have already committed FAO to providing all the assistance, in the form of information and statistics, that may be required to further the discussions" (FAO 1986b, Appendix D). The launch of the GATT Uruguay Round spurred the FAO secretariat to ramp up its production of analytical studies on agricultural trade with the intention of solidifying the scientific case for liberalization.

Developed Countries Attempt to Block the FAO's Involvement in the Negotiations

FAO officials viewed the Uruguay Round agriculture negotiations as a historic opportunity to roll back agricultural trade protectionism and thus improve the economic prospects of developing countries. Eager to ensure that the interests of developing countries were adequately reflected in the negotiations and aware of the historical negotiating weakness of developing countries at the GATT, the FAO secretariat made a request to GATT members for observer status in the agriculture negotiations (FAO 1986a). While the FAO already enjoyed observer status at the GATT Council, this was different—it would allow FAO officials to be present during actual negotiation sessions, which were typically limited to GATT member states. Observer status in the agricultural negotiations would permit FAO officials to be in the room during closed-door bargaining sessions among GATT members, provide them with access to unfiltered information about developments in the negotiations, and put them in a position to monitor bargaining in real time with the ability to directly comment and make suggestions on tabled negotiating proposals. The FAO's request for observer status to the GATT agriculture negotiations was a self-directed act. At no time prior to making this request did FAO or GATT members instruct the FAO secretariat to do so; there is also no evidence that the secretariat consulted states prior to making this request, which was consistent with Saouma's leadership style of taking independent actions often without states' prior approval (Davies 2013).

Many developed countries intensely objected to the FAO's request for observer status in the GATT agriculture negotiations and wanted the GATT membership to reject it outright. They presented various reasons as to why the FAO's request should be refused: Canada, for example, argued that "active involvement in these sensitive negotiations by any multilateral organization is inappropriate" (FAO 1987a, 45), while the US and Australia expressed the view that any involvement by the FAO secretariat in the GATT agriculture negotiations exceeded the organization's mandate (FAO 1987a, 45, 50; 1987c). Saouma was, however, able to secure the support of developing countries. After submitting the request to the GATT, he brought the issue up for debate in the FAO's main governing bodies, the Council and the Conference, where developing countries leveraged their numerical advantage to table and vote in favor of a resolution that called for the FAO secretariat "to play a more active supportive role in the multilateral trade negotiations" and urged "that every opportunity be taken to involve FAO in support of these negotiations" (FAO 1987f, para. 39).

Despite securing this resolution from the FAO's governing bodies endorsing its effort to gain observer status in the Uruguay Round negotiations, the FAO secretariat still faced resistance from developed countries at the GATT, where the final decision to approve its request had to take place. While the FAO had the support of developing-country GATT members, since decision-making in the trade regime is by consensus rather than majority vote, it was not possible for developing-country GATT members to simply impose their preference on developed countries (GATT 1987a, 1; 1987g, 3–4). Instead, the issue of whether IOs should be provided observer status in the agriculture negotiations was added to the GATT agenda and became itself a negotiating item (GATT 1987b, 1987c). Following lengthy talks, GATT members arrived at a compromise. Developed countries agreed to accept the FAO's request for observer status in the agriculture negotiations on the condition that equivalent status be given to other IOs, such as the World Bank and the IMF, in return (GATT 1987d, 1; 1987g, 5–6). Developed countries hoped that the World Bank and the IMF, over which they had strong control, would serve as counterweights to the FAO. In addition, as a result of the compromise reached, FAO officials (as well as officials of other IOs) were expressly forbidden from taking actions that could "prejudice the negotiating positions" of GATT members (GATT 1987g, 5). Given the fierce resistance from powerful states to the FAO's participation in the GATT agricultural negotiations, FAO officials were acutely aware of the risk of backlash from those states if they were seen to be interfering in the negotiations. As a result, when FAO officials did in fact decide to intervene later in the Uruguay Round, they chose to do so quietly, behind the scenes, specifically in order to avoid a direct confrontation with developed countries and reduce the risk of provoking backlash.

Concerns about Higher Future Food Prices

The GATT agriculture negotiations raised big questions about the expected winners and losers from trade liberalization. Many economists and policy makers stressed the financial "dividend" that agricultural trade liberalization promised, which referred to an estimated $200 billion in expected savings to governments, taxpayers, and food buyers from reducing protectionist policies such as agricultural subsidies and tariffs (Goldin and Knudsen 1990, 478). Developing-country agricultural exporters were projected to benefit most from liberalization, reflecting the fact that their economies were the most reliant on the agricultural sector for export earnings, employment, and food security. The World Bank's *World Development Report*, for instance, estimated that developing countries would earn an additional $922 million in export revenue from a reduction in developed countries' tariffs alone (World Bank 1986, 128). The FAO secretariat's own studies similarly projected that lowering developed countries' agricultural trade protections would greatly improve the economic prospects of developing countries (FAO 1985b, 1985a, 1987c, 1987d, 1987e).

As the agriculture negotiation progressed, however, it became evident that the agenda was being fashioned primarily to address the interests of the two most powerful players, the US and EU. Reforms proposed by the US and EU were intended to reduce their agricultural subsidies in order to generate higher prices and incomes for their farmers (Winters 1989, 34–35). But net food-importing developing countries (NFIDCs), which represented 90 of the 124 GATT member states, and which depended on cheap, subsidized Northern foods staples to meet domestic food needs, voiced concerns that proposed reforms could have adverse effects on their food security (Walch 2003, 170). NFIDCs' concerns were supported by a plethora of authoritative studies conducted by the FAO, as well as the World Bank, OECD, International Food Policy Research Institute (IFPRI), and US Department of Agriculture, which predicted that the agriculture negotiations could increase world food prices by as much as 18 percent for wheat, 25 percent for corn, and 21 percent for rice (World Bank 1986, 130–32; FAO 1987d, 21–23; Valdés and Zietz 1987). Indeed, studies suggested that NFIDCs as a group were expected to experience food import cost increases of 25 percent on average,[1] which was regarded at the time as "staggering" for a set of countries that were "already hard-pressed" to afford food imports because of declining terms of trade and high debt levels (T. Hertel 1990, 27). The poorest NFIDCs, for instance, spent between 50 and 80 percent of the foreign exchange earned from exports to import food (FAO 2004, 17). Some studies warned that agricultural trade liberalization under the GATT would therefore lead to higher rates of world hunger (Ballenger and Mabbs-Zeno 1992, 264–65). The expert consensus was that food price increases were likely to be primarily a short-term problem. It was assumed that higher prices would eventually incentivize increased supply and thus lead to a correction of prices. Even though higher food prices were expected to be transitory, FAO officials were nonetheless concerned about the immediate and harmful effects this would have for food-insecure populations in poor, food import–dependent countries.

The Food Price Problem: Framing and Agenda Setting
The potential negative effects of higher food prices for food security were a paramount concern for NFIDCs. These countries wanted the issue added to the agenda of the agriculture negotiations (GATT 1987f, 2, 5; 1987e, 1–4). Yet they faced difficulties getting their concerns onto the negotiating agenda. Although these countries made up the overwhelming majority of the GATT membership, NFIDCs were weak actors in the negotiations. The most powerful players—the US and EU—dominated the negotiating agenda and proposal development process (Steinberg 2002)

Most NFIDCs lacked full-time representation in Geneva and the technical capacity to effectively participate in the negotiations (Narlikar 2003). In addition, NFIDCs had diverse economic interests and lacked political unity to work as a group, which rendered them "incapable of articulating a common line, much less of pursuing it aggressively from a position of strength" (Walch 2003, 170). NFIDCs also had limited economic leverage to offer by way of trade concessions to shape the agenda. They were not in a position to offer to reduce agricultural subsidies, since they were not major users of subsidies (most could not afford them), or to offer greater market access, since most had already undertaken major unilateral tariff cuts as part of IMF-mandated structural adjustment programs. While developed-country negotiators privately acknowledged that NFIDCs could face higher food prices, those countries were primarily concerned with advancing their own economic interests in the negotiations. They accordingly downplayed NFIDCs' concerns by arguing that the potential gains in economic welfare from agricultural trade liberalization would more than offset any potential costs (GATT 1988b; Margulis 2017).

Because of their lack of bargaining power, NFIDCs adopted what Amrita Narlikar (2003, 150–51) has labeled a "strategy of resistance." They tried to disrupt the agriculture negotiations by issuing broad po-litical declarations that presented the GATT agriculture negotiations as a threat to their food security, national sovereignty, and domestic social and political stability (GATT 1988g, 1988a). NFIDCs criticized developed countries for seeking to unfairly shift the costs of liberalization onto them in the form of higher food prices (GATT 1988c, 2). They also threatened to walk away from the agriculture negotiations, stating that food security trumped "other agricultural policy objectives, such as those related to economic efficiency or to the optimal allocation of resources" (GATT 1988h, 5). NFIDCs' strategy of resistance thus focused on engaging in a rhetorical battle with rich countries, rather than in writing and tabling formal, concrete bargaining proposals, which are the main currency of influence in multilateral trade negotiations (Narlikar 2003, 150–53).

The FAO secretariat became increasingly concerned about both the effects of higher food prices on NFIDCs and these countries' weak bar-gaining position in the negotiations. The FAO's own analysis of developed countries' proposals concluded that such reforms, if agreed to, were likely to result in a net decrease in per capita food consumption in NFIDCs, especially among the urban poor (FAO 1987d, 8). Real-world events also gave FAO officials further pause. In 1987 and 1988, the combination of poor harvests in Asia and Europe and drought in the US caused world food prices to increase by 18 percent, which added $3 billion to the food import bill of poor developing countries and resulted in declining levels of food consumption and higher rates of malnutrition (FAO 1990, 5; 1991b,

17). For FAO officials, these events confirmed how vulnerable the food security of the populations of NFIDCs was to spikes in food prices.

In this context, senior FAO officials felt what they described as "a professional and moral responsibility" to take a more active role in the negotiations to protect the food security of NFIDCs.[2] Yet FAO officials were constrained by the requirements imposed by their observer status to the agriculture negotiations, which bound them to remain neutral and not take any action in favor of the position of some GATT members over others. Despite the risk of potential backlash from powerful states for breaking with the principle of neutrality, the FAO secretariat decided to insert itself into the agriculture negotiations at the GATT. This decision was taken by the FAO secretariat without any request or direction from its member states. Senior FAO managers discussed the matter internally and, with the approval of the FAO director-general, made protecting the food security of NFIDCs at the GATT a top priority for the organization (FAO 1991a, 521–22).[3] The FAO was the only nonstate actor that worked actively on creating new global trade rules to address the food price problem in the Uruguay Round negotiations. While NGOs later played an active role in the Doha Round agriculture negotiations, their engagement in the Uruguay Round was far more limited because of a lack of access to, and information about, the negotiations, which limited their ability to influence events, as well as a lack of technical capacity (M. Wilkinson 1996).

In inserting itself into the agriculture negotiations, the FAO chose a pragmatic approach. It decided that its involvement would be strictly behind the scenes in order to avoid a direct confrontation with developed countries. FAO officials concentrated their efforts on using the organization's resources to strengthen the bargaining capacity of NFIDCs at the GATT. To achieve this, the FAO dedicated more staff to work on analysis related to the agriculture negotiations and also stationed its "best and brightest" economist in Geneva in order to coordinate work to support NFIDC trade negotiators.[4] This was not an insignificant investment by the FAO given its dire budget situation at the time, which had almost led the organization to close its Geneva office in order to save desperately needed funds (FAO 1987b, 196). In Geneva, FAO officials organized and led strategy sessions for NFIDC trade negotiators, at which FAO officials presented econometric analyses of the impact of rich countries' proposals and proposed solutions to address the potential problem of higher food import bills (Wyles 1993). NFIDC trade negotiators welcomed the FAO's involvement, knowing that this would enhance their bargaining capacity given their weak position at the GATT.[5]

The FAO's actions went beyond merely providing technical assistance to NFIDC trade negotiators to actually steering their strategy in the negotiations. Until that point, NFIDCs' "strategy of resistance" had held little sway with developed countries and had failed to have any impact on the negotiations or to produce meaningful outcomes (Narlikar 2003). Stepping in, FAO officials provided NFIDCs with an alternative framing of the problem to bring forward in the negotiations: that future higher food prices threatened to create a balance-of-payments problem. In addition, FAO officials encouraged NFIDC trade negotiators to incorporate a demand for additional financing to respond to expected future balance-of-payment problems from higher food prices in the future.[6]

This new framing of the food price problem was first tested by Jamaica, one of the most active NFIDCs in the agriculture negotiations. With input from the FAO, Jamaica tabled a proposal in July 1988 demanding that developed countries provide NFIDCs with "appropriate compensatory measures, including, inter alia, food aid, IMF compensatory financing" if trade reforms eroded their balance-of-payments situation (GATT 1988d). Jamaica's paper was followed by a joint proposal tabled in September 1988 by Egypt, Jamaica, Mexico, Peru, Nigeria, and Morocco—all NFIDCs—which demanded financial compensation to respond to expected future balance-of-payments problems caused by higher food prices (GATT 1988e, 6). In the proposal, NFIDCs emphasized that they were not opposed to agricultural trade liberalization per se but that the "essential point was for developed country participants to take into account at each stage of the negotiations, not as an afterthought, the interests of those who could be forced to pay more for their food and could least afford to do so" (GATT 1988g, 2). By tabling these proposals, NFIDCs had thus changed their approach to the agriculture negotiations, dropping the strategy of resistance and instead opting to make formal demands at the bargaining table.

It is highly unlikely that NFIDCs would have chosen to focus their efforts in the agriculture negotiations on addressing the balance-of-payments problem without the FAO's involvement. This was an issue of significant interest for FAO officials, who had been working for over a decade on the relationship between food prices and the balance-of-payments situation in developing countries. The FAO secretariat's preoccupation with balance of payments had arisen from its frustrations with the IMF's Compensatory Financing Facility (CFF), a fund created in the wake of the 1974 World Food Crisis to provide financing on favorable terms to developing countries experiencing balance-of-payments problems due to rising costs of food imports (Kirkpatrick 1985). The FAO had been one of the leading advocates for the creation of the CFF (Adams 1983). However, the CFF proved to be greatly underutilized, despite many developing countries having major difficulties financing food imports. FAO officials had diagnosed the problem with the CFF to lie with the strict conditionality requirements imposed by the IMF, which they argued prevented most developing countries from drawing on the fund as originally intended (FAO 1983; 1984, 22–23; 1985c, vii, 52; Boughton 2001, 730–35). The FAO secretariat had previously—and unsuccessfully—lobbied the IMF Executive Board for changes to make the CFF more widely accessible to food import–dependent countries (Shaw 2007, 240–41).

FAO officials therefore saw the GATT agriculture negotiations as an opportunity to reopen debate on the nexus between food prices, imports, and balance-of-payments problems. It was a logical step for FAO officials to press NFIDCs to raise the issue of higher food prices and balance-of-payments problems at the GATT agriculture negotiations, given that the FAO secretariat saw this as a policy issue of outmost importance to food security for NFIDCs. The FAO's reframing of the problem of higher food prices as a balance-of-payments problem made the NFIDCs' request for additional financing fit better with economistic ways of thinking at the GATT. It also provided more traction on the issue at the GATT than NFIDCs' earlier political declarations. In the context of the 1980s developing world debt crisis and a global recession, demands that agricultural trade liberalization not amplify macroeconomic instability resonated with conventional economic thinking and the interests of developed countries. It was also a credible negotiating demand given the severe balance-of-payments difficulties experienced by NFIDCs in the years prior to the launch of the Uruguay Round (see table 2).

The NFIDCs' demand for compensation to address the risks that higher food prices could have for their balance of payments, a position that became widely supported by all GATT developing-country mem-

TABLE 2. Current account balance as percentage of Gross Domestic Product (selected countries and years)

Country	1980–85 average
Egypt	−5.1
Jamaica	−10.4
Morocco	−7.6
Mexico	−1.4

Source: IMF Balance of Payments Statistics Yearbook, World Bank, and OECD GDP estimates; author's calculations.

bers, persuaded developed countries of the need to add the issue to the negotiating agenda. This culminated with trade ministers agreeing at the 1988 Montreal Ministerial Meeting that "special attention should be given to the possible negative effects of short-term measures on net food-importing developing countries" and to prioritize work on the effects of food prices in the agriculture negotiations (GATT 1988i, 13). Getting their concerns about higher food prices onto the negotiating agenda was a significant win for the NFIDCs. It was also a win for FAO officials because it committed GATT members to take developing countries' food security concerns seriously in the agriculture negotiations, including examining the effects of higher food prices on food security.

Global Trade Rules to Safeguard Food Security

In spring 1989, the agriculture negotiations shifted into a critical stage of bargaining focused on designing new global trade rules for agriculture. Developed countries were first to put forward proposals for new global trade rules, but none of those proposals addressed NFIDCs' or FAO officials' concerns about the risks of higher food prices (GATT 1989b). As talks proceeded, NFIDCs came under immense pressure to produce a comprehensive proposal for new global trade rules to deal with the effects of higher food prices. This pressure came from developed-country trade negotiators, who had made clear to NFIDC negotiators that they would engage in substantive discussions on potential financial compensation only *after* NFIDCs tabled a proposal further specifying their demands (GATT 1988f, 3–6). This was a common bargaining tactic by developed countries to stymie initiatives by developing countries, since the latter rarely tabled proposal texts at the GATT (Steinberg 2002, 355).

NFIDC trade negotiators' failure to produce a joint comprehensive bargaining proposal was due to internal divisions and their lack of technical capacity (Walch 2003; Narlikar 2003). Troubled that NFIDCs were floundering in the agriculture negotiations, FAO officials stepped in to drive forward work by NFIDCs on a bargaining proposal.[7] Over the course of multiple meetings with NFIDC trade negotiators in Geneva, FAO officials presented in-depth research and analysis undertaken by the organization about the expected impacts of negotiating proposals tabled by the US, the EU, and other agricultural-exporting countries on food prices (Wyles 1993). Such analysis was intended to improve NFIDC trade negotiators' understanding of the ramifications of the various proposals on the bargaining table. These meetings also served to deepen NFIDCs' sense of shared interests and build political solidarity.

FAO officials did more than provide NFIDC trade negotiators with information. They also directly advised on bargaining strategy, provided feedback on formal statements to be made in the agriculture negotiations, and, most notably, became directly involved in the drafting of bargaining proposals. FAO officials, for instance, took the lead in formulating the draft of a proposal for pro–food security trade rules of their own design and presented this to NFIDC trade negotiators. In response, NFIDC trade negotiators deferred to FAO officials to hold the pen and lead on drafting their bargaining proposal. In interviews, FAO officials described this active role as "inevitable" given the lack of technical expertise among NFIDCs.[8] For their part, NFIDC trade negotiators stated that it "made sense for [FAO officials] to do the drafting of the bargaining proposal" because of their in-depth knowledge of agricultural policy and the food security problems facing food-importing countries.[9]

NFIDCs tabled their long-awaited joint bargaining proposal on food security in November 1989. In the proposal, NFIDCs emphasized that their goal was to "alleviate the burden of increased prices on the import bill and balance of payments" (GATT 1989d, 1). The bargaining proposal signaled the end of NFIDCs' earlier "strategy of resistance" centered on issuing broad political declarations and threatening to walk away from the negotiations; it marked an important shift to adopting a strategy that conformed to the GATT's "request and offer"–based negotiation process. NFIDCs' joint bargaining proposal also stood out for its technical sophistication. The proposal included a novel methodology for measuring the impacts of higher food prices on import bills (GATT 1989d, 2). In a further innovation, the proposal introduced the idea of a transitional multilateral fund that included a series of "offsetting measures"—ranging from concessional food sales to debt relief to additional aid for agricultural research and infrastructure—as potential forms of "compensation" for higher future food prices (GATT 1989d, 2–4). In presenting the proposal, NFIDCs stressed that these measures could easily be financed by developed countries from their expected future savings from reduced agriculture subsidy expenditures.

By leading the drafting of the NFIDCs' comprehensive proposal, FAO officials were no longer playing the role of neutral observers in the agriculture negotiations but had become active participants. The FAO's fingerprints were all over the NFIDCs' joint bargaining proposal. Some of its contributions were readily apparent, such as the three statistical annexes appended to the proposal, which had been produced by the FAO's trade division (GATT 1989d, 7–9). Less obvious was the fact that FAO officials had come up with, and written, many of the key elements of the proposal.[10] This included the proposed methodology to measure the impacts of food prices, which built on ideas that had been circulating within the FAO secretariat since the 1970s, with some floated earlier by the FAO during the creation of the CFF (Adams 1983). Similarly, the proposal's call for a transitional multilateral fund was a thinly veiled repackaging of the FAO's secretariat's 1979 Plan of Action on World Food Security. That plan had been one of Saouma's personal initiatives and was intended to make greater financial resources available to support agricultural research and infrastructure projects in developing countries (FAO 1979). However, the plan was never implemented because of a lack of support from developed countries at the time (Shaw 2007). With FAO officials leading in drafting the NFIDCs' proposal, many aspects of the plan were repurposed in the context of the Uruguay Round agriculture negotiations. While it was NFIDC negotiators that formally tabled the proposal, the joint proposal advanced many of the FAO secretariat's ideas and preferences.

Mobilizing NFIDCs at the GATT provided FAO officials with a unique opportunity to directly feed their own ideas about how best to protect food security into the agriculture negotiations. NFIDC trade negotiators accepted the active involvement of FAO officials because it was in their interest to do so. The FAO's participation not only helped NFIDCs to work more effectively as a bloc at the GATT but also resulted in a more effectual bargaining strategy and a more technically sophisticated proposal that significantly strengthened the position of the NFIDCs in the agriculture negotiations. The FAO also proposed measures, such as additional compensatory financing, that would be of direct material benefit to NFIDCs. By working with and through NFIDCs to formulate and table proposals in the agriculture negotiations, FAO officials inserted themselves into the politics of global trade rulemaking at the GATT.

An Agreement to Protect Food Security

The FAO's most significant action to influence the trajectory of global trade rulemaking occurred in the final stages of the Uruguay Round negotiations. In July 1990, the chair of the agriculture negotiations presented to GATT members the text of a draft agreement on agricultural trade liberalization, known as the Framework Agreement on Agriculture Reform Programme (GATT 1990b). The text had largely been written by the chair in an effort to overcome the deadlock in the negotiations caused by disagreement between the US and EU over the scope and pace of agricultural subsidy reform (Wolfe 1998). The 1990 Framework text outlined the main areas of consensus as well as the issues on which GATT members still remained far apart and required political guidance. The text was to be put forward for political decision by trade ministers at the Brussels Ministerial scheduled for December 1990.

Although GATT members had spent the previous eighteen months negotiating rules intended to address concerns about food security, there were no references in the 1990 Framework text to the issue of higher food prices or to any of the measures proposed by the NFIDCs (GATT 1990b, 6). NFIDC trade negotiators were outraged by this omission in the text. In negotiation sessions, Jamaica declared that the framework "was not an adequate basis for addressing NFIDCs' concerns," while Egypt accused developed countries of reneging on the 1988 Montreal Ministerial agreement to address the issue of higher food prices (GATT 1990c, 2–3).

NFIDCs were frustrated by these developments and signaled the readiness of their trade ministers to reject the framework at the upcoming ministerial, stating that they "were not prepared to accept a ready-made package agreed among the major trading partners and presented on a take-it-or-leave-it basis as a pretext for salvaging the [Uruguay] Round" (GATT 1990d, 3–4). FAO officials shared this view, fearing the food security situation of NFIDCs would deteriorate without adequate safeguards in future agricultural trade rules (FAO 1992, 154–55). FAO officials worked with NFIDCs to push for changes to the framework in the months leading up to the Brussels Ministerial, including working with NFIDC trade negotiators to produce a second bargaining proposal that further elaborated ways to operationalize the measures to offset the risks to food security set out in the earlier 1989 joint proposal (GATT 1990b, 1990e).

Though NFIDCs had threatened to walk out of the negotiations, the 1990 Brussels Ministerial Meeting actually broke down because the US and EU could not agree on a percentage cut to agricultural subsidies (Alons 2014). While most other bargaining areas of the Uruguay Round negotiations, such as industrial goods, services and intellectual property rights, were essentially completed by this time, it appeared as though disagreement on agriculture could lead to the failure of the round. With the Uruguay Round on the brink of collapse, GATT members tasked the GATT director-general, Arthur Dunkel, to broker a compromise solution. To break the impasse on agriculture, Dunkel adopted an exclusionary process that privileged small group negotiations among developed countries or bilaterally between the US and EU (Scott 2008; Alons 2014). Dunkel did, however, acknowledge that NFIDCs' concerns were unresolved and that they were unlikely to agree to an agricultural trade deal without a food security guarantee in place. As such, Dunkel stressed to developed countries that they would have to reach agreement on an offer to satisfy NFIDCs "should world prices rise significantly during the implementation period" (GATT 1990a, 154).

GATT members engaged in frantic and intense negotiations to get a last-minute deal on agriculture over the finishing line in the months that followed the failed Brussels Ministerial. During this time, NFIDC trade negotiators approached Dunkel with a text outlining a compromise solution for addressing the issue of higher food prices. In the text, they proposed that developed countries should make a commitment to provide NFIDCs with additional international food aid, export credits, and agricultural development assistance in exchange for their support of the other elements in the agriculture agreement, including reductions on agricultural subsidies and tariffs. FAO officials led the drafting of the text and worked closely with NFIDCs to ensure that they pressed other GATT members and Dunkel to get support.[11] Dunkel floated the NFIDC text and their demands to developed countries in bilateral and plurilateral consultations.

Dunkel's efforts eventually resulted in GATT members achieving a breakthrough agriculture deal in 1991. This deal included a Declaration on Measures Concerning the Possible Negative Effects of the Reform Programme on Net Food-Importing Developing Countries, which contained most of the elements to safeguard food security proposed and favored by NFIDCs and FAO officials. The declaration included a formal recognition by developed countries that agricultural liberalization could have "negative effects" on world food supply and the ability of NFIDCs to secure "adequate supplies of basic foodstuffs from external sources on reasonable terms and conditions, including short-term difficulties in financing normal levels of commercial imports" (GATT 1991, 213). It also committed developed countries to provide NFIDCs with additional international food aid, greater technical and financial assistance, and favorable access to agricultural export credits, as well as to establish new funding facilities as required to address expected higher food prices.

The 1991 Declaration thus signaled a significant change in the agriculture negotiations from no attention to NFIDCs' concerns about higher future food prices in the 1990 Framework text to a full-fledged political commitment by developed countries to safeguard NFIDCs' food security by 1991. NFIDCs were satisfied with the text of the declaration and saw it as a major negotiation victory, given that they had had no real bargaining leverage over developed countries (Walch 2003). The best-endeavor nature of the declaration made it agreeable to developed countries, which needed to secure NFIDCs' support for the Uruguay Round agriculture agreement. FAO officials were satisfied that their proposals were reflected in the agriculture agreement on the table.[12] The 1991 Declaration resolved the negotiation impasse between NFIDCs and developed countries in the agriculture negotiations.

The Uruguay Round agriculture negotiations effectively concluded some months later when the US and EU reached consensus on outstanding issues in agriculture at the Blair House meeting in 1992 (Meunier

1998). Trade ministers met in Marrakesh in 1994 to sign the Final Act Embodying the Results of the Uruguay Round of Multilateral Trade Negotiations, which formally concluded the Uruguay Round. The Final Act included the 1991 Declaration, which was retitled a "decision" (commonly referred to as the "Marrakesh Decision" or "NFIDC Decision") and became one of the founding legal texts of the WTO.[13] The food security safeguards built into the Marrakesh Decision, which had been heavily shaped by the FAO and reflected its goals to fight hunger, thus became part of global trade rules.

The FAO Intervenes in the WTO Doha Round

This section examines efforts by the FAO secretariat to steer WTO members to create a WTO-based food-financing facility during the Doha Round negotiations. The AoA was just the first step in a longer-term project of agricultural trade liberalization. WTO members returned to the bargaining table in 1999, as required under Article 20 of the AoA (see chapter 2), to negotiate further reductions in agricultural subsidies and tariffs. However, WTO members failed to launch a new round of negotiations at the 1999 Ministerial Meeting in Seattle because of disagreement between developed and developing countries on the negotiating agenda (R. Bernal 1999). Many developing countries were dissatisfied with the uneven outcomes of the Uruguay Round, claiming that the effects of trade reforms had primarily benefited developed countries (Finger and Nogués 2001; Ostry 2002; Gallagher 2007). WTO rules on intellectual property rights, for example, were estimated to have resulted in a net wealth transfer of $41 billion from developing countries to developed countries (Newfarmer et al. 2002). WTO members were able to successfully launch new negotiations at the Doha Ministerial Meeting in December 2001 only after a commitment by developed countries that the negotiations would prioritize the economic development of developing countries, accordingly naming the round the "Doha Development Agenda" (Wolfe 2004; Hopewell 2016).

The Food Import Bill Problem

A highly contested issue at the WTO in the lead-up the 1999 Seattle Ministerial Meeting was the effect of agricultural trade reforms on developing countries' food import bills. World prices for food staples increased rapidly between 1995 and 1997, coinciding with the start of the implementation of the AoA. The price of wheat, for example, increased from $135 per ton in 1994 to $190 per ton by 1995; this was equivalent to a 40 percent price increase and substantially higher than the projected increase estimated during the GATT Uruguay Round (Greenfield, de Nigris, and Konandreas 1996; FAO 1999a, 6). Higher food prices had a significant effect on the food import bills of least developed countries (LDCs) and NFIDCs, which rose by 83 percent and 61 percent respectively between 1995 and 1997 and made food less affordable for poor households (FAO 1999a, 12–13; WTO 1997a, 6).

FAO officials were instrumental in bringing attention to the problem of rising food import bills at the WTO as well as galvanizing states to work on the issue. It was the FAO's research that first identified, and disseminated knowledge about, the 1995–97 world food price shock and its effects on the food security of LDCs and NFIDCs. Concerns about the potential negative consequences of the AoA for food security led FAO officials to closely track the effects of agricultural policy reforms on world markets in general and food consumption in developing countries in particular (FAO 1999a). To bring attention to the issue at the WTO, FAO officials made a series of presentations during meetings of the Committee on Agriculture in which they warned WTO members about the "precarious" food security situation in NFIDCs and LDCs caused by their rising food import bills and declining ability to pay for food imports (WTO 1997a, 5; 1998a; 1999b, 2; FAO 1999b, 1999a).

While FAO officials acknowledged that poor harvests and unfavorable weather were key factors contributing to the spike in world food prices, they argued that WTO reforms were also to blame. The FAO brought attention to the overlooked fact that WTO-mandated agricultural trade reforms had resulted in the rapid drawdown of developed countries' surplus food stocks and a sharp decline in international food aid donations (FAO 1999b, 2000b). Northern surplus food stocks and food aid were traditionally key sources of food imports for most NFIDCs and LDCs. For most of the postwar period, government-held food surpluses in the global North had provided a food security guarantee to food import–dependent states; such stocks were sold by rich countries to other governments at discounted rates (known as "concessional sales") and/or donated as food aid (Uvin 1992). However, the shift in farm policy beginning in the 1980s toward liberalizing agricultural trade meant that major agricultural-producing countries were rolling back the very subsidies that had encouraged such surpluses in the past.

The FAO secretariat's analysis demonstrated that reduced surplus stocks in the US and EU had exacerbated an already-tight world food supply situation, resulting in upward pressure on world food prices (FAO 1999a, 2–4). In addition, since international food aid flows were inversely related to levels of surplus food stocks (Clay and Stokke 2000), the result was that food aid donations declined by nearly a third between 1995 and 1997. This had a drastic effect on LDCs and NFIDCs. Whereas international food aid had accounted for 22 percent of NFIDCs and 64 percent of LDCs' cereal consumption during the mid-1980s, by 1998 the levels dropped precipitously to 2 percent and 21 percent, respectively (FAO 1999a, 12). One trade expert described the situation facing LDCs and NFIDCs during the 1995–97 food price spike as follows: "World food prices go up, and the poor food-importing developing countries are unable to import as much, [and] food aid dries up."[14]

The result of dwindling Northern food surpluses and food aid donations was that NFIDCs and LDCs had to rapidly adjust their food procurement strategies and all of a sudden switch to importing a greater share of food through the commercial market.[15] This shift to the commercial market in turn required NFIDCs and LDCs to spend more of their foreign exchange reserves to pay for food imports. However, the supply of foreign exchange was scarce in these countries because of their high levels of debt-repayment obligations and generally poorly performing economies (FAO 1999a, 11–13; 1999b; 2001a, 5–8). Another challenge for NFIDC and LDC governments was that they could not easily obtain additional financing from the IMF, since the organization did not provide long-term loans to finance food imports. In addition, unlike rich country governments, LDCs and NFIDCs could not easily turn to private banks or capital markets for loans because of their poor credit ratings. These conditions led FAO officials to conclude that NFIDCs' and LDCs' food import problem was not a temporary one but likely to become even more acute in the future, increasing food insecurity in countries where reducing hunger was already a major challenge (FAO 2000b, 2001b).

Pre–Doha Round Food Fights over Import Bills at the WTO

Given the perceived threat to food security, FAO officials turned their efforts to mobilizing NFIDCs and LDCs at the WTO to put the issue of rising food import bills onto the agenda of the planned new negotiations on agriculture. Rising food import bills were not, however, initially a priority negotiating issue for NFIDC or LDC trade negotiators, who, representing the broader interests of their trade ministries, were preoccupied with other trade issues such as increasing market access for their exports.[16] Furthermore, NFIDC and LDC governments experienced and perceived the food import bill problem as a national one, rather than as a collective problem experienced by many other developing countries. In contrast, FAO officials, who produced and had access to the most comprehensive information about the scope and scale of the food import problem, identified it as a structural and collective problem. As such, FAO officials sought to make NFIDC and LDC trade representatives aware of their common challenges in paying for food imports and worked to forge shared interests among them by demonstrating how this collective problem was linked to structural changes caused by agricultural trade liberalization.[17] FAO officials inundated NFIDC and LDC trade representatives with the message about the importance of addressing rising food import bills via the WTO. They did so using a multitude of forms and channels, including during informal and formal meetings with trade negotiators at the WTO (WTO 1997a, 5; 1998a; 1999b, 2–3), in FAO-led training workshops on implementing the AoA (Healy, Pearce, and Stockbridge 1998; FAO 2000a, 2000b), and through briefings and reports produced for WTO members (Greenfield, de Nigris, and Konandreas 1996; FAO 1999a, 1999b, 2000a). As a result of the FAO's insistent efforts, NFIDCs and LDCs came to be convinced of the pressing nature of the issue and were persuaded to bring the issue forward in talks preparing for the new agriculture negotiations at the WTO. According to one NFIDC negotiator, the FAO had provided NFIDCs and LDCs with the "arguments and evidence" necessary to make the case that the food import problem was linked to global agricultural trade reforms and therefore that the problem had to be solved via the WTO.[18]

When NFIDCs and LDCs began to formally raise the issue of food import bills in the lead-up to the 1999 Seattle Ministerial, the question of whether WTO reforms were to blame for the problem led to political discord (WTO 1998b, 6; 1999a, 4, 6). On one side of the debate, NFIDCs and LDCs argued that the available evidence (compiled by the FAO) was sufficient to prove that there was a structural link between trade reforms and rising food import bills and that this obligated developed countries to provide assistance as committed to in the Uruguay Round Marrakesh Decision (WTO 1995a, 4–5; 1995b; 1996, 8–9). On the other side of the debate, the US, the EU, Australia, and Canada claimed a lack of conclusive statistical evidence to show the direct causation claimed by the FAO and the LDCs and NFIDCs; thus they argued that rising food import bills did not merit triggering the Marrakesh Decision (WTO 1995b, 6; 1996).

There was no simple solution to resolve this disagreement over the link between trade reforms and rising food import bills. FAO officials believed that, on balance, the evidence supported LDCs' and NFIDCs' demand for additional assistance. However, FAO officials acknowledged that the economic models available at the time were unable to adequately test every relevant causal variable, thereby "making it impossible to provide the irrefutable proof demanded by developed countries."[19] At the WTO, NFIDC and LDC trade officials called developed countries' position on rising food import bills organized hypocrisy, complaining that the burden of proof they demanded was impossible: "In order to receive assistance under the Marrakesh Decision, developing countries were asked to prove that they were negatively affected by the Agreement on Agriculture. We have seen that it is virtually impossible to isolate the effects of the Agreement, but developing countries were asked to prove a causal link between the Agreement and the difficulties they were facing."[20] In response, food import bills became a priority issue for LDCs and NFIDCs for future negotiations, both to address the problem of higher food prices and to receive the assistance promised to them in the Uruguay Round. These countries clamored for the issue to be put on the agenda of the Committee on Agriculture and the planned new round of agriculture negotiations (WTO 1998b). While WTO members subsequently agreed to put rising food import bills on the agenda of future agriculture negotiations, the collapse of the 1999 WTO Seattle Ministerial Meeting meant that the launch of a new trade round would wait.

At the WTO, it was known to all WTO members that the FAO had led the charge on the food import problem. After all, it had been FAO officials that brought attention to the issue at the WTO and publicly pressed for WTO members to address the issue. FAO officials recognized that the organization's efforts to press the issue and influence the agenda of future WTO negotiations carried a real risk of backlash from powerful developed countries, which did not agree with the FAO's prescriptions. Yet despite the risk of backlash, the FAO senior leadership team, including the director-general, as an FAO assistant director-general put it, felt that they needed to take action on behalf of food-insecure countries who were the "least resourced to defend their interests."[21]

A WTO-Based Food-Financing Facility

FAO officials were alarmed by the lack of urgency among WTO members to address the food security risks to LDCs and NFIDCs posed by rising food import bills.[22] The issue was of high importance for the FAO secretariat given its direct relevance to its mission to fight hunger, which led FAO officials to urge WTO members to take appropriate action. As part of their regular updates to the Committee on Agriculture on trends in world food security, FAO officials proposed to WTO members that they should create a new financial facility to mitigate NFIDCs' and LDCs' reduced ability to pay for food imports (WTO 1997b, 8–11, 17–18).

Senior FAO officials were convinced that a new WTO-based financing facility was a both technically and politically viable solution, arguing that WTO members had the scope under the Marrakesh Decision to establish such a facility (WTO 2001e; FAO 2001a, 2001b, 2002c).[23] They viewed this as the best available option. The FAO secretariat favored a new facility over alternative forms of assistance available to LDCs and NFIDCs under the Marrakesh Decision. FAO officials made the case to WTO members that international food aid had become far too unpredictable to guarantee food security and that IMF loans, which included additional and often onerous conditionalities for borrowers, such as forcing governments to cut social spending, would unfairly shift the burden onto food-insecure countries (WTO 2001a; FAO 2001a, 2001b).[24]

Following the collapse of the 1999 Seattle Ministerial, FAO officials glimpsed a window of opportunity at the WTO to put a new food-financing facility onto the agenda. The Seattle collapse had significantly altered the political dynamics at the WTO, resulting in a renewed impetus among members to cooperate; this included a readiness by states to consider LDCs' and NFIDCs' food import bills as part of the agenda of future agriculture negotiations (WTO 2000b, 4–6, 11–12, 17; 2000a, 10–

12, 19–20; 2000e, 4–8). Indeed, within the trade policy community, the food import bill problem took on symbolic importance; the issue came to be seen as a litmus test of how willing developed countries were to address trade-related aspects of food security (WTO 2000d, 2; Raghavan 2000a).

FAO officials expected that the renewed spirit of cooperation at the WTO would open up space for states to consider new ideas and solutions. In June 2000, FAO officials pitched to NFIDC and LDC delegates a fully fleshed-out proposal for a new WTO-based food-financing facility, now called a "revolving fund," intended to provide fixed-term loans to eligible developing-country WTO members that faced difficulties financing adequate levels of commercial food imports (FAO 2002c, 261). FAO officials presented their vision for the fund during a series of plurilateral meetings in Geneva.[25] The FAO's proposal was far advanced and reflected months of works by officials. In a working paper circulated to WTO members, FAO officials outlined the basic architecture of the revolving fund, proposing that it be time limited for up to three years and that donors be responsible for providing $600 million annually in working capital. Other technical aspects suggested by FAO officials included eligibility criteria for borrowers and a method for how the terms of interest rates and repayments should be set (FAO 2002b). By designing clear criteria and conditions for creating the fund, FAO officials sought to provide WTO members with a ready-made solution that could serve as the starting basis for further negotiations (FAO 2001b, 16–17). In advocating for the revolving fund, FAO officials did not seek to expand their organization's mandate or gain additional resources, since they proposed that the fund be established at, and controlled by, the WTO rather than their own organization.

To gain support for its proposal, FAO officials mobilized a diverse group of developing-country WTO members—including NFIDCs, small island developing states (SIDS), and the African Group—to bring forward the proposal for a revolving fund at the WTO (WTO 2001g, 9; 2001i; 2001j; 2001k). All of these countries faced food import bill challenges, and their delegates to the WTO were persuaded of the merits of the FAO's proposal, seeing the fund as being in their economic and food security interests.[26] Country representatives also appreciated the FAO's leadership and work, indicating that FAO officials did the "heavy lifting" for them in terms of developing the technical aspects of the fund, which most delegations lacked the capacity to do on their own.[27] Subsequently at the WTO, NFIDCs and LDCs jointly tabled a proposal for a revolving fund, the Proposal to Implement the Marrakesh Ministerial Decision in Favour of LDCs and NFIDCs (WTO 2001j), at the March 2001 meeting of the Committee on Agriculture.[28] NFIDC and LDC trade negotiators presented the rationale for the revolving fund to the wider WTO membership as follows: "The NFIDCs and LDCs need access to special financing facilities to maintain the normal volume of food imports during times of high market prices without further jeopardizing their balance-of-payments position. Experience has shown that the existing facilities under the Bretton Woods institutions, due to the conditionalities attached and other technicalities, have not been used by the countries in need of such financing" (WTO 2001j, 2). These countries argued that the proposed revolving fund was meant to "ensure that adequate financing at concessional terms is made available to the NFIDCs and LDCs in times of high world market prices" (WTO 2001j, 2–3).

WTO members subsequently debated the revolving-fund proposal at the Committee on Agriculture, as well as in the preparatory talks for the Doha Ministerial scheduled for November 2001. NFIDCs and LDCs were successful in garnering broad support from other WTO members for continued talks on the revolving-fund proposal, including from agricultural exporters, such as Argentina and Thailand, and developed countries, such as Norway and Japan (WTO 2001f, 6). Canada, Australia, and New Zealand signaled that they were open to further talks but requested additional technical details before agreeing to put the proposal forward for a decision by trade ministers in Doha. The US and EU were skeptical about the proposed revolving fund. American negotiators expressed their reluctance to pay for any new fund, while the EU stated that the WTO was not the appropriate forum to discuss multilateral financing and that the issue should instead "be dealt with by the IMF and the World Bank" (WTO 2001f, 6).

Despite the diverging views among WTO members, trade negotiators were under significant political pressure to bring forward something concrete for decision by trade ministers at the Doha Ministerial to address rising food import bills. In a show of how salient the issue had become for NFIDCs and LDCs, their negotiators signaled that they were prepared to block the launch of the Doha Round unless WTO members committed to establish the revolving fund (WTO 2001e). This position was put bluntly by the Honduran negotiator, who stated that it was difficult for developing countries "to consider the launching of a new round of negotiations" when "they were still waiting to obtain the [food security] benefits from the past round."[29] While threatening to block the launch of a new trade round was an extreme position, it was seen as a credible threat at the time given that developing countries had walked out of the Seattle Ministerial two years earlier over similar grievances (Raghavan 2000a). To avoid a repeat of the debacle of the Seattle Ministerial in Doha, WTO members reached a compromise to move forward work on the food import bill problem. They agreed to create an interagency panel of experts that would be delegated the task of providing actionable recommendations to WTO members on establishing a revolving fund (WTO 2001a, 3). The motion to create an interagency panel to examine the revolving fund was put on the agenda of the Doha Ministerial Meeting, where it was formally approved by trade ministers (WTO 2001h). Trade ministers instructed delegates to create a panel consisting of a select group of WTO members and IO representatives. The panel was given a six-month mandate to examine the feasibility of establishing a revolving fund and provide recommendations to the General Council, the WTO's second-highest-level decision-making body (WTO 2001c).

While many NGOs were active in lobbying WTO members on agricultural issues in the lead-up to the Doha Ministerial, their advocacy efforts focused on calls to eliminate rich countries' agricultural subsidies and other unfair trade practices that discriminated against developing countries' exports (Aaronson and Zimmerman 2007; Hopewell 2015b; Eagleton-Pierce 2018). NGOs were not active in the discussions or technical work led by FAO officials on the development of the revolving fund. NGOs, such as Oxfam, would later endorse the NFIDCs' and LDCs' demands for the revolving fund (Oxfam 2005a), but they did so only several years after the FAO's actions to place the issue on the negotiating agenda and its circulation of technical proposals to operationalize the revolving fund.

The FAO and the Interagency Panel
The decision by trade ministers to establish an interagency panel marked a significant departure for the WTO. Unlike other IOs, the WTO had no precedent for establishing ad hoc "expert commissions" or "blue-ribbon panels" that were delegated responsibility to work on complicated trade matters (Luck 2003; Madokoro 2019). The creation of the panel was a sharp aberration from standard practice at the WTO: it was a member-

driven organization, whose states rarely delegated work related to trade negotiations to others, even to the WTO secretariat (Elsig 2010).

The matter of which IOs should be invited to serve on the interagency panel became highly politicized. The key source of discord was the potential inclusion of the FAO. This was because the US, the EU, Canada, and Australia—WTO members that were lukewarm to the idea of the revolving fund because they were the most likely to have to pay for it—raised the prospect of excluding the FAO from sitting on the panel to other WTO members (WTO 2001j). Knowing that FAO officials were vocal champions of the fund led these states to try to stack the panel in their favor by arguing that only IOs with an official mandate and expertise in multilateral financing, such as the IMF and World Bank, should be invited to join the panel (WTO 2001a, 11). The US and EU both suggested to other WTO members that the FAO, which lacked a mandate to work on finance, was not competent to advise on the issue. These countries wanted to limit participation to the Bretton Woods institutions for strategic reasons, instructing IMF and World Bank officials to "kill the idea of a revolving fund" at the WTO.[30] In response to moves by developed countries to exclude the FAO from the panel, which would limit its ability to influence deliberations, FAO officials chose to mobilize like-minded WTO members to support its obtaining an invitation to sit on the panel.[31] This led NFIDCs and LDCs to come out strongly in favor of appointing the FAO. These countries' trade negotiators viewed the FAO's participation in the interagency panel as critical to improving the chance that the panel's work would address their food security concerns.[32] Ultimately, these countries' insistence, with support from other WTO members, that the interagency panel "be as inclusive as possible" forced the US, the EU, and others to capitulate and agree to allow the FAO to serve on the panel. WTO members agreed to permit the "full involvement of the FAO" on the interagency panel (WTO 2001b, 9–10; 2001j, 7, 11).

The interagency panel was formally established in March 2002 and included the representatives of five IOs: the FAO, IMF, World Bank, UNCTAD, and IGC. Records of the panel's work show that FAO officials were the most active participants; they played a vital role in steering the panel's working agenda, produced the vast majority of technical papers and proposals for discussion, and worked closely with WTO delegates to help them understand the intricacies of how food financing worked. In the course of their work on the panel, FAO officials also presented a series of refinements and innovations to their original 2001 revolving fund proposal; they proposed, for example, that access to the fund's resources be extended to borrowing by private food importers in developing countries in recognition of the major role these firms played in securing access to food (WTO 2002, 30; FAO 2003). The FAO's leadership and intense activity sharply contrasted with the far more limited engagement by World Bank and IMF officials, who, by comparison, offered few ideas and often only read prepared statements sent from headquarters back in Washington. The World Bank and IMF's apparent lack of interest in advancing the work of the panel can be explained by the fact that they viewed a WTO-based revolving fund as a potential competitor.[33] Indeed, during meetings of the panel as well the Committee on Agriculture, World Bank and IMF representatives repeatedly questioned the need for a revolving fund and stated firmly that they would not contribute financing toward it (WTO 2002).

Ultimately, it was FAO officials that most shaped the substantive content of the interagency panel's final report to the WTO General Council. Their influence is evident in the report's recommendations, which called on WTO members to hold further discussions on the revolving fund as part of the Doha Round agriculture negotiations and to use the proposed architecture for a fund—designed by the FAO—as the basis for future talks (WTO 2002, 43–44).[34] These recommendations were adopted by the General Council. As a result, trade negotiators were instructed to continue work on the revolving fund, thus keeping the issue on the WTO agenda despite resistance from powerful states. WTO members continued to work on the revolving fund throughout the Doha Round; however, the collapse of the round in 2008 led to negotiations on the revolving fund being put on hold. Despite the collapse of the Doha Round, WTO members have continued to debate the revolving fund initiated by the FAO, most recently in the context of responses to rising volatility in world food prices (WTO 2019a).

Conclusion

This chapter has demonstrated multiple interventions by the FAO secretariat intended to alter the trajectory and outcome of multilateral trade negotiations. The FAO secretariat's interventions were motivated by concerns that global trade rules could have negative consequences for food security. Its interventions were initiated by the FAO secretariat rather than undertaken on formal or informal orders of states. The FAO's interventions were intended, not to increase its own mandate or resources, or to achieve a joint regulatory goal with the GATT/WTO secretariat, but to insert itself into the interstate bargaining process in order to safeguard the food security of food import–dependent developing countries. In seeking to safeguard food security at the GATT/WTO, the FAO secretariat behaved in ways consistent with its social purpose to fight world hunger and defend the interests of food-insecure populations.

The FAO secretariat used the intervention strategy of mobilizing states, which provided the organization proximate access to decision-making by states at the GATT/WTO. Food import–dependent states were willing to let the FAO secretariat lead in the design of their approach to the agriculture negotiations, including drafting the text of bargaining proposals, because doing so strengthened their hand and their ability to defend their interests in multilateral trade negotiations. Yet the FAO's choice to intervene at the GATT/WTO carried with it significant risks of backlash from powerful states. To mitigate such risks, FAO officials worked primarily behind the scenes during the Uruguay Round, after efforts by powerful GATT member states to prevent the organization from being granted observer status in the agriculture negotiations and warn it against interfering in the business of states. The FAO's advocacy for a WTO-based food-financing facility in the Doha Round dissatisfied many powerful states, who in turn took steps to block the FAO's participation on the interagency panel.

Despite not having a formal seat at the bargaining table, by working with and through states, the FAO secretariat exercised influence over the discourse, agenda, and outcomes of multilateral trade negotiations. In the Uruguay Round, it was the FAO that developed the framing of higher food prices as a balance-of-payments problem, and its efforts were critical in getting the issue onto the negotiating agenda. The FAO secretariat also played an important role in global trade rulemaking by drafting what became the Marrakesh Decision, which is now part of WTO law. During the Doha Round, it was the actions by the FAO that brought the food import bill problem to the attention of WTO members and into the negotiations. Moreover, it was the FAO, not WTO members, that furnished a proposal to establish a food-financing facility, and its advocacy efforts and technical work were pivotal in driving forward deliberations at the WTO on its design and operationalization. It is unlikely that developing countries could have achieved similar progress on these issues without the interventions by the FAO. Not only was the FAO the originator of these proposals, but developing countries would have likely been less effective in the negotiations without the benefit of the FAO's active leadership, support, and expertise, especially when it came to writing bargaining proposals, which are an essential part of multilateral trade negotiations.

By mobilizing states, the FAO secretariat played an agentic and impactful role in shaping global trade rulemaking at the GATT/WTO. The FAO's influence on the discourse, agenda, and outcomes of multilateral trade negotiations far exceeds existing accounts that portray IOs as merely peripheral players in the trade regime. The next chapter considers a more visible and confrontational intervention strategy—public shaming—in which an IO exerts its moral authority to present a decision at an overlapping organization as being against the interests of the international community.

CHAPTER 4
Don't Take Food from the Starving

The WFP Publicly Shames WTO Members

CONCERNS THAT PROPOSED TRADE RULES could increase the number of food-insecure people worldwide spurred the WFP to launch a media campaign depicting the WTO as recklessly endangering the lives of hungry people. The WFP secretariat's use of public shaming as an intervention strategy to influence the outcomes of the WTO Doha Round negotiations is an illuminating case of how an IO can exert its moral authority to present a prospective decision at an overlapping organization as a violation of the values and interests of the international community. The WFP's use of public shaming generated international controversy and was a public relations disaster for the WTO. Its intervention provoked substantial backlash from WTO members, many of which were highly dissatisfied by the WFP's interference in the negotiations. The WFP secretariat's intervention at the WTO was, however, successful in blocking agreement on proposed new rules governing international food aid. Moreover, the WFP's public shaming of WTO members had a lasting effect on the trajectory of the Doha Round agriculture negotiations with the subsequent 2015 WTO Ministerial Decision on Export Competition, which included new rules on international food aid, incorporating the demands made by the WFP.

The chapter is organized as follows. The first section situates the WFP's role in the global governance of food security. The second section explains why international food aid has been a source of trade conflict and how it came to be governed by the WTO. The third section analyzes why and how the WFP secretariat chose to insert itself into the politics of global trade rulemaking at the WTO during the Doha Round, including the events that led to the WFP's decision to publicly shame WTO members. The fourth section assesses the impacts of the WFP's public shaming strategy on the trajectory and results of the WTO agriculture negotiations.

The WFP and the Political Economy of Food Aid

The WFP is the world's largest humanitarian agency and leads in coordinating and delivering food aid in emergency situations. The organization's mandate is to use food aid toward the eradication of hunger and to coordinate international food relief efforts (WFP 1996). Its role in fighting hunger on a world scale embodies the international norm that states have a responsibility to prevent starvation of not just their own citizens but also those of other nations (Uvin 1994). The WFP feeds approximately one hundred million people annually at risk of malnutrition and starvation in over eighty countries (WFP 2020c).

The WFP was created in 1961 as an initiative of the FAO director-general, R. B. Sen. It was initially a pilot project to redirect agricultural surpluses from North America for use in hunger relief and to trial new development programs in the global South, such as school feedings for malnourished children and food-for-work schemes (Shaw 2007; Rietkerk 2016). Part of the impetus to create the WFP stemmed from the problem facing the international wheat market caused by rapid increases in government-held surplus wheat stocks in the late 1950s. Because of a combination of technological innovation, government support, and the recovery of food production in postwar Europe, US surplus wheat stocks, for example, grew from 1.25 billion bushels in 1955 to over 2 billion bushels by 1961 (Shaw 2007, 48).[1] The growth in surplus wheat stocks led to a supply overhang, which undermined international efforts to stabilize world wheat prices and trade. The US and Canada responded to the problem by disposing of surplus wheat as bilateral food aid. Sen saw an opportunity to create a multilateral channel for food aid that would have the dual purpose of stabilizing the international wheat market while also assisting newly independent states that had hungry populations and lacked the foreign reserves to purchase adequate volumes of wheat on commercial terms (Schultz 1960; Talbot 1979; Friedmann 1982). The WFP's early successes in improving nutrition and fighting hunger in developing countries led to an international consensus to make it a permanent UN organization in 1965 (Faaland, Mclean, and Norbye 2000; Ross 2011). By the 1980s, the WFP was the second-largest multilateral aid agency after the World Bank, delivering upwards of $1 billion in food aid annually (Hopkins 1992, 230; Uvin 1992, 303).

Unlike most UN agencies, the WFP is not financed by assessed contributions from UN members. Instead, it is funded solely through voluntary contributions, including in response to the organization's periodic, public appeals for donations to respond to humanitarian emergencies (WFP 2020b). The WFP has a strong reputation among donor and recipient countries, and it consistently ranks among the best-performing IOs in terms of delivering value for money, with among the lowest administrative costs of any major IO (Lall 2017; MOPAN 2018). Donors' trust in the WFP's effectiveness is reflected in their financial contributions, which averaged a total of $6.5 billion annually between 2015 and 2019, making the WFP the second-best-funded UN agency after the Department of Peacekeeping Operations (UN 2020). Historically, the US, the EU, Canada, Japan, Australia, and the Nordic countries have been the WFP's largest donors. However, the composition of donors has changed over the past decade, with a number of emerging economies, such as Saudi Arabia, Brazil, and China, transnational corporations, and private individuals increasingly ranking among its donors (WFP 2020d).

The WFP secretariat is described as having a "results-oriented" organizational culture that is focused on the goal of feeding the maximum number of people and ensuring continual improvements in the efficacy of its food aid programs (Hopkins 1992; Clay 2003; WFP 2020a). The WFP secretariat, as a technical agency focused on the delivery of food relief, is widely seen as apolitical and therefore free of the South-North political conflict that characterizes many other UN bodies. Part of the reason for this is that the organization was designed to be insulated from states, with the WFP secretariat delegated wide authority to design and implement food assistance programs and with states largely limited to rubber-stamping their approval (T. Johnson 2014). Ranjit Lall (2017, 273) finds a strong link between the WFP's strong performance and the high level of independence enjoyed by its secretariat, which has allowed the WFP "to consistently resist state attempts to promote parochial national interests" and has "earn[ed] it a widespread reputation for political neutrality." The WFP has engaged in long-standing efforts to improve the effectiveness of food aid and to encourage states to adopt better food aid practices (Shaw 2011; Ross 2011).

James T. Morris was the WFP executive director (2002–7) during the WFP's intervention at the WTO analyzed in this chapter. Morris, an American citizen, spent half of his professional career working in the charitable sector, at one point serving as president of the Lily Endowment, one of the United States' largest philanthropic foundations. Initially tapped by the Bush administration to serve as the US ambassador to the UN Rome-based agencies, Morris was instead put forward as a nominee to lead the WFP when the position became available in 2002.

Morris's tenure as executive director occurred during one of the most challenging periods for the WFP, with a large number of natural and human-made disasters drastically increasing global demand for food aid. Morris was in charge when the WFP undertook its then largest humanitarian mission: feeding almost the entire population of Iraq—twenty-six million people—in 2003 when the country was on the brink of starvation following its invasion by the US. Among his other accomplishments as head of the WFP was bringing international attention to how the HIV/AIDS pandemic in African countries worsened food insecurity, especially among children, and increasing the WFP's network of donors to include emerging and transition economies. In interviews, Morris publicly spoke about the emotional difficulty of the job of WFP executive director, recounting how he often left country visits in tears after helping to nurse severely undernourished children that he knew were likely to die.

International Food Aid and Global Trade Politics

International food aid has been a perennial source of interstate trade conflict (Puchala and Hopkins 1978; Clapp 2012). The key source of this conflict lies in the origins of international food aid as a vehicle to dispose of agricultural surpluses and its potential to crowd out commercial food trade. The perception that food aid displaces food trade is most strongly held by major agricultural exporters, particularly Canada, Australia, Argentina, and Brazil. These states have regularly criticized certain types of US food aid under its Public Law 83–480 Food for Peace (PL 480) program.

US food aid under PL 480 includes fully grant donations but also sales of food aid on concessional terms, in which surplus stocks are sold below market prices and on long-term loans at favorable rates. Concessional sales of food aid have long been controversial and criticized by other donors as a type of hidden agricultural export subsidy (Barrett and Maxwell 2005). In addition, the US government is required under PL 480 legislation to provide the majority of its food aid as "in-kind" food aid; that is, US food aid must be procured from US producers as well as processed, bagged, and transported by US-based firms (Ball and Johnson 1996; Kneteman 2009). The practice of in-kind food aid was intended to generate a domestic political constituency of farmers, traders, and shippers in favor of US food aid. Competing agricultural exporters, however, have long argued that in-kind food aid provides an economic benefit and unfair trade advantage to US exporters. Another major source of criticism of US food aid is that it is driven by foreign and commercial policy goals; historically, the majority of US food aid went not to countries with the greatest need but to military allies and client states (Eggleston 1987; Diven 2001). Agricultural exporters that compete with the US in those countries have complained that US food aid has led them to lose out on commercial food sales.

States have repeatedly turned to international institutions to resolve trade-related conflicts over international food aid. In the 1950s, states negotiated a code of conduct at the FAO, the Principles on Surplus Disposal (known as the "FAO Principles"), in an effort to ensure that international food aid did not adversely affect commercial food trade (FAO 1954; Hasenclever, Mayer, and Rittberger 1998). Subsequently in 1965, states established the Food Aid Convention (FAC), a burden-sharing system intended to ensure the predictability of international food aid, which also committed donors to minimize distortions to international trade (Cathie 1982; Uvin 1992). In addition, national aid agencies, as well as the WFP, instituted a series of reforms in the 1980s to further prevent trade displacement in recipient countries (Hopkins 1992; Shaw 2011).

Despite these international efforts, agricultural exporters continued to be concerned about the trade-related effects of international food aid and put the issue on the agenda of the GATT Uruguay Round agriculture negotiations. On the one hand, agricultural exporters expected that proposed reductions in farm subsidies—historically a key driver of agricultural overproduction—would diminish surpluses in the US, and thus the need for food aid as a vehicle for surplus disposal (Josling, Tangermann, and Warley 1996; Wolfe 1998). On the other hand, agricultural exporters were also wary of the possibility that the proposed cuts to agricultural export subsidies would increase pressure on the US and EU governments to misuse international food aid as an alternative escape valve for uncompetitive farm exports (Margulis 2017). In the Uruguay Round, states (including the US) agreed on the need for stricter food aid disciplines to ensure that donors provided only "bona fide food aid" and avoided distorting normal patterns of commercial food trade (GATT 1989a, 6).

The AoA included new trade rules governing international food aid. Article 10.4 of the AoA required donors to ensure that international food aid was not "tied" to conditions requiring purchases of other agricultural products by recipient countries; was carried out in accordance with the FAO Principles; and was provided in fully grant form or on terms consistent with the FAC (GATT 1994a, 9–10). Food aid transactions that did not meet the criteria set out in Article 10.4 would be classified as an agricultural export subsidy and thus count toward a WTO member's subsidy reduction commitments.[2] In addition, donors were required to report all of their international food aid transactions to the WTO Committee on Agriculture on an annual basis in order to be reviewed for consistency with global trade rules. While the food aid disciplines in Article 10.4 were not *de novo* rules, since they referenced existing provisions in the FAO Principles and the FAC, they were significant because they "hardened" what had previously been soft law arrangements into binding, enforceable international law under the WTO's rules-based system (Zhang 2004). As a result, the AoA expanded the trade regime's authority in the governance of international food aid and made the WTO the final arbiter for deciding whether international food aid transactions were genuine development assistance or a hidden agricultural export subsidy (Shaw and Singer 1996; Margulis 2017).

Cooperation between the WFP and WTO Secretariats

The WFP has formal observer status at both the regular and "special" (i.e., negotiating) sessions of the WTO Committee on Agriculture. As an official observer, the WFP's main role is to provide WTO members with information on international food aid transactions, as well as demand-driven inputs to inform trade policy debates (WFP 1995). For example, the WFP secretariat has, on the request of WTO members, organized special information sessions to provide trade negotiators with briefings and expert advice on technical food security matters (WTO 2011c; WFP 2017; WTO 2019b). The WFP has also cooperated with WTO members to ensure that international food aid containing genetically modified crops complies with global trade rules (WFP 2004). The WFP has a permanent liaison office in Geneva; its director represents the WFP at WTO meetings and has the right to convey the organization's views to WTO member state representatives.

The WFP and WTO secretariats have a cooperative relationship. This relationship goes beyond the provision of information. The two secretariats cooperated on designing the multilateral response to the 2008 Global Food Crisis (High Level Task Force on the Global Food Security Crisis 2008) and have jointly advised the G8 and G20 on trade and food security matters (FAO et al. 2011; Margulis 2012; Clapp and Murphy 2013). There is limited functional overlap between the WFP and WTO secretariats. The WTO is not in the business of delivering international food aid, which is the WFP's core function. The WFP as an organization is committed to ensuring that food aid deliveries do not displace local or regional production or commercial trade. As a result, there is limited scope for potential rivalry among officials given that the WFP and WTO do not directly compete for mandates, members, resources, or policy influence.

Negotiating Food Disciplines in the Doha Round

The launch of the WTO Doha Round negotiations in 2001 put international food aid back onto the negotiating agenda. This development was not spurred by any pressing food aid–related trade conflict but was automatically required by Article 20 of the AoA. Article 20 committed WTO members to return to the bargaining table to resume negotiations to further liberalize agricultural trade, which included the rules disciplining food aid (GATT 1994a). States agreed that the objective of the Doha Round agriculture negotiations would be to "substantially reduce trade-distorting farm support and tariffs" and, in particular, to reduce, with the view of phasing out, all forms of agricultural export subsidies (WTO 2001d, 3).

Eliminating agricultural export subsidies was a priority for nearly all WTO members. Agricultural export subsidies are considered the most "trade-distorting" type of state intervention, since they artificially boost the competitiveness of subsidized agricultural products on the international market (Josling 2005).[3] In fact, export subsidies for all other goods had been prohibited under the GATT since the 1950s. While states agreed to reduce agricultural export subsidies in the AoA, major subsidizers retained the right to provide significant volumes of such subsidies. Most WTO members therefore saw the Doha Round negotiations as a historic opportunity to end "agricultural exceptionalism" by eliminating agricultural export subsidies once and for all (de Gorter, Ingco, and Lilian 2002; Stoler 2010; Trebilcock and Pue 2015). Agricultural export subsidies were part of the "export competition" pillar of the agriculture negotiations, which also included the issues of agricultural export credits, international food aid, and state trading enterprises as negotiating items.[4] Progress on reducing agricultural export subsidies was linked to strengthening trade disciplines on these other issues to prevent WTO members from using export credit, food aid, and state trading enterprises to provide hidden agricultural export subsidies (L. Young, Abbott, and Leetmaa 2001; Peters 2008).

Dissatisfied with the food aid disciplines in the AoA, the Cairns Group of major agricultural exporters called for stricter food aid disciplines to restrict the use of surplus disposal–driven food aid and to stop the sale of food aid.[5] These were both food aid practices predominately used by the US. Yet disciplining international food aid was not generally regarded by other WTO members as a high priority in the agriculture negotiations. Most WTO members believed that the AoA had been successful in severing the link between agricultural surpluses and international food aid, which had been the lightning rod for earlier trade conflicts (Barrett 1998, 570). Indeed, by the launch of the Doha Round in 2001, the US government had largely phased out its programs to stockpile agricultural surpluses (Daugbjerg and Swinbank 2009; Winders 2009; Graddy-Lovelace and Diamond 2017). WTO members at the time signaled that in terms of food aid, their reform goals were modest and their focus would likely be on improving the transparency and reporting of international food aid transactions (WTO 2001b).

The dynamics of the agriculture negotiations changed dramatically, however, in May 2004, when the EU tabled an offer to eliminate its agricultural export subsidies (EU 2004). The EU's offer was considered a surprising and important development in the negotiations, since the EU accounted for nearly 80 percent of agricultural export subsidies provided by all WTO members (WTO 2000c). Its offer came at a time when the agriculture negotiations were stalled because of growing South-North disagreement over the negotiating agenda that emerged at the 2003 Cancun Ministerial Meeting (Narlikar and Wilkinson 2004; Narlikar and Tussie 2004; Matthews 2005). The EU's offer was intended to restart the moribund negotiations by dangling a major carrot for other WTO members—a promise to eliminate its much-vilified agricultural export subsidy scheme. The EU was in a position to make such an offer because it had initiated a major reform of its Common Agricultural Policy (CAP) in 2003 that paved the way for the eventual elimination of its export subsidies (Daugbjerg 2017; Garcia-Duran, Casanova, and Eliasson 2019). The issue for the EU was not so much if, but when, it would eliminate its agricultural export subsidies.

The EU's offer in the WTO agriculture negotiations proved controversial among some EU member states. Most notably, the agriculture ministers of France and Germany, whose countries received the lion's share of the EU's agricultural export subsidies, publicly declared the EU's offer a "massive tactical mistake" (Deutsche Welle 2004). France and Germany accordingly put pressure on EU trade negotiators to obtain an equivalent "political scalp" in the agriculture negotiations, which led EU officials to decide to target US food aid (Margulis 2018, 377). EU negotiators thus informed WTO members that in exchange for eliminating agricultural export subsidies, the EU expected "strict parallelism" in export competition. In particular, EU negotiators insisted that they expected the Americans to "fully match the EU [in disciplining] the forms of export support they use," including the "abuse of food aid" (EU 2004).

The EU's demands for concessions from the US on food aid drew on the long-standing criticism that the US "misused" and "abused" food aid to achieve commercial objectives. In its 2004 bargaining proposal on export competition, for example, the EU demanded that all "food aid should be given in fully grant form and that it should not be used as a market promotion tool." EU negotiators singled out the United States' PL 480 program, which had an explicit market development objective written into its statutes, and questioned whether the US practice of concessional sales really counted as genuine food aid (EU 2000, 4). American negotiators responded by insisting that their food aid programs were not up for negotiation. They told other delegations that their hands were tied because of pressure from the powerful US food aid lobby—known as the "Iron Triangle"—which included American farmers, millers, traders, shippers, and NGOs that benefited financially from US food aid programs, and which had strong cross-party ties and for decades had blocked efforts to reform US international food aid programs (Clapp 2012; Lentz 2014). Yet the US position on food aid at the WTO softened over the course of the agriculture negotiations, especially after it came to light that the US government had shipped record-level quantities of skim milk powder as food aid to Asia through a subsidiary of Land O'Lakes, one of the United States' largest commercial dairy producers. It was well known at the time that the US was sitting on mounting dairy surpluses with no commercially viable outlet. At the WTO, US officials claimed that its skim milk powder food aid was to improve child nutrition. But its actions ignited controversy as other agricultural exporters, including the EU as well as Canada and Australia, accused it of deliberately flouting WTO rules (ICTSD 2004). While the US had signaled at the beginning of the round that it did not wish to negotiate new food aid disciplines at the WTO, it later reversed its bargaining position in order to lock in the EU's offer on export subsidies. Eliminating the EU's agricultural export subsidies was the top US priority in the agriculture negotiations (Clapp 2004, 1443–44).

The EU's offer was thus successful in restarting the negotiations. By July 2004, WTO members had agreed to a so-called framework paper outlining the contours of the negotiating agenda on agriculture. On food aid, the July framework paper committed WTO members to negotiate new food aid disciplines with the objective "to prevent commercial displacement" and to examine "the question of providing food aid exclusively in fully grant form" (WTO 2004a, 3). The framework paper also imposed a deadline on trade negotiators to complete work on new food aid disciplines by June 2005, in order to allow sufficient time for a final text to be prepared in advance of the Hong Kong Ministerial Conference scheduled for December 2005. The July framework text was a significant development with important implications for the global governance of international food aid, introducing the possibility that future WTO rules could come to restrict and prohibit certain types of food aid transactions (Konandreas 2007, 325).

The WFP in Food Aid Debates at the WTO

The WFP secretariat engaged in a very limited way in the early stages of the Doha Round agriculture negotiations. Despite food aid taking on greater importance in the negotiations following the EU's offer on agricultural export subsidies, WFP officials chose initially not to make statements concerning the status of the agriculture negotiations at meetings of the WTO Committee on Agriculture special sessions or at the Doha or Cancun Ministerials. Instead, WFP officials adopted what they described as a "discreet approach" that focused on holding informal bilateral meetings with key WTO members to better understand negotiators' positions on new food aid disciplines.[6] The main reason the WFP chose this approach was that officials were reluctant to be seen as directly interfering in the agriculture negotiations and were wary of putting the organization in the middle of the brewing political battle between its two largest donors—the US and EU—over new food aid disciplines.[7] Instead, WFP officials focused on technical consultations and information sharing in support of the negotiations.

Following the 2004 July framework, trade negotiators turned to technical work on devising rules to prevent commercial displacement by food aid. The talks focused on disciplines for three types of US food practices: concessional sales, monetization, and in-kind donations. The US was the sole donor that continued to sell food aid on concessional terms. Though the volume of concessional sales by the US government was at record low levels by the early 2000s, other WTO members saw the agriculture negotiations as an opportunity to "shut the door" on concessional sales permanently.[8] There was also broad support among WTO members to create additional disciplines to address the practice of monetization. Monetization involves the sale of food aid in the open market *after* it has been delivered to the recipient country. While some part of the food aid do-nation is used directly to feed hungry people, other parts of the delivery are "monetized" in order to generate cash to pay for the transport and storage of food aid or to fund other development projects. The practice of monetization became increasingly common among American NGOs in the early 2000s in response to changes in US aid policy and cuts to its foreign aid budget, which spurred NGOs to sell US food aid to generate much-needed cash. However, monetization was widely criticized at the WTO, with many states arguing that it displaced local agricultural pro-duction and distorted food prices in recipient countries (WTO 2004b; S. Murphy 2005).

The issue of in-kind food aid received the most attention in the nego-tiations. While all donors had provided in-kind food aid in the past, by the early 2000s nearly all major donors, with the exception of the US, had reformed their food aid policies to "untie" donations from the purchase of domestically produced commodities (Barrett and Maxwell 2005; Clapp 2012). Most donors had switched to providing cash donations, which were then used by the WFP, other UN agencies, or NGOs specializing in food relief to purchase food on the world market and cover logistical costs (Singer 1994; Kneteman 2009).

In the agriculture negotiations, the EU took an especially hardline po-sition on in-kind food aid. Its negotiators demanded that all international food aid be provided exclusively in cash, effectively pressing for a ban on in-kind food aid at the WTO. The EU signaled to other WTO members that it would not agree to eliminate its agricultural export subsidies unless it secured a ban on in-kind food aid in return. Other agricultural export-ers, including the bulk of Cairns Group members, signaled their support for the EU's position. As Jennifer Clapp (2012, 129) argues, as a result of the EU's approach of hinging progress on eliminating agricultural export subsidies to achieving highly restrictive food aid rules, "Food aid effec-tively became a bargaining chip among donor countries in the context of the broader agricultural trade negotiations."

The WFP secretariat signaled to WTO members that it supported new additional disciplines on concessional sales and monetization. Indeed, WFP officials were themselves critical of these practices; the WFP itself does not engage in concessional sales of food and, as a policy, prefers to avoid monetization and instead distribute food directly to beneficiaries

(WFP 1997).[9] WFP officials also indicated that in principle the organization preferred cash contributions over in-kind donations, since cash contributions are the most cost-effective for procuring food and paying for transportation in emergency situations (Shaw 2007). But they informed trade negotiators that in a context of an increasing number of humanitarian emergencies, paired with dwindling food aid resources, the WFP and other humanitarian agencies needed to be pragmatic and flexible in how they sourced food aid and thus keep the in-kind option on the table. While acknowledging that in-kind food aid was less efficient, WFP officials told trade negotiators that the organization was experienced enough to know how to "move as quickly with an in-kind donation as with most cash donations" (WFP 2005a, 4).

WFP officials were concerned by the potential negative implications of the proposed WTO rules to limit in-kind food aid. The WFP's main concern was that any prohibition on in-kind food aid at the WTO could significantly reduce the supply of international food aid, without an assurance by donors to make up the shortfall with other resources (WFP 2005b).[10] The US was the world's largest food aid donor, and the WFP secretariat estimated that a WTO ban on in-kind food aid would result in a 25 percent drop in international food aid supply.[11] WFP officials feared what the proposed rules could mean for political support for US food aid. Providing food aid in kind was pivotal to maintaining political support from Congress, farmers, processors, shippers, and NGOs for US food aid programs. In fact, a bipartisan group of members of Congress warned that they were unlikely to support equivalent levels of future food aid if new WTO rules forced the US to shift to a "cash-only" model (Barrett and Maxwell 2005, 87).

The prospect that new WTO rules could induce a massive reduction of food aid alarmed the WFP's senior leadership, especially given that donations had already fallen by nearly 40 percent in recent years (see figure 3), leaving the organization struggling to meet the needs of a growing number of humanitarian emergencies around the world, such as the war in Darfur (UN News Centre 2005b).[12] While the supply of food aid had already dropped precipitously, demand was skyrocketing: in the early 2000s, the number of people affected by humanitarian emergencies—a key indicator of the need for emergency food aid—increased by 50 percent, or an additional one hundred million people (Lentz 2014). Indeed, throughout 2004 and 2005 the WFP made numerous appeals to donors citing insufficient food supplies to combat mounting hunger and malnutrition (H. Young 2007).

WFP officials were also concerned that prohibiting in-kind food aid would undermine the organization's efforts to expand donations from new middle-income donors, such as Brazil, China, and India, which, because of their lower level of economic development, primarily provided in-kind donations rather than cash contributions (WFP 2005a, 2013). The WFP's executive director, James Morris, summed up the organization's position at the time as follows: "The issue for WFP is simple. We need more resources—cash and food—to feed the growing number of hungry, seriously at-risk people" (WFP 2005a).

There was intense pressure on WTO members to reach a deal on agriculture, with stalemate in the agriculture negotiations seen to be holding back progress in other negotiating areas. As the negotiations on new food aid rules advanced, disagreement intensified among WTO members over how to treat in-kind food aid, with the issue becoming increasingly politicized. At the bargaining table, EU trade negotiators went on the

FIGURE 3. International food aid deliveries, 2000–2004 (in millions of metric tons)

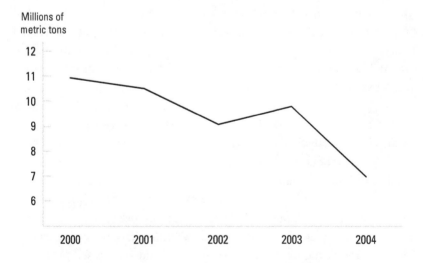

Source: WFP Food Aid Information System (FAIS), author's calculations.

attack by arguing that the United States' in-kind food aid was self-serving and could not be considered genuine humanitarian assistance (ICTSD 2005a). In response, US negotiators challenged the EU's attempts to take the moral high ground, arguing that the EU provided too little food aid, while the burden of feeding the world fell largely on the US.[13]

NGOs also became increasingly active in the food aid debate at the WTO, although they were split on the issue. Many NGOs, such as Oxfam, IATP, and Action Aid, called for more stringent WTO disciplines to prevent food aid from harming local farmers in recipient countries. A highly publicized Oxfam report (*Food Aid or Hidden Dumping?*) that documented how US in-kind food aid damaged the livelihoods of poor farmers abroad was influential in bringing international public attention to the issue (Clapp 2012). However, other NGOs, including CARE, Catholic Relief Services, and World Vision, that were largely dependent on US in-kind donations and the monetization of food aid to fund their development programs objected to new disciplines. These latter NGOs worked with US firms with a commercial interest in food aid to lobby the US government and other WTO members to oppose any new WTO rules (Kripke 2009).

At this point, the increasing politicization of food aid at the WTO spurred WFP officials to become more active in the agriculture negotiations. WFP officials became more proactive, for instance, in communicating the organization's concerns directly to trade negotiators in bilateral meetings. At such meetings, WFP officials indicated that there were serious risks for world food security with the EU and other WTO members' push for prohibiting in-kind food aid.[14] WFP officials also informed trade negotiators that prohibiting in-kind food aid would constrain their organization's operational flexibility to deliver food aid in emergency situations and thereby reduce their capacity to feed hungry people.[15] Indeed, WFP officials stressed to WTO members that it was incumbent on them to ensure that "any text dealing with food aid should at least reiterate the commitment by members to ensure the continuation and increase levels of food aid" (Belgasmi 2006, 179). However, WFP officials came away from their bilateral meetings with trade negotiators even more dismayed, fearing that trade politics were riding roughshod over humanitarian concerns and that WTO members were seeking to use food aid disciplines as a makeweight to secure a deal on agricultural export subsidies.[16]

The WFP Attempts to Persuade WTO Members to Alter Course

By spring 2005, there was a growing consensus among the EU and other major agricultural exporters on the need for new global trade rules that would prohibit in-kind food aid, potentially even in emergency situations (ICTSD 2005b; WTO 2005h). In response, the WFP secretariat redoubled its efforts at the WTO.[17] WFP officials organized a series of high-level workshops with WTO members in Geneva, with the aim of persuading trade negotiators about the risks for world food security posed by prohibiting in-kind donations. This included flying the WFP executive director in to Geneva to make the case for rethinking the scope of the proposed rules in the hope that trade negotiators might change their position if the message came directly from the UN's chief for food aid.

At a meeting held in May 2005 at the WTO, WFP executive director James Morris told an audience of delegates that he supported the goals of trade liberalization and was not there to tell them "what kind of disciplines you should place on food aid from a commercial perspective" but that, as the head of the WFP, he had a mandate to prevent any unintended consequences that could impede the fight against hunger (WFP 2005b). Morris communicated his concerns that the proposals on the table in the agriculture negotiations could restrict food aid supply when global demand was at a record high, telling WTO members: "The simple truth is that food aid commitments and deliveries are nose-diving, while the WTO is discussing their discipline. Please remember that simple fact and that the world's hungry children are paying the price" (UN News Centre 2005d). Morris also expressed concerns that "clumsily drafted" rules would discourage in-kind donations from emerging donors, while excluding traditional donors such as the US, but also Japan, which was a major donor of rice. Morris offered the assistance of the WFP secretariat to work jointly with WTO members to help them design food aid disciplines with "a firewall between commercial food transactions and food aid" to achieve a "win-win" solution. In the same instance, Morris emphasized that the WFP was "absolutely opposed" to any new WTO rules that would discourage donations of agricultural commodities by new and traditional donors, which he warned would "cut off hungry people from life-saving food aid" (WFP 2005a, 2, 6).

Morris's forceful words did give some trade negotiators a moment of pause, encouraging them to take seriously the potential negative consequences of prohibiting in-kind food aid.[18] Most trade negotiators recognized that they had a limited understanding of international food aid and agreed to the WFP's offer to hold further technical meetings in Geneva. At such a meeting, a technical workshop held at the WTO and led by WFP deputy executive director John Powell, the WFP reaffirmed that they supported strong food aid disciplines but wanted to ensure that "genuine" humanitarian aid would not be adversely affected. Powell expressed the challenge facing WTO members as follows:

> WFP feels that the most workable solution for WTO is not to focus on the *source* of food aid—cash versus in-kind, surplus versus non-surplus—but on its use. The question then is: *Is this food aid donation being used to address bona fide emergencies or to assist vulnerable groups with clearly defined food security problems?* Is food aid to a rural community where half the children are chronically malnourished and suffering from micronutrient deficiencies commercial displacement? Obviously not. These children and their families are not real participants in the commercial market. (WFP 2005a, 6, italics in original)

From the WFP's perspective, to avoid negative consequences for world food security meant that WTO members would need to build into new rules a commitment by donors to maintain adequate levels of food aid. Powell reminded WTO members that the WFP was willing to work closely with trade negotiators in drafting new rules. But he also warned them that protecting world food security trumped any trade agreement and that the failure to accomplish this would harm the WTO's reputation, stating that "a Doha Round Agreement on Agriculture that inadvertently undermines assistance to the needy would be both a moral and public relations disaster" (WFP 2005a, 2).

The high-level meetings between senior WFP leaders and WTO member state representatives did not, however, yield the result hoped for by the WFP—that states would reconsider the proposed ban on in-kind food aid. Nor did WTO members take up the WFP secretariat's offer to provide their expertise and assist in the design of new food aid disciplines. On the contrary, many trade negotiators did not welcome the WFP's warning, with several EU and Cairns Group negotiators suggesting that WFP officials were not being impartial and were improperly interfering in the negotiations.[19]

Despite the new information provided by WFP officials to WTO members about the risks for world food security of restricting in-kind food aid, the main priority for trade negotiators was to get a deal done in order to lock in the elimination of agricultural export subsidies. For trade negotiators, who represented their national ministries of trade and/or agriculture and had little practical experience with food aid policy, humanitarian considerations were not at the top of their list of bargaining priorities. They expected the US to make a major concession on food aid, including possibly agreeing to cash-only food aid, in order to complete work on the export competition pillar and thus move the agriculture negotiations closer to completion (WTO 2005c, 8).[20]

As the July deadline approached for negotiators to finalize a new text on food aid, the work on concessional sales and monetization was nearly complete. According to the chair of the agriculture negotiations, Tim Groser, the main outstanding point of disagreement was whether in-kind food aid "might constitute genuine emergency food aid" (WTO 2005b, 2). While the WFP insisted that it did, EU and Cairns Group trade negotiators expressed an opposing view, keeping up the pressure in an effort to extract greater concessions from the US in the agriculture negotiations.

The WFP Publicly Shames Trade Ministers

By late November 2005, with only days remaining until the Hong Kong Ministerial Meeting, Morris and other senior WFP officials recognized that they had failed in their efforts to persuade WTO members to alter course and drop the proposal to prohibit in-kind food aid.[21] The ban on in-kind food aid remained on the bargaining table, with the final draft ministerial declaration circulated in advance of the ministerial stating that there was an "emerging convergence" on "some elements regarding the disciplines on food aid necessary to eliminate commercial displacement" and the goal that WTO members "should (albeit gradually) move towards untied" food aid (WTO 2005g, 1, A-4). Trade negotiators had also arrived at draft text to prohibit in-kind food aid, but given the issue's political sensitivity for the US, they left the final, political decision to be hashed out by trade ministers at Hong Kong (WTO 2005a, 2005e). While WTO members signaled that they did not want the WTO to "stand in the way of the provision of genuine food aid," there was a general expectation among negotiators that trade ministers would agree to declaring a "move towards untied, in-cash food aid only" (WTO 2005e, 4).

To lay the groundwork for the political decision in Hong Kong, the EU trade commissioner, Peter Mandelson, increased his public criticism of in-kind food aid. Mandelson repeatedly called it "fake food aid" and "trade distorting" in media interviews and press releases in the weeks leading up to the ministerial (Mekay 2005). The political balance at the WTO appeared to tilt heavily in favor of the EU's preferred position to place major restrictions on in-kind food aid, especially after the Australian and Canadian governments introduced legislative changes to end any remaining vestiges of their earlier in-kind food aid programs and declared themselves ready to switch to a cash-only model (Clapp 2012). The signals coming out of the agriculture negotiations therefore suggested the strong likelihood that trade ministers would agree to prohibit in-kind food aid in Hong Kong.

This spurred the WFP executive director to conclude that it was time for the organization to take a public stance against the proposed WTO rules.[22] Up to this point, the WFP had only communicated its concerns directly to states and had remained reluctant to go public with its concerns. One of Morris's first steps was to organize a joint press conference with Antonio Guterres, the UN High Commissioner for Refugees (UNHCR), and Anne Veneman, the executive director of the UN Children's Fund (UNICEF), to voice concerns about the prohibition on in-kind food aid. It was the idea of senior WFP officials to enlist the UNHCR and UNICEF, the two other UN agencies involved in the delivery of food assistance to the hungry. WFP officials believed their concerns would carry more weight and attract greater international media attention if the message came in unison from three high-profile UN chiefs.[23] In addition, enlisting the other UN agencies would give the WFP greater political cover from potential backlash from WTO members compared to going public on its own.

At the joint press conference, held the week prior to the ministerial, the three UN chiefs called on WTO members to protect the interests of food-insecure people in the agriculture negotiations. They affirmed their support for a rules-based trading system but flagged their concerns for world food security, stating:

> We strongly believe reform of international agricultural trade is vital and can help overcome poverty in the developing world . . . This may well include disciplines on some types of food aid. But reforms should be carefully designed to protect millions of the world's children, refu-

gees and malnourished people who count on donations of food aid for their survival, nutrition and health. The needs of hungry women and children should take priority if the Doha Round is to be the pro-poor trade round we all hope for. . . . We appeal to negotiators at the World Trade Organization to put humanitarian considerations first when they address food aid. (UN News Centre 2005c)

For the WFP to go public with its concerns, as well as enlist other UN agencies to its cause, marked a major change in the WFP's approach to the WTO negotiations. This shift was driven by the failure of its earlier strategy to privately persuade negotiators to change course.

Tensions between the WFP and WTO members reached fever pitch at the December 2005 Hong Kong Ministerial. Believing that he had exhausted all other alternatives, Morris took the extraordinary step of publishing an advertisement in the *Financial Times* on the opening day of the 2005 WTO Ministerial that openly criticized the WTO's proposed food aid rules.[24] This time, Morris partnered with Jean Ziegler, then UN SRRTF, who was also critical of a ban on in-kind food aid (UN News Centre 2005a). Emblazoned with the title "Will WTO's Negotiators Take the Food out of Their Mouths?," the WFP's advertisement depicted four starving children, followed by the message: "Trade reform is good, but restrictions on donations of food aid to the United Nations could leave these children hungry. Sadly, millions who rely on food aid to survive have no voice at the negotiating table in the Doha Round. Who will fight for them?" (WFP 2005e).

The WFP's message was unmistakable—WTO members were depicted as recklessly endangering the lives of vulnerable and hungry people. The WFP employed a strategy of public shaming in the hope that going public with its concerns, and exercising its moral authority as the UN agency charged with feeding the world's hungry, would trigger public outrage and pressure WTO member states to change course.[25] The advertisement ignited international controversy, as the world's media ran with coverage that the UN was claiming the WTO wanted to starve millions of innocent children (Clapp 2012). The WFP's claims were a public relations disaster for the WTO and were seen to reinforce the perception that trade was skewed against the interests of the global poor.

The WFP's advertisement in the *Financial Times* subsequently became the flashpoint of a political blame game among WTO members at the

Hong Kong Ministerial. The EU, which was under pressure to commit to an end date for eliminating its agricultural export subsidies at Hong Kong, went on the attack against US food aid, releasing a "fact sheet" and statements in the press alleging that US in-kind donations were not genuine humanitarian aid but instead worked primarily to benefit US agribusiness and shipping companies. The US responded with its own "fact sheet" that argued that the EU proposal would lead to a decline in international food aid and, in an effort to sow doubt about the proposed ban on in-kind food aid, claimed that the EU's own donations had been cut in half after adopting a cash-only model (Mekay 2005). The WFP's advertisement in the *Financial Times* came as a total shock to WTO members, including the WFP's main donors, as they had no prior knowledge of the WFP's plans (Heri and Häberli 2011). Indeed, few states could have predicted the WFP's actions, since only just a couple of weeks earlier, Morris had told donors that he was concerned about "the potential impact of WTO decisions on the ability of WFP to attract additional resources" but "emphasized that WFP had no interest in a central role in trade debates" (WFP 2005c, 1).

The WFP's intervention at Hong Kong provoked intense backlash from states. Trade ministers were incensed with the WFP's advertisement and expressed the view that "a UN agency should not be so publicly and directly involved in lobbying on a sensitive WTO negotiating issue" (Khor 2005). The strongest rebuke came from the EU trade commissioner, who stated, "I find it shocking that United Nations agencies should be financing an advertisement in *The Financial Times* that is designed to support the US' trade distorting policies on food aid" (EU 2005). EU members also responded to the WFP advertisement in an op-ed in the following day's *Financial Times* entitled "UN Agencies' Advert Is an Insult to All WTO Members," in which they accused the WFP of being part of a group of "entrenched interests" who were not ready for a change to a cash-only food aid regime (Mandleson and Fisher Boel 2005). The US, which also had been unaware of the WFP's plans to intervene at the Hong Kong Ministerial, responded by distancing itself from the WFP's advertisement. In a press conference, the US trade representative, Rob Portman, stated: "First, the United States did not put in any ad or article in *The Financial Times*. That was the United Nations agencies that did it. . . . It's a free world. If people want to put ads in the newspaper, they can do that. We didn't put any ads in anywhere" (US Department of State 2005). Morris refuted the EU's accusation that the WFP had acted in support of "entrenched interests" in his own follow-up letter in the *Financial Times*. He wrote that the purpose of the WFP's advertisement had not been to support any particular WTO member's position but to prevent an outcome at Hong Kong in which the "humanitarian needs of our beneficiaries would be diminished in the quest for a trade agreement" (Morris 2005). The highly public spat among the EU, US, and WFP over proposed WTO food aid rules dominated international press coverage of the ministerial. As a result of the WFP's intervention, food aid became the most contested issue by states at the ministerial.

The Impact of the WFP's Intervention at the WTO

The WFP's public shaming of WTO members had a significant impact on the negotiating agenda and outcomes of global trade rulemaking. The expectation among WTO members going into Hong Kong was that the ministerial would be a key decision point for finalizing the negotiation agenda and would give trade negotiators the green light to move forward with the proposed food aid rules. However, the WFP's public shaming of WTO members and its claims that WTO rules would increase world hunger made it politically impossible for trade ministers to agree to prohibiting in-kind donations—and to risk being seen as knowingly producing more hunger-related deaths. Instead, the WFP's intervention forced trade ministers to rewrite their declaration to acknowledge the potential risks of the proposed food aid disciplines and commit themselves to ensuring that trade rules did not result in negative effects on the delivery of food aid. The Hong Kong declaration ultimately stated: "On food aid, we reconfirm our commitment to maintain an adequate level and to take into account the interests of food aid recipient countries. To this end, a 'safe box' for bona fide food aid will be provided to ensure that there is no unintended impediment to dealing with emergency situations" (WTO 2005d, 2). Trade ministers' decision to instruct trade negotiators to create a "safe box" for food aid was in direct response to the concerns expressed by the WFP that any WTO rule that prohibited in-kind donations in emergency situations would constrain its ability to provide food aid.[26] Most importantly, the WFP's intervention forced WTO members to take the proposal for prohibiting in-kind food aid off the agenda.

The WFP's intervention altered the trajectory of global trade rulemaking at the WTO. When WTO members returned to the bargaining table after Hong Kong, one of the first steps trade negotiators took was to roll back the idea of prohibiting in-kind food aid. The shift in bargaining position was most notable among the Cairns Group countries, such as Canada, Brazil, Australia, New Zealand, Argentina, and Thailand. Prior to Hong Kong these states had signaled their support for prohibiting in-kind food aid, but in their follow-up proposals after the ministerial they each affirmed that there should not be a prohibition on in-kind food aid at the WTO (WTO 2007a). Even the EU, the strongest advocate for the prohibition, softened its previously hardline position in the agriculture negotiations (ICTSD 2007).

WTO members eventually converged around the idea that in-kind donations in emergency and nonemergency situations would be given "safe harbor" under new WTO rules (WTO 2007b, 13). There was also a shift in trade negotiators' approach to the WFP, as they began to consult closely with the WFP secretariat on the design of the new food aid disciplines in order to prevent any adverse effects.[27] Several trade negotiators stated that their change in position was an acknowledgment that they had earlier been "too hasty" in dismissing the WFP's concerns and had "underappreciated" the potential negative effects that WTO rules could have on the availability of international food aid.[28]

By February 2008, following two years of intensive negotiations in Geneva, trade negotiators reached consensus on a draft text of new WTO food aid rules to replace Article 10.4 of the AoA in a new agriculture agreement. Under the new rules, WTO members would be required to provide all food aid in fully grant form (meaning that concessional sales by the US would no longer be permitted) and to ensure that food was "needs-driven" and not linked to states' market development objectives. The new rules also largely prohibited monetization except under very specific conditions in emergencies (WTO 2008c). Crucially, the draft text did not prohibit in-kind donations. Rather, WTO members were "encouraged" to refrain from using in-kind food aid and instead to procure food aid in other markets, and also to make "their best efforts to move increasingly towards more untied cash-based food aid" (WTO 2008c, 72–73). In-kind food aid would, furthermore, continue to be explicitly permitted under specific conditions, including if there was a declaration of emergency by the recipient country government and/or the UN secretary-general, or following an appeal or needs assessment by the WFP or other relevant humanitarian organizations (WTO 2008c, 74). In addition, the draft text included a commitment by WTO members "to maintain an adequate level of international food aid" and to ensure that the disciplines "do not unintentionally impede the delivery of food aid provided to deal with emergency situations" (WTO 2008c, 72).

WFP officials were delighted by the food aid rules contained in the 2008 draft text. From their perspective, the new rules allayed their main concern by ruling out the possibility of a general ban on in-kind food aid. As one WFP official put it, the organization was "very satisfied" with the draft text because "WTO rules would not prevent the WFP from drawing on food commodities to feed vulnerable populations."[29] It was the WFP secretariat that had pressed WTO members to ensure that any future rules would continue to provide the WFP flexibility to receive in-kind food aid donations, especially to fight hunger in emergency situations (WFP 2005a, 2005b, 2005d, 2005e). That flexibility was now explicitly built into the rules. WFP officials were also pleased with the commitment by WTO members to maintain adequate levels of food aid. This had, in fact, been a key demand made repeatedly by WFP officials to WTO members throughout the agriculture negotiations, in an effort to ensure that new global trade rules did not result in a decline in international food aid supply (Belgasmi 2006).

According to the chair of the agriculture negotiations, the draft text on new food aid disciplines was "ripe and ready to go" to trade ministers for approval (WTO 2008b, 4). The new food aid rules were incorporated into the full draft agriculture agreement presented by the chair to trade ministers in July 2008. Ultimately, however, trade ministers were unable to reach agreement on agriculture and other trade issues at the 2008 Geneva Ministerial Meeting, which led to the collapse of the Doha Round (Blustein 2008; Stewart-Brown 2009; Ismail 2009). Yet despite the collapse of the Doha Round in 2008 and WTO members' official acknowledgment that the round was dead in 2011, the agriculture negotiations resumed in 2013. Rather than seeking to conclude a comprehensive agreement on agriculture, WTO members instead chose to focus on fast-tracking parts of the draft agriculture agreement where there was greatest consensus. One of the areas of the agriculture negotiations that was chosen by WTO members for an "early harvest" was export competition, which included food aid (WTO 2013a).

When resuming the negotiations on food aid, WTO members worked from the food aid rules set out in the final draft of the agriculture agreement (Revised Draft Modalities for Agriculture) from 2008 (known as "Rev.4" in reference to its status as the fourth—and last—revised version of the agriculture text). The negotiations on export competition were swiftly and successfully completed in time for the 2015 Nairobi Ministerial. In the 2015 Ministerial Decision on Export Competition, WTO members agreed to impose new disciplines on international food aid and to eliminate agricultural export subsidies by 2018 (R. Wilkinson, Hannah, and Scott 2016). Speaking about the new food aid disciplines, then WTO director-general Roberto Azevêdo explained that the decision "will provide a better framework for international food aid—maintaining this essential lifeline, while ensuring that it doesn't displace domestic producers" (WTO 2015a). The food aid disciplines contained in the 2015 Ministerial Decision on Export Competition reproduced the key provisions of the 2008 food aid text, including stipulating that WTO members could continue to provide in-kind international food aid and restating the commitment by states "to maintain an adequate level of international food aid" (WTO 2015b, 6–7). The decision thus satisfied all of the WFP's concerns.

The WFP's decision to intervene in the WTO agriculture negotiations was driven by the organization's social purpose to feed vulnerable people. WFP senior officials firmly believed that if trade ministers approved the proposed food aid rules at Hong Kong, those rules would have disastrous consequences for world food security. While a reduction of in-kind food aid could have sharply decreased the WFP's access to food aid supply, it would not have been of consequence to the organization's authority, survival, or budget, which is financed through voluntary financial contributions from states, not through in-kind food aid. Access to in-kind food aid simply enabled the WFP to feed more hungry people. Furthermore, the WFP's actions cannot be interpreted as direct support for the US position in the agriculture negotiations. The WFP clearly indicated that it supported eliminating concessional sales and the monetization of food aid, positions that put it at odds with US negotiators and the "Iron Triangle" of American firms and NGOs that benefited financially from US food aid programs.

The WFP's use of a public shaming strategy was a calculated risk. WFP officials were cognizant that vilifying WTO members not only was controversial but would be seen by many WTO members as undermining their economic interests and likely lead to backlash.[30] However, WFP officials indicated that they believed their actions to influence WTO trade rules were consistent with their organizational mission and values to protect the interests of hungry people.[31] While the WFP's intervention at the Hong Kong Ministerial resulted in significant criticism from its major donors, these states did not punish the WFP secretariat by, for example, reducing their donations of food aid. Doing so would have likely led to widespread international condemnation and been counterproductive, because it would have only further worked to paint those countries as behaving irresponsibly by taking lifesaving food aid away from starving people in order to make a point to UN bureaucrats. Instead, states waited and exacted retribution in a more discreet and personal manner: the EU blocked the reappointment of Morris for a second term as WFP executive director in 2007, in a move widely seen as retaliation for his actions at Hong Kong.[32]

Conclusion

The WFP secretariat intervened at the WTO by publicly shaming trade ministers, portraying them as recklessly endangering the world's hungriest people. Although the WFP secretariat was in favor of stricter global trade rules to prevent food aid from displacing commercial trade or adversely affecting food production in recipient countries, its officials were concerned that the proposed WTO rules to prohibit in-kind food aid would put the lives of millions vulnerable people at risk. The WFP turned to publicly shaming WTO members only after its earlier efforts to privately persuade them to change course had failed. The WFP's intervention at the WTO was primarily driven by the principled beliefs of its staff and the mission of the organization to feed the hungry and avoid the preventable loss of life. Despite not having a formal seat at the bargaining table, the WFP secretariat inserted itself into the politics of the WTO agriculture negotiations. In spite of significant backlash from states, its actions were influential in blocking WTO members from agreeing to prohibit in-kind food aid at the 2005 Hong Kong Ministerial Meeting, and its core demands were subsequently incorporated into new global trade rules in the 2015 Ministerial Decision on Export Competition.

CHAPTER 5

The OHCHR Invokes Human Rights at the WTO

THE OHCHR INTERVENED AT the WTO to ensure that global trade rules would not undermine human rights.[1] This chapter shows that the OHCHR used the strategy of invoking an alternative international legal framework to challenge proposed trade rules by presenting them as potentially violating established international human rights law. Two separate episodes of intervention by the OHCHR at the WTO are examined: the first occurring in 2002 when it proposed that WTO members adopt a right-to-food approach for the Doha Round negotiations on agriculture, and the second in 2003 when the OHCHR made an "unofficial" submission to trade ministers in the context of the WTO Ministerial Meeting in Cancun. In both these episodes, the OHCHR not only raised the specter that prospective global trade rules could potentially lead to the violation of human rights, but also introduced its own proposals for new trade rules intended to protect the right to food of vulnerable populations.

The OHCHR's choice to intervene at the WTO was taken independently and not ordered by its member states or requested by those of the WTO. Indeed, quite the opposite, states repeatedly signaled their preference to keep human rights talk out of multilateral trade negotiations. The OHCHR was driven to intervene at the WTO out of concern that prospective global trade rules could have adverse impacts on the food security of vulnerable groups. Since the OHCHR does not have observer status to the WTO, meaning it lacks formal access to both negotiating sessions and general meetings of WTO members, it was creative in choosing to invoke human rights law in an effort to exercise influence over global trade rulemaking. Most significantly, intervention by the OHCHR changed the discourse about trade and human rights at the WTO, and its proposals for new trade rules to protect the right to food of vulnerable groups were incorporated by WTO members into the text of a new agriculture agreement.

The chapter is organized as follows. The first section contextualizes the role of the OHCHR in the regime complex for food security and the political debates concerning potential conflicts between global trade rules and human rights. The second section examines the OHCHR's intervention in the lead-up to the launch of new agriculture negotiations at the WTO and its proposals for a human rights approach to global trade rules. The third section analyzes the OHCHR's "unofficial" submission to the 2003 WTO Ministerial in Cancun. The fourth section discusses the impacts of the OHCHR's interventions on global trade rulemaking at the WTO.

The Mandate of the OHCHR

The OHCHR, the UN human rights treaty bodies,[2] the Human Rights Council (HRC),[3] and the HRC's Special Procedures mechanism[4] make up what is commonly referred to the "UN human rights system" (Hunt 2017). The origins of the UN human rights system date back to the 1945 UN Charter, which made promotion of human rights a key goal of the postwar liberal international order. Although the idea of a "human rights attorney general" had been considered in the early 1950s, the post of High Commissioner for Human Rights was established only in 1993, largely in response to growing mass violations of human rights following the end of the Cold War and the advocacy efforts of global civil society organizations for a central UN agency in charge of human rights (Gaer 1995; Alston 1997).

The High Commissioner for Human Rights (hereafter "High Commissioner") is the UN's senior human rights official and holds the rank of

UN under-secretary-general. The formal mandate of the High Commissioner is to be the chief official with principal responsibility for UN human rights activities (UNGA 1994). The High Commissioner is charged with various tasks, including promoting, protecting, and monitoring human rights; coordinating the UN's work on human rights; dialoguing with, and making recommendations to, states on human rights standard setting; and providing technical assistance and expertise to states and other institutions (UNGA 1994, 2–4). As a result, the High Commissioner straddles many roles, including manager, politician, diplomat, norm generator, and "moral conscience" for the world (Gaer and Broecker 2013). The High Commissioner also manages, and is supported by, a secretariat, the OHCHR, which carries out the day-to-day work of the UN human rights system, such as assisting states to implement international human rights treaties and cooperating with other IOs and national human rights institutions.

The OHCHR's mandate covers "every imaginable aspect of human rights work," from the prevention of torture to the social consequences of aid conditionality (Clapham 1994, 565). Such a "combination of vagueness and comprehensiveness" reflected the preferences among states, and also many senior UN officials, to limit the power of the organization (Alston 1997, 326). While the OHCHR lacks enforcement powers and is severely underfunded, the High Commissioner enjoys significant discretion and independence in their work due to an ambiguous, open-ended mandate and the moral authority associated with the position (Seiderman 2019). This allows the OHCHR to undertake work that states are unable or unwilling to do (Subedi 2017). For example, High Commissioners have interpreted their mandate creatively to strengthen human rights accountability mechanisms (often in the face of resistance by states), as in the case of advocating for the creation of the Universal Periodic Review, which is a peer-review mechanism that scrutinizes UN members' human rights practices (Ramcharan 2004).

The OHCHR has an activist organizational culture. Unlike most other IOs, the OHCHR operates in what is essentially a confrontational system because it is states that are typically the violators of human rights. Although the OHCHR is formally accountable to UN member states, in practice, OHCHR officials see their responsibility as being foremost to the victims of human rights abuses, and thus a core part of their work is to hold states that violate human rights to account, with the result that "public confrontations between the High Commissioner and rights-violating governments are frequent" (Pegram 2014, 603). High-profile examples of the OHCHR's advocacy include that of Louise Arbour (High Commissioner between 2004 and 2008), who denounced the US's practice of "extraordinary rendition," and Navi Pillay (High Commissioner between 2008 and 2014), who urged the UN Security Council to refer the gross human rights violations by the Syrian regime to the International Criminal Court (Foot 2007; Gaer and Broecker 2013).

Many of the events analyzed in this chapter took place during the tenure of Mary Robinson, who served as High Commissioner between 1997 and 2002. Robinson—the first female president of Ireland and a respected constitutional lawyer and well-known human rights activist—was recruited to the post by UN secretary-general Kofi Annan in order to advocate the protection of international human rights. With the OHCHR a relatively new organization when Robinson took the helm, she made advancing economic, social, and cultural rights—including the human right to food—a priority for the organization's mission. Robinson's long experience in global affairs and credibility as a former head of state brought gravitas to the position of High Commissioner (Alston 1997). In addition, her charismatic leadership and personal relationships with many world leaders empowered her to frequently take strong, public positions on human rights issues. This included, for example, publicly criticizing numerous states for failing to respect human rights, including the US, Russia, Rwanda, East Timor, and Mexico, which helped to establish the OHCHR's activist organizational culture.

The OHCHR and World Food Security

The OHCHR's contribution to world food security has been through its role as a norm generator and diffuser. In particular, the OHCHR contributed to making the human right to food an established international norm. At the 1996 World Food Summit, UN members tasked the OHCHR to clarify the legal content of the human right to food as well as states' obligations under this international human right (FAO 1996). The OHCHR played a direct role in the creation and implementation of several new international instruments designed to promote and protect the right to food.[5] Within the regime complex for food security, the

OHCHR diffuses the norm of food as a human right; leads human rights "mainstreaming" across the UN system, Bretton Woods institutions, and regional organizations; and monitors the coherence of states' policies with their commitments under international human rights treaties to respect, protect, and fulfill the right to food and other human rights relevant to achieving world food security (Mechlem 2004; Rae, Thomas, and Vidar 2007).

Trade Liberalization and Human Rights: Friends or Foes?

There is significant international debate about the compatibility between international human rights and global trade rules. The creation of the WTO and its expanded authority into many areas of social and public regulation resulted in growing concerns about potential norm and treaty conflicts between WTO law and human rights law (A. Lang 2011; Ratner 2015; Kanade 2017). Debates about trade and human rights conflicts have been the subject of extensive scholarship (e.g., F. Abbott, Kaufmann, and Cottier 2006; Joseph 2011; H. Andersen 2015; Ferguson 2018; Langille 2020). Rather than rehash those debates here, I highlight the political dynamics most relevant for contextualizing intervention by the OHCHR at the WTO.

Shortly after the establishment of the WTO, several developments culminated in creating international political discord about the coherence between the trade and human rights regimes. First, a controversy emerged after the US and France proposed in 1999 to insert a "social clause" at the WTO, which was intended to permit WTO members to refuse trade benefits to other states that violated labor rights (Leary 1997; R. Wilkinson 1999). While this proposal had strong support among developed countries and labor and social justice NGOs, most developing countries regarded the proposed social clause as new protectionism by rich countries intended to diminish developing countries' competitive advantage in cheap labor (Hughes and Wilkinson 1998). Interstate disagreement over the social clause was one of the principal causes of the collapse of the 1999 WTO Ministerial Meeting in Seattle (R. O'Brien et al. 2000; Chan 2003; J. Smith 2005). Second, a series of controversial trade disputes, including the 1998 US-EU beef hormone case (in which a WTO panel ruled that the EU's ban on hormone-treated beef imports was not justified on public health grounds) and the high-profile global access-to-medicines campaign, intended to reform parts of the WTO's Agreement on Trade-Related Intellectual Property Rights (TRIPS) that limited the right of states to produce generic versions of essential medicines, spurred major international debate about whether global trade rules adequately accommodated social priorities such as public health and human rights (Helfer 1999, 2003; Sell 2001; Muzaka 2011).

Political battles about WTO rules and human rights were not confined to the WTO but spread into other global forums, including the UN General Assembly (UNGA), where the issue was debated extensively by UN members (Therien 1999; Ruggie 2003). Indeed, political discord among the UN membership concerning potential conflicts between trade and human rights was an important catalyst leading to the creation of the Millennium Development Goals (MDGs) and the Global Compact, both of which were efforts to foster economic globalization "with a human face" (Uvin 2007; McArthur 2014).

Debate concerning the coherence between global trade rules and human rights was taken up not only by the UNGA but by states in the UN human rights system, including the Commission on Human Rights (CHR, which preceded the HRC) and in the treaty bodies. As a result, the UN human rights system became a source of considerable legal and analytical work on the relationship between human rights and trade, with much of this work led by independent human rights experts appointed by UN members. Some of this work has been highly controversial. For example, one report commissioned by the CHR that concluded that the WTO was a "veritable nightmare" for human rights drew considerable criticism from many WTO members (Ala'i 2001; Raghavan 2000b). NGOs, which hold consultative status in the CHR/HRC, have also been influential in bringing attention to, and contesting, the impacts of global trade rules on human rights.[6] For example, NGOs highly critical of WTO agreements, such as the Habitat International Coalition, the International NGO Committee on Human Rights in Trade and Investment, and the Lutheran World Federation, were instrumental in lobbying member states of the CHR in the late 1990s to adopt the position that international human rights treaties trumped the WTO's rules on intellectual property rights when it came to the protection of traditional indigenous knowledge and common ownership of plant seeds (Weissbrodt and Schoff 2003). The CHR (and its successor, the HRC) has frequently been a site for high-profile criticism of WTO rules, both by UN member states and by independent experts, resulting in the view among many in trade policy circles that the UN human rights system has an "anti–free trade bias" (Petersmann 2004, 614; A. Lang 2006; WikiLeaks 2011).

The OHCHR and the WTO

The expanded authority of the WTO and concerns about potential conflicts between trade and human rights have also spurred cooperation between the WTO and OHCHR secretariats. Although international human rights are not directly referenced in WTO law and there is no formal linkage between the two organizations, cooperation between the OHCHR and the WTO is focused on better understanding the interface between international trade and human rights law, especially as it relates to legal interpretation and agreement implementation (Marceau 2002; Cottier 2002; Pauwelyn 2003; F. Abbott, Kaufmann, and Cottier 2006). Cooperation between the OHCHR and the WTO is not formalized but takes place on a purely ad hoc basis; there is no signed memo of understanding that defines the scope of cooperation between these two IOs comparable to what exists, for instance, between the WTO and the IMF or the World Bank (Grabel 2007). Unlike the FAO and WFP, the OHCHR does not enjoy formal observer status at the WTO. This means that OHCHR officials do not have the right to attend or make statements at WTO meetings or to receive privileged information about multilateral trade negotiations. The OHCHR therefore lacks an established channel to communicate its views and concerns on trade issues directly to WTO members. But while lacking observer status at the WTO, the OHCHR has a unit in its Special Procedures and Right to Development Division that closely monitors developments at the WTO that it deems relevant for international human rights.[7]

Most cooperation between the two secretariats is in the form of expert consultations on technical and legal matters. For example, senior legal experts from both organizations have organized workshops and coauthored books and reports to guide the interpretation of human rights norms in the implementation of international trade law (OHCHR 2004, 2005). While most cooperative activities are among working-level officials, there is also executive-level cooperation between the High Commissioner and the WTO director-general.[8] This includes frequent participation by High

Commissioners at the WTO Public Forum and cooperation in the context of the UN Chief Executives Board, which coordinates work among IOs.

The OHCHR's "Right to Food Approach" to Agricultural Trade Liberalization

This section examines the first episode of intervention by the OHCHR at the WTO to alter the trajectory of global trade rulemaking. In the months leading up to the launch of the WTO Doha Round negotiations in 2001, the High Commissioner, Mary Robinson, began to publicly express concern that global trade rules failed to "take sufficient account of the food security of the poor and vulnerable such as poor farmers and farm workers" (OHCHR 2002b, 12). The High Commissioner's concerns echoed increasing attention at the time to the fact that approximately 70 percent of the world's food-insecure people lived in rural areas of developing countries (FAO 2002a, 3). This is because most farming households in low-income developing countries are generally poorer and more likely to live in poverty than the population as a whole, thus making farming households more likely to count among the food insecure (L. Smith, El Obeid, and Jensen 2000; FAO 2002a). The problem of food-insecure farming households was especially acute among least developed WTO country members, where poverty was widespread and on average 32 percent of the population was undernourished.[9] There was a growing consensus in development policy circles that reducing rural food insecurity and poverty in lower-income developing countries required enhanced government support and investment in the agricultural sector (Rahman and Westley 2001), which came to influence the design of the 2000 UN Millennium Development Goals targets on poverty and hunger (Fukuda-Parr and Orr 2014). However, there were growing concerns that low-income developing countries might be pressured by rich countries to take on new liberalization commitments at the WTO that could limit their policy space to address rural poverty and food insecurity (Clapp 2006). The High Commissioner stated her concerns about the risk to poor, food-insecure farming households in the context of an address to UN member states about the main challenges to achieving the full realization of the human right to food. In her address, she called on states to review their agricultural trade policies and to adopt a "right to food approach" such that global trade rules would be designed in ways to emphasize "the human rights principle of non-discrimination and consequently encourage affirmative action for the poor" (OHCHR 2002b, 12–15).

The concern that the Doha Round negotiations could lead to adverse effects for food security was what spurred the High Commissioner to use her authority to intervene at the WTO.[10] The High Commissioner was strongly committed to advocating for the human right to food and combating world hunger. Upon accepting the position of High Commissioner, Robinson had made clear that the focus of her mandate would be to promote and protect "second-generation" economic, social, and cultural rights, such as the right to food. Robinson was also a well-known advocate of the right to food, having played a leading role in developing the normative content of the human right to food early on in her tenure as High Commissioner and later championing the creation of a UN Special Rapporteur on the Right to Food (Boyle 2004; MacNaughton and McGill 2018). In sum, food security was a priority issue for the High Commissioner.

A challenge for the High Commissioner, however, was that she did not have the formal right to present her concerns directly to WTO members because the OHCHR lacked observer status to the WTO. Though the OHCHR and WTO headquarters are physically located just a few short blocks away from one another in Geneva, without observer status OHCHR officials could not attend or speak at meetings of the relevant WTO bodies and committees, including the General Council, the Committee on Agriculture, and the special sessions of the agriculture negotiations. The right to attend any of these bodies requires a formal invitation approved by the entire WTO membership. Such an invitation to the High Commissioner was, however, unlikely to be forthcoming because of the politics at the time. The US delegation to the WTO made it clear that it would block any such invitation; Robinson was considered persona non grata after naming and shaming the Bush administration for its illegal use of torture in the "war on terror."[11]

Since the High Commissioner was unable to secure a direct audience with WTO members in a decision-making forum, she instead chose to express her concerns through other means. In particular, she decided to author and release a report examining the human rights implications of agricultural trade liberalization. Reports issued by the High Commissioner differ substantially from those commonly produced by other IOs, in that their primary purpose is not simply to communicate information but to put forward recommendations to states, which, under the procedures of the UN human rights system, must be debated and voted on in formal resolutions (Gaer and Broecker 2013). Reports by the High Commissioner carry considerable political and moral weight, as they are one of the main mechanisms through which a High Commissioner alerts UN member states and the public to important and pressing human rights issues. Reports issued in the name of the High Commissioner are thus taken seriously by states, as well as human rights bodies, jurists, and global civil society (Hannum 2006). Indeed, such reports have a significant impact on international human rights practice; they are seen as an authoritative position on human rights issues and are often taken up by international and national bodies to inform norm development and legal interpretation of human rights (Knox 2009; Dudai 2009).

The High Commissioner's choice to author a report on agricultural trade liberalization was taken independently and not on the order of member states. Although states often use formal resolutions of the HRC or the UNGA to instruct the High Commissioner to issue reports on specific human rights topics, this did not occur in this instance. UN members never discussed or tabled any resolution instructing the High Commissioner to write a report on the WTO and agricultural trade liberalization. Instead, Robinson exercised her discretion as High Commissioner in choosing to author a report without consulting states or even notifying them in advance (Weissbrodt and Schoff 2003). Moreover, Robinson was fully cognizant that a report examining the WTO agricultural trade negotiations was likely to be controversial and to prompt a backlash from some WTO members.[12] First, it was highly unusual for a top UN official to comment on an ongoing multilateral trade negotiation. Any effort by the High Commissioner to weigh in on the WTO negotiations would be seen as unwanted political interference. Second, WTO members had already signaled that they were strongly against bringing human right considerations into the WTO, arguing that doing so would "unduly complicate" trade negotiations that were already politically contentious (Petersmann 2004, 607). Indeed, an early attempt by Norway and Mauritius to raise human rights concerns in the agriculture negotiations was quickly shut down by the rest of the WTO membership (Hawkes and Plahe 2013).

The anticipation of backlash from states is evident in the unusually lengthy discussion by the High Commissioner in the report's introduction, in which she went to great lengths to explain and justify her choice to author a report on agricultural trade liberalization at the WTO. The High Commissioner made three arguments to states in this regard. First, she argued that undertaking the report was broadly consistent with her mandate, stating that states had previously encouraged her not only to examine the impacts of economic globalization on human rights in general but also "to define better the right to food and to propose ways to implement and realize the right to food as a means of achieving the commitments and objectives of the 1996 World Food Summit" (OHCHR 2002a, 4). Therefore, although states had never formally asked for this particular report, the High Commissioner argued that it fell broadly within the parameters of earlier directives from the international community asking her to lead on realizing the human right to food and thus "that an examination of the liberalization of agricultural trade will be a further step in fulfilling her mandate" (OHCHR 2002a, 4).

Second, the High Commissioner argued that undertaking the report was essential to providing states with more information about the interaction between trade liberalization and human rights. She stated that "in order to focus the report in a way that allows meaningful analysis, the High Commissioner has chosen to examine the human rights dimensions of one of these processes in particular, namely trade liberalization. The focus on trade liberalization is based on a perceived need to continue filling a gap in information on human rights and globalization" (OHCHR 2002a, 4).

Last, the High Commissioner argued that the importance of agricultural trade liberalization for food security necessitated her involvement on this policy issue given the linkages to human rights, stating, "The High Commissioner believes that a focus on the liberalization of agricultural trade will also build upon work of the special mechanisms and treaty bodies of the human rights system. The international human rights machinery is increasingly looking at the link between international trade rules and the right to food and the right to development" (OHCHR 2002a, 3–5). By employing these arguments, the High Commissioner justified her decision to insert herself (and the OHCHR) into the politics of global trade rulemaking.

Not only did the High Commissioner act independently from states, she also did not inform states in advance of her intention to produce the report. The report was released by the High Commissioner a full three months *before* states would have a formal opportunity to discuss the report and debate its recommendations at the next meeting of the CHR.[13] In the period prior to the report's release, the High Commissioner did not directly consult states or solicit their views on the topic, which is often a standard practice with such reports.[14] Keeping states unaware of the potential content of her report prior to its publication was a strategic choice by the High Commissioner to prevent dissatisfied states from potentially acting to block the report's publication. Although the High Commissioner did not consult states, she did consult with other IOs, including UNCTAD, the FAO, the WTO, and the OECD. Consulting the "trade experts" at other IOs was important, both for informational reasons and to signal to WTO members skeptical about the relevance of human rights to trade that the High Commissioner was not "antitrade" or captured by NGOs or other pressure groups critical of the WTO.[15]

The High Commissioner's Report: Bringing in Human Rights

The High Commissioner's report, entitled *Globalization and Its Impact on the Full Enjoyment of Human Rights*, was publicly released in January 2002, just weeks after the 2001 WTO Doha Ministerial Meeting at which WTO members agreed to launch a new round of multilateral trade negotiations. Rather than echo a growing chorus of criticism from civil society that the WTO was a threat to human rights, the High Commissioner's report was widely seen as offering a highly nuanced assessment of the relationship between agricultural trade rules and the right to food (Petersmann 2004; A. Lang 2011).

In the report, the High Commissioner emphasized that the WTO had established a transparent, rules-based and fairer trading order, but she also drew attention to the fact that agricultural trade liberalization could result in greater vulnerability to food insecurity for certain groups. She argued that agricultural trade and human rights were intrinsically linked, stating, "Given the important role that agriculture plays for food security and development in many countries, the design and implementation of WTO rules concerning agriculture could affect the enjoyment of human rights, in particular the right to food and the right to development, and also the right to health, the right to social security, as well as the rights of particular groups such as children, indigenous peoples or migrants" (OHCHR 2002a, 10). Robinson also argued that the Doha Round provided WTO members with an opportunity "to review and improve trade rules" to liberalize agricultural trade while simultaneously promoting and protecting human rights such as the right to food and the right to development (OHCHR 2002a, 10).

The report, which was widely read by WTO members and trade experts, provided Robinson with a platform to seek to influence global trade rulemaking by invoking international human rights norms. In particular, the High Commissioner declared that all WTO members—as parties to human right treaties—had a prior legal obligation to ensure that the agriculture negotiations did not result in any adverse effects on the food security of vulnerable groups (OHCHR 2002a, 5). The High Commissioner made the case to WTO members as follows:

> The legal basis for adopting human rights approaches to trade liberalization is clear. All WTO members have undertaken obligations under human rights law. All 144 members of the WTO have ratified at least one human rights instrument. . . . Further, those areas of human rights law recognized as customary international law take on universal application, which means that trade rules should be interpreted as consistent with those norms and standards whatever the treaty commitments of States in trade matters. In other words, whatever the human rights treaty obligations undertaken by particular States, WTO members have concurrent human rights obligations under international law and should therefore promote and protect human rights during the negotiation and implementation of international rules on trade liberalization. (OHCHR 2002b, 8)

The report also provided detailed analysis of the relevant international human rights treaties and standards that the High Commissioner argued WTO members had a legal duty to take into account when entering into negotiating new global trade rules for agriculture.

The High Commissioner used the report to claim that international human rights law *required* states to adopt what she called a "human rights-approach" to multilateral trade negotiations on agriculture. This approach, the High Commissioner argued, required WTO members to make adequate consideration of the human right to food when formulating their bargaining proposals and designing global trade rules, including undertaking ex ante human rights impact assessments of trade agreements, rather than solely considering human rights implications after a deal was completed. In addition, the High Commissioner recommended to WTO members to incorporate discussions of impact assessments in the WTO Committee on Agriculture and in the agriculture negotiations in order to inform global trade rulemaking.

In making the case for a human rights approach to global trade rulemaking, the High Commissioner invoked a series of international human rights norms and standards that she argued resulted in WTO members having a duty to consider, when entering into trade negotiations, not only the human right to food of their own citizens but also that of other states (OHCHR 2002a, 7–8). The High Commissioner stressed to WTO members that states that failed to put in place such mechanisms could be considered to be in violation of the right to food under international law and that it was thus incumbent on WTO members to adequately consider the right to food in formulating the bargaining proposals they presented at the agriculture negotiations.

Not only did the High Commissioner tell WTO members they had a preexisting legal duty to protect human rights in trade negotiations, she also made her own proposals to WTO members for a set of new global trade rules that she argued were consistent with a human rights approach to agricultural trade liberalization. Invoking established international human rights law again, the High Commissioner called on WTO members to incorporate a series of food security safeguards into a new agriculture agreement, including special and differential treatment (SDT) targeted at vulnerable people and groups and SDT to promote food security. She also made additional recommendations calling for targeted financing for developing countries to implement policies to protect the right to food and the development of mechanisms allowing effective and minimally trade-distorting protection of food security crops in food-insecure countries (OHCHR 2002a, 18–19).

These recommendations marked the first time that a senior UN official publicly and directly proposed to WTO member states a set of new global agricultural trade rules. Moreover, in advocating for these new global trade rules, the High Commissioner reiterated that these proposed food security safeguards were not simply new options for WTO members to consider but were consistent with and required by states' existing obligations, under human rights treaties, to respect, fulfill, and promote the right to food of their citizens and those of their trading partners (OHCHR 2002a, 18).

While some of the High Commissioner's proposed food security safeguards lent support to ideas already under discussion by some WTO members and NGOs—such as that developing countries be granted additional flexibility to provide subsidies for crops essential to domestic food security beyond the level agreed to in the AoA (A. Lang 2011, 122)—others were entirely novel. Most notable was the High Commissioner's recommendation for a new form of SDT to protect the food security of specific communities of vulnerable groups, such as subsistence farmers, agricultural laborers, and rural communities (OHCHR 2002a, 17). SDT is one of the core principles of the multilateral trade system, which permits more flexible rules for developing countries in recognition of their lower levels of economic development (Chang 2006; Ho 2008; Toye 2014).

At the WTO, SDT is typically operationalized in the form of lower overall levels of tariff and subsidy reductions and longer implementation periods for developing countries compared to developed countries. The High Commissioner's proposal for new global trade rules to safeguard the food security of vulnerable groups significantly departed from existing conceptualizations and practice of SDT at the WTO. She called for a new form of SDT targeted at *specific groups of persons* rather than for general country categories (e.g., "developing countries" or "least developed countries" [LDCs]) based on their relative levels of income or development. The idea of exceptions for categories of persons (rather than categories of countries) had not previously existed in the trade regime. The High Commissioner argued that the establishment of new global trade rules to protect food-insecure persons was consistent with and required by international human rights: "The AoA currently does not make a distinction between different types of agriculture—such as commercial agriculture or subsistence agriculture—and different players—from low-income and resource-poor farmers on the one hand, to national and international agrobusiness on the other. . . . A human rights approach to trade liberalization therefore focuses on protecting vulnerable individuals and groups—in particular, low-income and resource-poor farmers, as well as farm laborers and rural communities" (OHCHR 2002a, 17–18).

In recommending SDT for subsistence farmers, agricultural laborers, and rural communities, the High Commissioner invoked one of the core principles of international human rights—the principle of *nondiscrimination* (Picciotto 2007). The legal basis for nondiscrimination is specified in Article 2 of the International Covenant on Economic, Social and Cultural Rights (ICESCR), a key international human rights treaty, which establishes that states have a legal duty to protect vulnerable individuals and groups from unlawful discrimination (Nifosi-Sutton 2017). The High Commissioner argued that WTO members had a prior legal duty under international human rights treaties to provide affirmative action in the form of SDT to protect vulnerable groups, noting that "even where the net social benefit from trade liberalization favors the majority in a certain country, the principle of non-discrimination under human rights law requires immediate action to protect the human rights of those who do not benefit. In the case of the AoA, this means that States should use existing flexibilities in the Agreement where they exist, and WTO members should consider improving or adding flexibilities where appropriate" (OHCHR 2002a, 16). Such flexibilities, she argued, would permit developing countries the right to raise their bound tariffs or to offer additional subsidies to improve the food security of subsistence farmers and poor rural communities beyond what was permissible under the AoA.

The High Commissioner's report on agricultural trade liberalization was well received by most WTO members, who appreciated its "careful and moderate tone" and balanced assessment of the benefits and costs of agricultural trade liberalization (A. Lang 2011, 121). Importantly, the High Commissioner's report reflected a reformist approach to global trade rules when compared to the more radical and rejectionist positions of many NGOs working at the nexus of human rights and trade at the time, including the International NGO Committee on Human Rights and the Food First Action Network (FIAN), which were aligned with La Via Campesina and advocated getting the "WTO out of agriculture" (Claeys 2015).

One of the key effects of the High Commissioner's report and its proposals for new global trade rules was that it created uncertainty for WTO members about whether their negotiating positions could be inconsistent with their obligations under international human rights treaties.[16] The prospect that the WTO negotiations could produce an outcome that

contravened international human rights law had not previously been seriously considered by WTO members. Whereas trade negotiators might
have been quick to dismiss claims by civil society groups that the WTO
was a threat to human rights, an authoritative report by the UN's most
senior human rights official was treated differently and prompted many
WTO members to seek clarification from legal experts in their own capitals and from the WTO secretariat.[17] The High Commissioner's report
also generated considerable interest and impact outside the WTO and was
taken up among international lawyers, human rights advocates, NGOs,
and parliamentarians to call on the responsibility of governments to protect human rights in trade negotiations (A. Lang 2011). Indeed, the High
Commissioner's right-to-food approach to trade came to inform advocacy
by development NGOs, such as Oxfam and IATP; while their initial advocacy strategy in the Doha Round had focused on the reform of US and
EU agricultural subsidies, following the OHCHR's interventions these
NGOs increasingly took up human rights discourse in their efforts to
influence WTO rules on agriculture (Aaronson and Zimmerman 2007).
The High Commissioner's specific recommendations for additional food
security safeguards for developing countries were, however, viewed un-
favorably by powerful agricultural exporters such as the US, the EU,
Canada, and Brazil, which sought more aggressive trade liberalization
in the Doha Round.[18] The US and other developed countries signaled
their displeasure with the High Commissioner's attempts to influence the
agriculture negotiations, both during private discussions with the High
Commissioner[19] and in their votes against the resolution tabled at the
CHR to endorse the report's recommendations (UN 2002, 471).

The OHCHR's "Unofficial" Submission
to the WTO Negotiations

The OHCHR continued its efforts to influence WTO rulemaking during
the 2003 WTO Ministerial Meeting in Cancun. The ministerial was
widely expected to be a key decision-making event in the Doha Round negotiations, with trade ministers meeting to settle the negotiation agenda.
Among the issues for decision-making by trade ministers was the scope of
SDT and how food security issues were to be addressed in the agriculture
negotiations (Weissbrodt et al. 2002, 2003).[20]

In advance of the 2003 Ministerial, the US and EU agreed to a draft agriculture agreement that many observers expected would be forced on the rest of the WTO membership as a fait accompli (Hopewell 2016, 80–81). OHCHR officials had analyzed the draft US-EU agreement and had been concerned by the absence of adequate safeguards to protect the right to food of vulnerable groups.[21] The deal on the table going into the Cancun Ministerial was widely viewed by OHCHR officials as highly unfavorable from a human rights perspective in that it lacked, in their view, sufficient flexibilities to protect the food security of poor populations.

In response, the OHCHR took the extraordinary action of making an "unofficial" submission directly to WTO trade ministers. Under the official procedures of the WTO, only WTO member states have the right to table submissions for consideration by trade ministers at a ministerial meeting. The WTO secretariat thus accordingly refused to distribute the OHCHR's submission as part of the official package of ministerial meeting documents. Instead, the OHCHR distributed its "unofficial submission" on the first day of the Cancun Ministerial Meeting by sending copies directly to national missions to the WTO and trade ministers in capitals, as well as by posting a copy on its website for the public and media. In putting forward its own submission to the ministerial, the OHCHR not only broke with convention but intentionally bypassed the procedural rules of the WTO.

The OHCHR had toyed with the idea of making a submission directly to a WTO ministerial prior to 2003. While the High Commissioner's report on agricultural trade liberalization had been widely discussed by states and NGOs, there was a desire among OHCHR officials to push the envelope further to bring greater attention to human rights in global trade rulemaking at the WTO.[22] The original idea for a submission by the OHCHR for trade ministers was first suggested by the Sub-Commission on the Promotion and Protection of Human Rights, a committee of twenty-six appointed human rights experts, which served as a think tank for the UN human rights system (Sub-Commission on the Promotion and Protection of Human Rights 2002, 2).[23] However, the subcommission's suggestion that the High Commissioner make a submission to the WTO was only symbolic and had no binding authority. Only requests issued by states through formal resolutions are considered obligatory by the High Commissioner. The actual decision to make a submission to WTO trade ministers was taken by senior OHCHR officials with support from the High Commissioner. UN member states did not have a hand in determining the OHCHR's decision to issue the submission or have any influence over its content. Indeed, the OHCHR's "unofficial" submission to the WTO was never presented or tabled for discussion by UN members.[24]

The OHCHR's submission to WTO trade ministers, entitled *Trade and Human Rights*, was styled as a primer "to assist policy makers who might not be familiar with the international human rights system" by providing illustrative examples of how trade liberalization could infringe on human rights (OHCHR 2003, 2). The submission was designed by the OHCHR to bring trade ministers' attention to the linkages between global trade rules and human rights and their countries' legal obligations to protect human rights under international law. While IOs often use their expertise to "teach" states new norms (Finnemore 1993; Risse 1999; Risse, Ropp, and Sikkink 1999), in this instance the OHCHR's unofficial submission to trade ministers was a creative form of instruction that sought to shape state behavior by informing trade ministers that they had responsibilities and obligations as human rights duty bearers and that this duty extended to global trade rulemaking.

Similar to the High Commissioner's 2002 report, the OHCHR's submission invoked international human rights law. Citing the obligations of WTO members as parties to international human rights treaties, the OHCHR argued that this meant that WTO members "should promote and protect human rights in the processes of negotiating and implementing trade law and policy" (OHCHR 2003, 4). The first section of the submission explained the basic relevance of human rights norms and treaties to various trade issues on the bargaining table in the Doha Round (not just agriculture but also intellectual property rights and services). The claim that WTO members had "concurrent obligations" to respect human rights while liberalizing trade and had a legal responsibility to protect the interests of the most vulnerable was strongly emphasized, in effect reminding trade negotiators that they could not simply choose to ignore human rights in the context of multilateral trade negotiations, or later claim that they were unaware that they had responsibilities as human rights duty bearers.

The OHCHR's submission included a number of illustrative examples of how human rights standards applied to WTO rules. Each example identified a specific trade policy issue and clearly outlined the relevant "human rights angle" that WTO members needed to understand. For example, the text considered the potential negative effects of food import surges on the livelihoods of poor farmers and agricultural laborers. In this example, the OHCHR alerted WTO members to the fact that in such cases they were required to consider how existing flexibilities in the AoA, or other forms of social safety nets, could be utilized to prevent situations that diminished the economic and physical accessibility to food by poor populations (OHCHR 2003, 9–10). The submission concluded with a reference guide for WTO members that listed all the relevant human rights treaties, UNGA and CHR resolutions, and reports and studies produced by the OHCHR that could be used to ensure that human rights principles were properly taken into account in the context of multilateral trade negotiations. This approach was consistent with the OHCHR's goal of ensuring that its submission served the purpose of giving notice to WTO trade ministers and their negotiators of the linkages between global trade rules and human rights, and their obligation, as parties to human rights treaties, to protect human rights, such as the right to food, in trade negotiations.

All trade ministers and national delegations to the WTO received copies of the OHCHR's submission at the start of the Cancun Ministerial. Bitter disagreement among WTO members over what issues should be on the agriculture negotiating agenda ultimately led the ministerial meeting to collapse. In the buildup to Cancun, developing countries, led by Brazil, India, and China, had formed a new bargaining coalition on agriculture known as the Group of Twenty (G20),[25] in an effort to block the US-EU proposal on agriculture (Narlikar and Wilkinson 2004; Hopewell 2013). One of the main issues of contention in the agriculture negotiations was the scope of SDT, with developing countries demanding major cuts to rich countries' agriculture subsidies before they would entertain further liberalization of their own policies. With both sides dug into their positions, the Doha Round agriculture negotiations at the WTO experienced their first deadlock (Hoekman, Michalopoulos, and Winter 2004; Narlikar and Tussie 2004). WTO members spent most of their time and energy trying to find a compromise between the US-EU and G20 positions on agriculture. As a result of the breakdown in talks, WTO members missed reaching consensus on the agriculture negotiating

THE OHCHR INVOKES HUMAN RIGHTS AT THE WTO   141

agenda. There was therefore no window of opportunity for the OHCHR to further engage WTO members during the ministerial on the relationship between WTO rules and human rights, since rather than moving forward with the agriculture negotiations to finalize the agenda, WTO members were now in lifesaving mode seeking to prevent a collapse of the Doha Round.

Assessing the OHCHR's Impacts on Global Trade Rulemaking

Interventions by the OHCHR in the WTO Doha Round agriculture negotiations have had meaningful impacts on the trajectory of global trade rulemaking. By invoking international human rights law, the OHCHR's actions contributed to changing the discourse on trade and human rights at the WTO and to shaping new rules intended to protect the food security of vulnerable groups.[26]

A key objective of the OHCHR's interventions was to ensure that WTO members took human rights into account in trade negotiations to ensure the coherence between international human rights and international trade law. Recall that in the late 1990s and early 2000s, there was palpable concern among states and global civil society about potential incoherence and conflicts between human rights and global trade rules. A schism erupted at the WTO, in which some states saw human rights being used as a "sword" against them whereas others sought to appropriate human rights as a "shield" to protect them from additional concessions (A. Lang 2011, 106; see also Rajagopal 2005). The OHCHR's interventions were instrumental in resetting the terms of the debate about human rights and trade. In particular, the OHCHR sought to change WTO members' understanding about the linkages between the two regimes by framing human rights, not as a strategic bargaining chip that WTO members could use as they pleased, but instead as an international legal obligation that all WTO members were obliged to actively protect in the context of multilateral trade negotiations. This idea, that states had "concurrent" obligations to protect human rights while liberalizing trade, was new to WTO members, most of whom had not been previously aware of, or had not previously considered, the relevance of international human rights law for trade.[27]

The way in which the OHCHR reframed the linkages between global trade rules and human rights was also significant. Many actors critical of the WTO agreements, including even some WTO member states, frequently portrayed global trade rules, by sheer dint of favoring trade liberalization and freer markets, as antithetical to economic and social human rights. This framing of trade and human rights often dominated popular discourse on the issue, making many in the trade policy community averse to engaging with the human rights regime. However, the OHCHR's forays into global trade rulemaking changed this perception. The OHCHR's authoritative claim that there was not any inherent doctrinal conflict between WTO agreements and human rights treaties, and that instead the relationship between global trade rules and human rights was context and issue specific, and could be in some cases be "mutually reinforcing," offered a new way to think about trade and human rights. This framing was especially important to changing perceptions among trade negotiators, who as a group had been the most skeptical about the relevance of international human rights to WTO trade negotiations. The OHCHR's efforts helped change the terms of the debate from one of antagonism to one of potential synergism between trade rules and human rights and provided states with a framework for how to weigh the positive and negative effects of specific global trade rules. In this way, the OHCHR presented a new way for WTO members to think through how human rights could be considered in global trade rulemaking. Its interventions are attributed with significantly improving the quality of the debate about trade and human rights at the WTO and with being central to alerting trade negotiators to the complex legal issues at stake (A. Lang 2006, 338).

Whereas initially human rights were viewed with deep skepticism at the WTO and were often seen as a code for protectionism, that is no longer the case. Human rights have "seeped slowly" into the multilateral trade system (Aaronson 2007; Aaronson and Abouharb 2011).[28] WTO members are far more aware of, and responsive to, the importance of ensuring coherence between global trade rules and human rights than ever before. The WTO has also taken more steps to increase information exchange and cooperation with the UN human rights system, and human rights issues now feature prominently at the WTO Public Forum.[29] Furthermore, trade dispute settlement panels have considered international human rights standards in the application of WTO law (Hestermeyer 2019). While these changes do not mean that WTO members have arrived at a general agreement on how best to incorporate human rights into international trade law, the premise that WTO members have a legal duty to protect human rights in global trade rulemaking—an idea that was at the heart of the OHCHR's intervention in global trade rulemaking—is now part of the standard discourse of WTO members.

The OHCHR's interventions have also influenced the design of proposed new global trade rules to safeguard the food security of poor populations in developing countries. Recall that the High Commissioner's 2002 report had proposed that WTO members use SDT and other new mechanisms to protect the food security and livelihoods of specific groups of persons. In 2004, WTO members began talks on new mechanisms to address food security. They agreed to develop a particular measure, known as "Special Products," which is intended to allow developing-country WTO members to exempt certain crops that are deemed essential for "food security, livelihood security and rural development needs" from deeper tariff reductions (WTO 2004a). Special Products have been championed in the WTO agriculture negotiations by the G33, a bargaining coalition of countries with food security concerns.

In the negotiations, one of the key debates among WTO members has been how to establish criteria determining which crops should be eligible to be designated as a Special Product. Initially, WTO members focused on standard quantitative measures usually used in trade negotiations when determining a particular crop's economic importance, such as a crop's contribution to national employment, food consumption, or value of production (Deep Ford et al. 2005; Hoda 2005). In 2005, the G33 proposed a set of new indicators, which were not limited to the usual quantitative metrics but for the first time also included qualitative indicators. In particular, the G33 proposed that a crop should be eligible to be designated as a Special Product when "the product contributes to the livelihood of vulnerable populations such as tribal communities, women, aged people, or disadvantaged producers" (WTO 2005f). The proposal was notable in that it was the first time that states had put forward text in the context of multilateral trade negotiations justifying exemptions to trade liberalization based on specific categories of persons. Not only did the G33's 2005 reference to "vulnerable groups" echo the recommendations in the High Commissioner's earlier 2002 report, but the choice of term was also a clear invocation of the human rights discourse that the OHCHR had injected into the negotiations (Moon 2013). The term *vulnerable groups* is a core concept in human rights law affirming the responsibility of states to protect poor and marginalized populations and persons; it is widely used in the texts of international human rights standards, national human rights legislation, and human rights jurisprudence (Morawa 2003; Nifosi-Sutton 2017).

By referencing "vulnerable groups" in their proposal, the G33 brought human rights into the WTO agriculture negotiations. The OHCHR did not have a direct hand in drafting the G33's 2005 proposal. But the OHCHR's recommendations that WTO members design global trade rules to focus on the groups and individuals most likely to be negatively affected by agricultural trade liberalization did inform discussions among G33 trade negotiators and with their advisers, including officials from think tanks such as the South Centre and ICTSD, as well as NGOs such as Oxfam and the Third World Network (Oxfam 2005b; Mably 2009). Indeed, the G33's 2005 proposal was notable in marking the group's shift in focus from the issue of which crops should be eligible for Special Products toward an emphasis on the intended beneficiaries—poor farmers and households—of greater trade flexibilities intended to protect food security (L. Bernal 2005).

The Doha Round negotiations broke down in 2008, largely because of disagreement between the US and large emerging economies, such as India and China, over agriculture (Hopewell 2016). Although the round was never concluded, by that point WTO members had reached consensus on the majority of the elements for a new agreement to replace the AoA. The Rev.4 agreement included a stable text (i.e., one that had wide consensus among WTO members) setting out new global trade rules to operationalize Special Products.[30] The Rev.4 text confirmed that WTO members were in agreement that developing countries would be entitled to self-designate Special Products guided by a set of indicators based on the criteria of food security, livelihood security, and rural development (WTO 2008c). The text stipulated that developing countries might designate 5 to 8 percent of all tariff lines as Special Products, some of which would be eligible for a 0 percent cut and the remainder eligible for a lower overall tariff cut. The draft rules set out an illustrative list of twelve indicators that would determine the eligibility criteria for designating Special Products.

Most relevant to this study is indicator number 6, which formalized the idea of SDT for specific groups of persons. Under this indicator, a crop can be designated as a Special Product when "a significant proportion of the producers of the product, in a particular region or at the national level, are low income, resource poor, or subsistence farmers, including *disadvantaged or vulnerable communities and women*" (WTO 2008c, 55–56, italics added). This indicator in the draft agreement is significant because it is the first time that the text of a multilateral trade agreement referred directly to the concept of "vulnerable groups." Moreover, the indicator further specified and listed a series of categories of persons that would qualify as "disadvantaged or vulnerable," such as low-income subsistence farmers, disadvantaged communities, or women farmers. This marks the first time in the history of the trade regime and in international trade law that protecting particular groups or categories of persons—rather than types of countries or countries based on official levels of economic development—was taken as an acceptable justification for states to receive additional flexibilities under a trade agreement and to be allowed to take lesser liberalization commitments.

The rules on Special Products in Rev.4 are widely regarded as a victory for WTO members with food security concerns (Matthews 2014). The inclusion of the human rights concept of "vulnerable groups" in the draft text of the Doha Round agriculture agreement was not an oversight or an accident. WTO members are highly exacting when it comes to the wording of trade agreements, given that this becomes international law and sets out their binding commitments under WTO rules. It is notable that even in the highly publicized 2001 TRIPs waiver on public health, WTO members could not agree to insert a reference to specific vulnerable groups, such as HIV/AIDS-infected persons (Correa 2002; Feichtner 2009). In contrast, in no small part because of the efforts of the OHCHR, WTO members embedded in the 2008 text on Special Products a core human rights principle—the responsibility of states as duty-bearers to protect vulnerable groups—into proposed global trade rules. Although the Doha Round ultimately collapsed and never reached a conclusion, Rev.4 remains the basis for continued negotiations today and forms the foundation of any future WTO agreement on agriculture (Hopewell 2019). While certain parts of Rev.4 remain hotly contested by states, the elements of the text that reflect the intervention of the OHCHR have been broadly accepted by WTO members.

Conclusion

This chapter has analyzed interventions by the OHCHR at the WTO. Despite having no mandate to make global trade rules and no observer status to the WTO—and in the face of resistance by most WTO members to linking trade and human rights—the OHCHR took self-directed action in an effort to influence the Doha Round negotiations on agriculture. The OHCHR was driven to intervene out of a firm belief that the outcome of agriculture negotiations could worsen the food security of vulnerable populations, which was counter to its mission to promote and protect the human right to food. It intervened at the WTO by invoking an alternative legal framework–international human rights law—and utilizing its moral authority as the international community's voice for human rights to call on states to fulfill their legal duty to protect human rights. By invoking human rights and telling WTO members that they could potentially violate international human rights law, such as the human right to food, unless they incorporated protections for vulnerable populations into global trade rules, the OHCHR created uncertainty for states by suggesting the possibility of norm and treaty conflicts. The OHCHR's efforts reframed how trade negotiators understood the relationship between global trade rules and human rights, presenting these as potentially mutually reinforcing rather than as diametrically opposed. The OHCHR's unorthodox practices, including the 2002 report on agricultural trade liberalization and its unofficial submission to the 2003 Cancun Ministerial, demonstrate the creative means the organization used to insert itself into the politics of rulemaking at the WTO. Ultimately, the OHCHR's proposals for safeguarding the food security of vulnerable groups were incorporated by WTO members into the text of the proposed new agreement on agriculture.

CHAPTER 6

The UN Special Rapporteur on the Right to Food

"Food Security Hostage to Trade"

THE UN SPECIAL RAPPORTEUR on the Right to Food (SRRTF)[1] intervened at the WTO by taking sides with a group of states demanding greater flexibilities in trade rules to implement pro–food security policies. This last chapter examines how, by siding with some WTO members over others, the SRRTF sought to sway the debate and tilt the balance of power in multilateral trade negotiations in favor of food-insecure states. In taking sides, the SRRTF not only endorsed the bargaining positions of some WTO members but burnished those positions with greater legitimacy by declaring them to be consistent with the goals of the international community to end hunger. The actions taken by the SRRTF to exercise influence in multilateral trade negotiations challenged the interests of powerful WTO members, who saw its intervention as unwanted political interference. Several WTO members, who viewed the SRRTF's actions as a threat to their economic interests, pushed back by seeking to discredit the SRRTF and restrict their mandate. Nevertheless, despite backlash from powerful states, the SRRTF's intervention at the WTO had a meaningful impact on global trade rulemaking. Of greatest consequence were the SRRTF's proposal and advocacy efforts to create a legal waiver to protect public food stockholding programs by developing countries from legal challenge, which served as the basis for new WTO rules to protect food security. As this analysis shows, the SRRTF's actions were self-directed, driven by the conviction that seeking to shape global trade rules to protect food security was consistent with its mandate to promote the full realization of the human right to food.

The first section of the chapter situates the role of the SRRTF within the UN human rights system and identifies its contribution to debates about the relationship between agricultural trade liberalization and the human right to food. The second section analyzes the SRRTF's 2008 mission to the WTO, including its cooperation with the WTO secretariat as well as the backlash that the mission generated. The third section examines the actions of the SRRTF to influence decision-making at the 2011 WTO Ministerial Meeting, including its proposal for a legal waiver for public food stockholding. The next section assesses the SRRTF's impacts on global trade rulemaking by tracing how its proposal for a legal waiver was taken up in the WTO negotiations and became the basis for the 2013 Ministerial Decision on Public Stockholding for Food Security Purposes.

The SRRTF in Global Food Politics

The SRRTF is part of a unique category of institutions under the Special Procedures mechanism of the UN human rights system (Alston 1992; Nifosi 2005). Similar to UN independent experts, working groups, or special representatives of the secretary-general, the SRRTF is an independent human rights expert appointed by UN members in a competitive process for a maximum term of six years (Limon and Power 2014). The main functions of UN human rights experts are to analyze and report on human rights situations; alert the HRC and UNGA to gross human rights violations; elaborate international norms; and develop human rights standards (OHCHR 2008). At present, there are over forty independent experts/working groups assigned to "thematic" mandates (i.e., responsible for a specific human right, such as the right to food) and a dozen country-specific mandates to examine the situation in countries where the international community deems human rights are most at risk (e.g., Syria, Myanmar, North Korea). Post holders are not paid a salary but are provided administrative support by the OHCHR, travel on a UN *laissez-passer* (a passport that confers diplomatic rights), and have access to special funds to cover travel and other expenses related to fulfilling their mandates. While independent human rights experts receive administrative support from the OHCHR, there are no formal linkages between them and the UN High Commissioner for Human Rights. Independent human rights experts are accountable to UN member states, not to the High Commissioner.

The CHR (predecessor to the HRC) established the role of the SRRTF in 2000. While the human right to food was first recognized in the 1948 Universal Declaration on Human Rights and was further elaborated in 1966 in the ICESCR, it was the 1996 World Food Summit that catalyzed deeper legal institutionalization of the right to food. At that summit, states affirmed "the right of everyone to have access to safe and nutritious food, consistent with the right to adequate food and the fundamental right of everyone to be free from hunger" (FAO 1996).[2] It was in this context that lobbying efforts by the UN High Commissioner for Human Rights, with the support of like-minded states, such as Norway, were successful in persuading the UN membership to create the position for an independent expert dedicated to working on the right to food (OHCHR 2000; Kent 2005; Ziegler et al. 2011). Established under Resolution 2000/10 of the CHR, the mandate of the SRRTF is to gather information and report on all aspects of the human right to food; cooperate with states, IOs, and NGOs; and recommend ways to improve the promotion and implementation of the right to food (CHR 2000, 3).

While UN member states set the mandate for independent human rights experts, in practice the vagueness of such mandates provides post holders with significant discretion to interpret their mission, including discretion to choose their issues of focus (R. Smith 2011). UN human rights experts are often referred to as the "crown jewel" (Alston 2011, 571) of the international human rights system and play a key role in catalyzing the improvement of human rights performance by states (Piccone 2012; Nolan, Freedman, and Murphy 2017). Their UN affiliation provides post holders with considerable visibility and media attention, as well as access to political elites, which enables them to bring attention to human rights situations and pressure the international community into action (Naples-Mitchell 2011). In addition, since UN human rights experts operate at arm's length from states, they "have greater freedom of action, greater flexibility, and fewer political constraints on speaking their minds" (Subedi 2011, 209). The influence of UN human rights experts is often surprising, given that they lack judicial or enforcement powers, operate in a highly constrained environment in which they are engaged in a constant balancing act of maintaining independence while seeking to engage and confront states, and work with inadequate budgets and levels of administrative support (Pinheiro 2011; Subedi 2011). The effectiveness of independent experts in changing the behavior of states depends heavily on their individual skills, reputations, and media savvy (Lesser 2010; Bode 2018).

The SRRTF and Global Trade Rules

Since the inception of the mandate, multiple SRRTFs have made significant efforts to influence debate on the relationship between global trade rules and food security. This is clearly evident in the work of the first two special rapporteurs, Jean Ziegler (2000–2008) and Olivier De Schutter (2008–14), who both authored multiple reports examining the AoA and the Doha Round agriculture negotiations (Ziegler 2001a, 2001b, 2002, 2004, 2005; De Schutter 2009c, 2009d, 2009b, 2011).[3] As SRRTF, Jean Ziegler, a former Swiss politician and author, was one of the most high-profile critics of the WTO, arguing, for instance, that global trade rules perpetuated malnutrition and hunger in developing countries (Ziegler 2001a, 2001b). A highly controversial figure, Ziegler used his UN platform to support the position of La Via Campesina, a transnational social movement of peasants and small-scale farmers calling for food sovereignty and the rollback of the WTO's agenda of free trade (Ziegler 2004, 13; A. Lang 2011; Claeys 2015). Ziegler was succeeded by Olivier De Schutter, a professor of international law at the Katholieke Universiteit Leuven and a former secretary-general of the International Federation for Human Rights, a major human rights NGO. As SRRTF, De Schutter took a legal doctrinal approach to the WTO that focused on using legal reasoning to assess the coherence between global trade rules and international human rights law (Häberli 2012; Cismas 2015).[4] Both Ziegler and De Schutter chose to devote significant parts of their mandates to influencing multilateral trade negotiations out of concern about the potential negative consequences of global trade rules for food-insecure populations. As special rapporteurs, both Ziegler and De Schutter argued that states' human rights obligations trumped their international trade commitments. They also called on states to ensure that WTO negotiations did not result in outcomes that created food insecurity for their own citizens or those of their trading partners (Joseph 2011; Fakhri 2015, 69). Unlike the FAO or WFP, the SRRTF lacks observer status to the WTO and cannot attend official meetings or negotiating sessions; given these constraints, SRRTFs have sought to leverage their moral authority to claim the right to be heard by trade negotiators. This chapter focuses on the efforts by Olivier De Schutter during his term as SRRTF to illustrate the intervention strategy of taking sides.[5]

Mission to the WTO

De Schutter's first official fact-finding mission as SRRTF was not to a UN member country but, atypically, to the WTO headquarters in Geneva in May 2008.[6] The choice to undertake a mission to the WTO was made by the SRRTF and was not on the order of states. According to the SRRTF, there were strategic and pragmatic reasons to begin with a mission to the WTO.[7] Like most observers, the SRRTF anticipated that the WTO "mini-ministerial" scheduled for July 2008 in Geneva was likely to result in a decision by states consequential for food security.[8] At the time, the world was in the midst of the 2008 Global Food Crisis, characterized by record-high food prices and a rising number of hungry people (FAO 2009a, 2009b). The crisis was high on the international political agenda, with skyrocketing food prices spurring food riots and generating political instability in many developing countries; the crisis also exacerbated geopolitical tensions as Russia, India, and Vietnam imposed food export bans, to the shock of food importers globally (Clapp 2009a; Conceição and Mendoza 2009; Bush 2010; L. Sneyd, Legwegoh, and Fraser 2013). The WTO director-general, Pascal Lamy, presented the July 2008 mini-ministerial as an opportunity for the WTO to help "solve" the Global Food Crisis, stating:

> The reasons why we must conclude the Round this year are visible to all of us and they are becoming more critical by the day. . . . [We] have also witnessed an unprecedented escalation in food prices worldwide which has had negative effects particularly on developing countries that depend on imports for their food security or are net food buyers. . . . [A] WTO deal could help soften the impact of high prices

by tackling the systemic distortions in the international market for food. (WTO 2008a)

The SRRTF was alarmed by the "lack of international coordination" on agricultural trade policy and deeply concerned that many developing countries were "not in a position to feed their populations" because of the rising costs of food imports (De Schutter 2008, 6, 10–11). With the expectation that the 2008 mini-ministerial would address trade-related dimensions of the food crisis, the SRRTF believed that this made it an "urgent matter" for him to meet with WTO members to better understand the "impacts of new global trade rules in agriculture for realizing the right to food."[9] The SRRTF was also encouraged by having received assurances from WTO secretariat officials and the Bolivian ambassador to the WTO (a member of the G33, a coalition, led by India, of developing countries with food security concerns) that they would assist in securing access to relevant trade officials.[10]

The SRRTF's choice to kick off his mandate with a mission to the WTO was regarded by many trade policy experts as a "bold move," given many WTO member states' mistrust of, and hostility toward, his predecessor, Jean Ziegler, whom they perceived as antitrade and too publicly critical of the WTO.[11] The SRRTF's fact-finding mission to the WTO consisted of a series of face-to-face meetings with numerous WTO member state representatives, the WTO director-general, and other stakeholders, including trade experts from academia, NGOs working on trade and development issues, and farmer organizations (De Schutter 2009c, 2–3).[12]

The WTO secretariat played an enabling role by helping to arrange meetings with multiple ambassadors to the WTO and technical experts from the secretariat. In addition, WTO secretariat officials provided written feedback on the draft report produced by the SRRTF.[13] This was a high-water mark of cooperation between the UN human rights system and the WTO secretariat. The SRRTF praised "the cooperative spirit" of WTO secretariat officials for their assistance in undertaking the mission (De Schutter 2009a, 3). The cooperation between the WTO secretariat and the SRRTF, as well as the willingness of many WTO member state representatives to meet with the SRRTF, was a significant development given the previously acrimonious relationship with Jean Ziegler, whom many WTO members regarded as a "loose cannon" and "overt in promoting socialist policies."[14] In sharp contrast, many WTO members described De Schutter as a "credible" and "serious" figure because he struck a moderate tone in his public statements, affirmed the importance of a rules-based trading system, and did not "castigate the WTO at every turn like other [UN independent] human rights experts."[15]

The SRRTF Takes Sides at the WTO

The SRRTF presented the report on the mission to the WTO at the Tenth Session of the HRC in March 2009.[16] In setting out the report's aims to UN member states, the SRRTF emphasized that his goal was to promote greater coherence between trade and food security by providing guidance to "assist States in the negotiation and implementation of their commitments under the multilateral trade framework, in order to ensure that their commitments under trade agreements will support, rather than undermine, their efforts to realize the right to food at domestic level" (De Schutter 2009c, 4). The report offered a detailed assessment of the obligation of states to respect the human right to food in international human rights treaties and their commitments under WTO agreements, the effects of agricultural trade liberalization under the AoA, and the impacts of the AoA for achieving the human right to food.

In the report, the SRRTF took sides with the position of food-insecure developing-country WTO members. By this point, the Doha Round agriculture negotiations were strongly split along South-North lines, with food security increasingly a wedge issue (Hopewell 2016; Singh 2017). Despite being an EU citizen from Belgium who relied on the endorsement of EU member states to be elected to the post, the SRRTF chose to side with food-insecure developing countries at the WTO. In explaining the reasons for taking sides, the SRRTF argued that the mandate required him to prioritize the needs of the most vulnerable people, the majority of whom resided in the global South. The SRRTF expressed this principled position as follows:

> The majority of hungry people in the world are located in developing countries, live in rural areas, and depend on agriculture directly or indirectly for their livelihoods. They are hungry because they are poor: they are often net buyers of food, and their incomes, which are on average significantly lower than those of the non-rural populations, are insufficient to buy the food which they do not produce themselves. Fifty per cent of the hungry are smallholders, living off 2 hectares of

cropland or less; 20 per cent are landless laborers; 10 per cent are pastoralists, fisherfolk, and forest users; the remaining 20 per cent are the urban poor. Any trade regime which does not benefit these categories or affects them negatively is likely to lead to further denial or violation of the right to food. These groups need to be protected. (De Schutter 2009c, 6)

In short, the SRRTF argued that achieving the right to food required that global trade rulemaking not be focused narrowly on economic efficiency and aggregate welfare but that it include prioritizing the food security of the most vulnerable groups in society in trade negotiations.

Beyond emphasizing that WTO members needed to prioritize the interests of food-insecure populations, the SRRTF actively endorsed the positions taken by most developing countries in the agriculture negotiations. This included endorsing the starting position of the majority of developing countries: that the outcomes of the AoA were unequal and skewed toward the interests of developed countries. The SRRTF, for instance, criticized the inherent asymmetries in the AoA, noting that global trade rules provided developed countries with an advantage by enabling them to retain high levels of subsidy spending not available for developing countries. Indeed, the SRRTF critiqued the idea that the WTO had created a level playing field, calling this "illusory," given that the ability of developed countries to maintain high levels of subsidies locked in their competitive advantage over other agricultural exporters (De Schutter 2009c, 9–10). The SRRTF's assessment was thus that existing WTO rules were skewed against developing countries. The SRRTF called on developing countries to decrease their "excessive reliance" on trade for food security and instead to obtain greater trade flexibilities to pursue rural development and food security goals.

The SRRTF's report also supported developing countries' position on multiple issues that were on the bargaining table at the WTO and the subject of intense South-North disagreement. On agricultural tariffs, for example, the SRRTF supported developing countries' demands that developed countries be required to significantly reduce their tariffs, while developing countries should be subject to lesser tariff cuts. In the negotiations, developing countries resisted demands from developed countries that they undertake substantial tariff reductions, arguing that they had effectively taken comparatively larger tariff cuts than developed countries in the Uruguay Round. The SRRTF concurred in the report that the Uruguay Round tariff reductions had "not worked for the benefit of developing countries" and argued that additional tariff cuts could potentially violate the human right to food:

> Encouraging these countries to open up their agricultural sector to competition by binding themselves to low rates of import tariffs may therefore constitute a serious threat to the right to food, particularly if we take into account that food insecurity is mostly concentrated in the rural areas and that a large portion of the population in the countries which are most vulnerable depends on agriculture for their livelihoods. (De Schutter 2009c, 6, 10)

The SRRTF also weighed in on the issue of tariff escalation, when developing countries face higher tariffs on their exports of semiprocessed or processed commodities compared to lower tariffs on unprocessed versions of the same commodity. The SRRTF argued, echoing the position of developing countries at the WTO, that tariff escalation by developed countries discouraged poorer countries from diversifying into higher-value-added production and thereby increased their vulnerability to "brutal" fluctuations in commodity prices (De Schutter 2009c, 12).

The SRRTF also took sides on the most politically contentious issue in the agriculture negotiations: the creation of a Special Safeguard Mechanism (SSM) (Wolfe 2009; Ismail 2009). The SSM was the chief negotiation demand by the G33 (Clapp 2006). In proposing the SSM, the G33 sought additional flexibilities in global trade rules that would permit developing countries to raise tariffs above their bound-level commitments in the AoA in situations where a flood of subsidized imports threatened the food security and/or livelihoods of poor farmers (Valdes and Foster 2003; L. Bernal 2005). From the G33's perspective, the proposed SSM corrected the imbalances of the AoA, which had left most developing countries without access to the "special agriculture safeguard," a similar mechanism that was provided almost exclusively to developed countries. However, the US, the EU, Brazil, and other major agricultural exporters strongly opposed the SSM. These countries were concerned that the SSM could be used to diminish their market access gains as well as to roll back the progress in tariff liberalization achieved during the Uruguay Round (Margulis 2014).

By publicly endorsing the G33's proposal for the SSM, the SRRTF inserted himself into the politics of the WTO agriculture negotiations. The

SSM was one of the major stumbling blocks holding up the conclusion of the Doha Round, and the SRRTF chose to weigh in directly on the issue. In the report, as well as in accompanying public statements, the SRRTF argued that developing countries needed access to an SSM in order to "retain the freedom to take measures which insulate domestic markets from the volatility of prices on international markets," since otherwise they would be at risk "that local producers will be driven out by import surges" (De Schutter 2009c, 21). The SRRTF further argued that trade measures, such as the SSM, that help protect vulnerable groups such as poor, small-scale farmers worked to support achieving the human right to food. This led the SRRTF to make recommendations to WTO members that they should agree to "maintain the necessary flexibilities and instruments" in the form of the SSM (De Schutter 2009c, 23).

The SRRTF took sides in the agriculture negotiations to support the bargaining positions of food-insecure developing countries, in particular the G33, against those of the major agricultural exporters. By taking sides, the SRRTF waived any claim to be acting as a neutral observer, since he publicly supported one group of states over another in global trade rulemaking. The SRRTF's endorsement also conferred greater legitimacy on the bargaining positions of developing countries by claiming that, for instance, establishing the SSM was consistent with the goals of the international community to reduce hunger and achieve the human right to food. Knowingly taking sides on the most controversial issue in the WTO agriculture negotiations, the SSM, indicated the SRRTF's willingness to act against the interest of agricultural exporters in an effort to tilt the political balance in the negotiations in favor of the G33.

While both the SRRTF and the OHCHR intervened with the goal of increasing the policy space for food-insecure developing countries at the WTO, it was only the SRRTF that publicly took sides with one group of WTO members over another in the agriculture negotiations. Indeed, the OHCHR explicitly avoided taking sides, and its approach was viewed by WTO members as balanced and neutral (see chapter 5). Their contrasting approaches were likely shaped by the fact that the OHCHR and the SRRTF intervened at different stages of the negotiations. The OHCHR's intervention took place between 2001 and 2003, and the SRRTF's between 2008 and 2013. Seeking to inject a human rights framework into the Doha Round negotiations, the OHCHR intervened during the agenda-

setting stage, when the scope of bargaining issues had not yet been final-
ized and when there was no concrete text on the table on which to take
a firm position in favor or against. By contrast, the SRRTF intervened
when the negotiations were at an advanced stage, with a comprehensive
draft agricultural agreement (i.e., Rev.4) on the table, in which specific
food security issues, such as the SSM, were key sticking points to concluding the Doha Round. By this time, the negotiations were deeply split
between the major agricultural exporters and food-insecure developing
countries. In this context, the SRRTF chose to side with food-insecure
developing countries, endorsing many of their demands for specific measures to promote food security.

Backlash from States at the Human Rights Council

The SRRTF's report on the mission to the WTO drew fierce criticism from
major agricultural-exporting nations at the HRC (Joseph 2011; Ferguson
2018). Although the formal presentation of the report was scheduled for
the afternoon plenary session of the Tenth Session of the HRC and was
preceded by a high-level panel on policy responses to the Global Food
Crisis, several states used their allotted time during the earlier session to
make formal statements commenting on the SRRTF's report.[17] Representatives from India, Chile, Nepal, Bangladesh, and the Philippines, for
example, supported the SRRTF's conclusions, arguing that trade distortions contributed to food insecurity and that developing countries should
prioritize increasing domestic food production. The report also received
statements of support from NGOs with observer status to the HRC, including FIAN, World Vision International, and the Asian Legal Resource
Centre, which endorsed the SRRTF's assessment of agricultural trade liberalization. In sharp contrast, the representative from Brazil—the world's
third-largest agricultural exporter—was highly critical of the report and
stated that the SRRTF had paid insufficient attention to the negative effects of developed countries' agriculture subsidies on food security. The
Brazilian representative argued that agricultural subsidies were the principal culprit behind the "difficulties of many countries to grow their own
food" and "the main underlying causes of the [Global Food Crisis]."[18]

Brazil also led in criticizing the SRRTF during the formal presentation of the report in the afternoon plenary session. While the majority
of states—primarily developing countries—indicated their support for

the report, Brazil attacked the SRRTF's recommendations and credibility. The Brazilian delegate accused the SRRTF of being inaccurate and biased in the analysis of global trade rules, stating that the report suffered from "critical problems of balance and a selective use of information."[19] In addition, Brazil questioned the SRRTF's neutrality and accused him of supporting the protectionism of developed countries:

> The difficulty of many countries in growing their own food was due to decades and sometime centuries of distortions in the international agricultural market. It was unacceptable to blame international trade negotiations for the challenges they faced regarding the realization of the right to food. For a long time now, the developing world had faced difficulties in the World Trade Organization negotiations on agriculture due to the resistance posed by the developed world. That intolerable protectionism weakened and disorganized production in other countries, particularly the poorest. Those distortions had created dependency, when they had not simply dismantled entire production structures in developing countries.[20]

Brazil's harsh criticism of the SRRTF was endorsed by other agricultural exporters at the HRC. The Uruguayan delegate stated that his country supported Brazil's statement, arguing that "ensuring the right to food of an increasing world population was linked to a free and fair agricultural trade" and to helping developing countries by "allowing them better access to food."[21] Similarly, the Australian representative told UN members that "a Doha outcome would greatly assist in alleviating the global food security problem" and that liberalizing agriculture trade "would expedite rational supply responses and the allocation of resources towards more efficient producers, thus lifting productivity and global output."[22]

HRC delegates remarked that they were surprised by the ferocity of Brazil's attack on the SRRTF, given that the consensus view among most delegates was that the SRRTF produced high-quality reports and was not "political" like other independent experts.[23] The SRRTF was "taken aback" by Brazil's attack on the report, noting that Brazil had sent a trade official from its Permanent Mission to the WTO instead of the usual delegate from its Permanent Mission to the UN to attend the HRC session and that this official had provided a scathing critique of the report on a "paragraph by paragraph basis."[24]

Brazilian trade officials explained that their attacks were prompted by their belief that the SRRTF had "undermined the interests of Brazil."[25] Brazil is one of the world's largest and most efficient agricultural exporters and has pursued aggressive trade liberalization at the WTO (Hopewell 2013). Staunch free traders, Brazilian officials regarded the SRRTF's recommendations for countries to be less reliant on food trade as "preposterous."[26] Moreover, they claimed that the SRRTF was "dangerous" and a "threat" because he lent legitimacy to positions taken by WTO members critical of agricultural trade liberalization. Brazilian trade officials insisted that the SRRTF "was not neutral" and that his position on the SSM in the report sounded "too much like India's" and that of other interest groups that "endorsed policies to increase production levels that led to major distortions in world markets."[27] Notably, however, Brazilian officials, in their public statements at the HRC, carefully chose to accuse the SRRTF of being an agent of *developed countries*. This was because Brazil's power at the WTO was due to its leadership in the G20, a bargaining coalition of developing countries in the agriculture negotiations that includes India and China. To maintain its position of influence at the WTO, Brazil must frequently compromise its preference for aggressive agricultural trade liberalization and instead support the demands of other G20 members that prefer far less liberalization (Hopewell 2015a). This situation made it difficult for Brazil to publicly attack the SRRTF for taking sides with the G33 and endorsing the SSM, as doing so would have alienated India and China and thus undermined the political unity of the G20 alliance.[28]

Beyond the formal plenary session, states also clashed during the subsequent open-ended informal meeting at the HRC to draft the resolution on the SRRTF's report.[29] A key point of disagreement among states in drafting the resolution was how to refer to the SRRTF's recommendations in the report. Brazil, the US, Australia, and Canada, all major agricultural exporters, expressed concerns about developing countries' insertion of text in the resolution that "endorsed" the SRRTF's recommendations on the issues under active negotiation at the WTO.[30] In addition, agricultural exporters indicated that they wanted to signal in the resolution their dissatisfaction with the SRRTF's efforts to insert himself into the politics of the WTO, which they saw as unwanted interference in sensitive trade negotiations. Canada, for example, made a proposal to include text in the resolution ordering the SRRTF to avoid analyzing the "international economic architecture" in future reports, arguing that WTO trade issues were beyond the scope of the SRRTF's mandate.[31] Canada's suggestion was endorsed by the US and the Czech Republic (representing the EU in the open-ended informal meeting). Developing countries, led by India and Mauritius, stated that they were opposed to Canada's proposal to order the SRRTF to steer clear of international trade issues.[32]

The ensuing meeting was characterized by acrimonious exchanges among delegates, which led the chair to admonish delegates for acting in a "disruptive manner" and "breaking with the norms" of HRC open-ended informal meetings.[33] Interviews with several state representatives to the HRC confirmed that the tenor of the meeting was far more "antagonistic" and "politicized" than was "normal for exchanges among delegates in informal meetings."[34] Such meetings were attended primarily by working-level staff rather than ambassadors and thus tended to be freer of the political theater typically associated with HRC plenary sessions (Weiss 2009).[35]

Despite their dissatisfaction with the SRRTF's efforts to insert himself into the WTO agriculture negotiations, the representatives of Brazil, the US, Australia, and Canada eventually agreed to the text favored by developing countries, which "encouraged" the SRRTF to continue to work on the impacts of global trade rules on the right to food.[36] The reason that agricultural-exporting countries did not reject the resolution (for example, by calling for a roll-call vote and formally voting against the text) was that the political costs were seen as being too high. At the HRC, states will choose the option for a roll-call vote only when there is an irreconcilable disagreement on the substantive content of a resolution as in the case of resolutions critical of Israel's occupation of Palestinian territories) or if a resolution promotes a contested international norm (Marin-Bosch 1987; Öberg 2005). Despite pressure from their trade ministries to reject the report, these countries did not want to appear to be against the human right to food at the HRC, especially when a Global Food Crisis was going on and when their governments had already supported international calls to increase food production in developing countries.[37] A Canadian diplomat explained that it would have been poor diplomacy and costly for their country's reputation to reject the resolution, stating: "Here, in Geneva, you have to go along because even if your department of trade has a major problem, you can't have Canada objecting to a [HRC] resolution. So, Canada has problems with the language but in the end agrees by consensus to adopt it. . . . That's the way the game is played here at the HRC."[38] The SRRTF emphasized the importance of the 2009 HRC resolution as a watershed moment for the mandate. Had agricultural exporters been successful in inserting text into the resolution with instructions to cease work on international trade issues, the SRRTF stated, he "would have quit right then," since any such restrictions on his independence would have made it impossible to carry out the mandate.[39]

Backlash from States at the WTO

Despite the backlash from agricultural-exporting countries to the report at the HRC, the SRRTF was determined to present it directly to WTO members. The mission to the WTO had led the SRRTF to conclude that there was "willful isolation" between human rights and global trade rules because of a lack of joined-up thinking by government departments responsible for human rights policy and those for trade policy.[40] The SRRTF sought to engage with WTO member state representatives directly, since this community of officials wielded influence in shaping their governments' bargaining positions but were also the least knowledgeable about the right to food. However, lacking observer status to the WTO, the SRRTF required a formal invitation from states to present his report at the WTO. To obtain such an invitation, the SRRTF made informal requests to several WTO ambassadors and also raised the issue with the WTO director-general.[41] Ambassadors from several G33 members countries agreed to bring forward the request to the WTO membership. The director-general also offered the WTO secretariat's support to facilitate any such meeting.[42]

Discussions among WTO members revealed differing views on extending an invitation to the SRRTF. Unsurprisingly, major agricultural exporters—the US, Brazil, Canada, the EU, Australia, Argentina, and New Zealand—were lukewarm to the idea, fearing that doing so would lend the SRRTF "too much credibility" and that his arguments would be "taken up at the WTO and give fuel to India and the G33 position."[43] One representative of a major agricultural-exporting WTO member expressed their unease with inviting the SRRTF to the WTO as follows: "The problem is that he is calling for things that developing countries themselves do not want. De Schutter is limited by a Western perspective. He comes from a country of subsidies, oversupply, and butter-mountains. Consumers are in need of lower prices, and history has shown that trade helps to bring down prices, therefore, saying we need to limit trade, this argument embedded in pushing for self-sufficiency is all wrong."[44] Continued disagreement between agricultural exporters and the G33 on the SSM was also a consideration for the former group, whose trade negotiators feared giving the SRRTF a platform at the WTO where he might tell them, on the record, that they should agree to the G33's SSM proposal, thereby strengthening the G33's hand in the agriculture negotiations at their expense.[45]

Despite the hesitancy of agricultural exporters, however, denying an invitation to the SRRTF to the WTO was not a realistic option. Support from developing-country WTO members was too widespread for agricultural exporters to block the prevailing consensus. Indeed, agricultural exporters anticipated that if they blocked the invitation, other WTO members would leak their opposition to the press, with the likely outcome being that they would be painted in the media as being "against human rights" and thus providing the SRRTF with even more attention and publicity.[46] Instead, agricultural exporters agreed to invite the SRRTF to the WTO but sought to exercise control over the choice of venue and timing. Whereas the G33 proposed having the SRRTF present during the June 2009 meeting of the WTO General Council—the high-profile venue of the WTO's second-highest decision-making body, after ministerial meetings—agricultural exporters pushed back, calling the date "too early" and "short of notice" to prepare. They countered with a proposal to hold the SRRTF's presentation following the November 2009 meeting of the Committee on Agriculture, arguing that this was the most appropriate venue, since the meeting would be focused on food security issues.[47] WTO members arrived at a compromise and issued an invitation to the SRRTF to present the report during a closed, informal session following the regular July 2009 meeting of the Committee on Agriculture. This format was strongly preferred by agricultural exporters, since no motions could be tabled for decision by WTO members in an informal meeting, nor would there be an official record of the meeting. Agricultural exporters had strongly insisted on these conditions.[48]

The SRRTF accordingly met with trade negotiators at WTO headquarters directly following the meeting of the Committee on Agriculture on July 2, 2009. The meeting was unusually well attended by WTO member state representatives and lasted for over three hours, which was exceptionally long for this type of meeting. During the meeting, the SRRTF highlighted the key themes of the report on his mission to the WTO and emphasized the need for global trade rules to protect poor and food-insecure small-scale farmers in developing countries from import surges, including declaring his support for establishing the SSM.

The presentation was followed by questions and comments from trade negotiators, which, according to officials present at the meeting, including the SRRTF, were frequently hostile and antagonistic.[49] The SRRTF received a lengthy barrage of criticism from Brazil, Uruguay, Australia, Paraguay, Pakistan, Argentina, Costa Rica, South Africa, and the EU. Trade negotiators from these countries argued, for example, that his recommendation "to allow countries to protect against imports was too sweeping" (WTO 2009b). The representatives from Brazil, Uruguay, and Australia were the most critical; they questioned the SRRTF's neutrality, criticizing him for "aligning with the positions taken by some WTO members but not that of others."[50] In addition, they challenged his expertise and right to speak on international trade matters, arguing that he "failed to understand the benefits trade brought to poor consumers" (ICTSD 2009; WTO 2009a). Not all WTO members were critical of the SRRTF, with many G33 members (including India, Tanzania, Bolivia, Cuba, and Mauritius), Ecuador, and Luxembourg expressing statements of support. India, in particular, welcomed what it described as the "first time that the right to food and trade were discussed at the WTO" (WTO 2009b). Despite this, the discussion was driven by WTO members critical and dismissive of the SRRTF's report and its recommendations.

Much of the criticism of the SRRTF came from the Cairns Group of agricultural exporters, whose members made similar statements arguing that the SRRTF was too focused on the negative aspects of agricultural trade liberalization and failed to sufficiently condemn the agricultural protectionism and subsidies of the US and EU. This similarity was not a coincidence but, according to several officials, part of a "clearly organized and orchestrated attack."[51] Cairns Group members' officials met in advance and decided on a common strategy with the goal of specifically discrediting the SRRTF.[52] One Cairns Group member explained that the group planned the coordinated attack because the SRRTF "had lost credibility by speaking out so harshly against the status quo" (ICTSD 2009). The SRRTF described himself "shell-shocked" by the barrage of criticism and surprised by "the viciousness of the political attack" by Cairns Group countries.[53] While he had anticipated some resistance based on what had previously occurred at the HRC, he had not expected WTO members to attack his credibility and question his right to speak on trade matters in such an aggressive manner.[54]

That Cairns Group countries felt obliged to make a coordinated attack on the SRRTF is significant. Their actions suggest more than just a passing dissatisfaction with the SRRTF's views. The intensity of their attack suggests that they feared the influence of his intervention in trade negotiations. Several Cairns Group members openly stated in interviews that they viewed that the SRRTF as a significant threat to their bargaining positions at the WTO.[55] Attacking the SRRTF would have been unnecessary if Cairns Group countries believed that the SRRTF's actions were harmless or inconsequential. If that was the case, they could have simply dismissed or ignored the SRRTF, as they had done previously with his predecessor, Jean Ziegler.

Making the WTO "Compatible" with Food Security

The SRRTF decided to intervene again in the lead-up to the December 2011 Ministerial Meeting in Geneva. This was the first WTO ministerial meeting to be held following the collapse of the Doha Round in 2008. Most WTO members regarded the ministerial meeting as a final chance to salvage the round, thus making the outcome particularly high stakes (R. Wilkinson 2012).

It was widely expected that trade ministers would address the trade-related aspects of world food security at the 2011 Ministerial Meeting (ICTSD 2011). The ministerial was to be the first time trade ministers would discuss both the effects of the 2008 Global Food Crisis and a new food crisis. By 2011, food security was again high on the international political agenda because of a second global food crisis, with food prices surpassing 2008 levels (Torero 2012). The second food crisis also had significant trade-related consequences, with a number of states, including the Ukraine and Russia, initiating export bans on wheat. The crisis also drew attention to the plight of NFIDCs, whose food import bills reached a record high of US$1.29 trillion in 2011—an increase of US$250 billion alone from the preceding year (WTO 2011f). The food crisis led to renewed interest in public food stockholding by governments across Asia, Africa, and the Middle East as a policy tool to reduce their vulnerability to food price shocks (Wright and Cafiero 2011; Demeke et al. 2014; Fouilleux, Bricas, and Alpha 2017).[56] India, for instance, was developing the largest food-stockholding program in the world, which would make two-thirds of its 1.2 billion citizens eligible to purchase food at subsidized prices—in a country where undernutrition rates among children were 45 percent (S. Hertel 2015). Given these important developments in world food security, WTO members were under political pressure to show that the WTO was capable of addressing problems caused by the food crises.

In the months preceding the 2011 Ministerial, WTO members were highly divided on how global trade rules should contribute to addressing the consequences of the food crises. There was significant momentum among developed countries to tighten existing rules in the AoA regulating the use of food export bans (Headey 2011; Karapinar 2012; P. Abbott 2012). Disciplining food exports bans, however, became highly politicized at the WTO, as efforts to create tougher rules had strong geopolitical overtones, with the EU and US aggressively targeting Russia's policies (WTO 2011a, 2011e). Concerns about the declining affordability of food led NFIDCs to reintroduce the idea of a new multilateral fund that would help NFIDCs finance food imports (see chapter 2) to address the "devastating situation" these countries faced in terms of their food security (WTO 2011g, 3; 2011h, 2011l). Many developing countries also voiced their dissatisfaction with WTO rules, complaining that these constrained their ability to implement public food-stockholding programs. In particular, they argued that the AoA's subsidy rules, which required them to count government purchases of foodstuffs used to feed poor populations as agricultural subsidies, were unfair and created uncertainty regarding the legality of their food security programs under WTO law (Das 2016). WTO members also discussed the possibility that the 2011 Ministerial could serve as an opportunity to make progress on other outstanding food security issues in the agriculture negotiations, including the SSM and Special Products.

The expectation that world food security would be a priority item on the 2011 Ministerial agenda spurred the SRRTF to resume efforts to influence global trade rulemaking. The SRRTF believed that the 2011 Ministerial would provide an important opportunity to press WTO members for changes to global trade rules needed to achieve world food security.[57] The SRRTF intervened by publishing a new report, *The World Trade Organization and the Post-Global Food Crisis Agenda: Putting Food Security First in the International Trade System,* focused exclusively on food security issues on the WTO's agenda. The report was accompanied by a media campaign, including internationally syndicated opinion-editorials and interviews in print, on the radio, and on television.

The release of the report was carefully timed and occurred on November 18, 2011, to correspond with a key meeting of the WTO Committee on Agriculture at which negotiators were expected to finalize a series of food security–related proposals to be put to trade ministers for decision (WTO 2011f). The report was also specifically written for WTO trade negotiators and ministers, rather than for consideration by UN members at the HRC or UNGA (De Schutter 2011, 20). It was distributed directly to WTO member state representatives in Geneva, journalists, and over ten thousand subscribers to the SRRTF's newsfeed.[58] The report received major press coverage, aided by the fact that the SRRTF was by 2011 a well-known public figure and had become "something of an international phenomenon" as the most vocal and visible UN figure calling for more effective global governance to address rising food insecurity (Orford 2015, 7; Sage 2014). It was widely circulated across, and discussed by, NGO networks working on trade, human rights, and food security, which supported the positions taken by the SRRTF on agricultural trade liberalization at the WTO and in UN bodies including the HRC, UNGA, and CFS (McKeon 2009; Fakhri 2015).

The SRRTF called the 2011 report a "compatibility review" intended to examine whether global trade rules were coherent with the post–global food crises policy consensus favoring increased public and private investment and foreign aid to expand food production in developing countries (Clapp 2009b; Wise and Murphy 2012). To this end, the report examined "the question of whether existing WTO rules, or the framework that could result from the completion of the Doha Round of trade negotiations, support measures that states are putting in place to improve food security" (De Schutter 2011, 4). It focused on the adequacy of existing and proposed global trade rules to support several post–global food crisis policy objectives that fell under the WTO's authority, including rules on investment in domestic food production, income support measures for small-scale farmers, and public food stockholding. The report also offered a series of recommendations to WTO members on the bargaining positions they should take with respect to these issues to ensure that global trade rules supported achieving food security.

Like the SSRTF's previous report, this report again took sides with the positions favored by many developing countries, including the G33. The SRRTF, for example, called on trade ministers to "strengthen and materialize the proposed [SSM]" (De Schutter 2011, 9). Among the most contentious issues the SRRTF took sides on was public food stockholding. The SRRTF was especially concerned about the lack of legal certainty for developing-country WTO members seeking to implement public food holding, which he feared was discouraging states from pursuing pro–food security policies out of fear of violating WTO rules.

The problem faced by many developing countries was that while the AoA permitted public food stockholding, it required that government purchases of foodstuffs from producers be made at market prices (GATT 1994a, 16). However, most developing countries implementing public food-stockholding programs, such as India, wanted to intentionally purchase foodstuffs at so-called administered prices—that is, at fixed prices *above* the market price—in order to incentivize domestic food production among poor farmers, while also selling food *below* market prices to consumers so as to make food more affordable for lower-income groups. Under the rules of the AoA, the difference between the market price and the administered price provided to farmers counted toward a country's agricultural subsidy spending. Since developing countries agreed in the AoA to very relatively low caps on their agricultural subsidy spending levels, most found that their food-stockholding programs were likely to put them at risk of violating WTO rules. This mattered because WTO rules are hard law: if governments exceed their agricultural subsidy spending limits, they can be deemed to be in violation of international trade law and thus vulnerable to trade sanctions carrying significant economic costs (Scott 2017; Nakuja 2018).

That developing countries' public food-stockholding programs could be at risk of violating their agricultural subsidy commitments spending was a historical artifact of previous multilateral trade negotiations. Unlike developed countries, which had agreed to cap and (moderately) reduce their high levels of farm spending under the AoA, most developing countries had agreed to very low spending limits on their agricultural subsidies. At the time of the Uruguay Round, most developing countries had been too highly indebted and engaged in structural adjustment to have imagined the need for space under WTO rules to provide agricultural subsidies in the future. Developing countries operating public food-stockholding programs argued that the problem lay not with their policies, which they maintained were legitimate measures to achieve food security, but instead with the rules of the AoA (Correa 2014). Developing countries had almost secured a fix to this problem by proposing technical changes to how agricultural subsidies were calculated for public food stockholding, but this proposal was not agreed to because the negotiations collapsed in July 2008 over North-South disagreement on other aspects of agriculture (Montemayor 2014; Das 2016).

In the report, the SRRTF argued that the complexity of WTO rules remained a significant impediment to implementing public food stockholding. In addition, he argued that the proposed technical fixes for recalculating agriculture subsidies in the AoA were insufficient. Instead, the SRRTF proposed a legal waiver to end any uncertainty in existing WTO rules, suggesting that states should "simply adopt a statement that procurement rules do not apply to public stockholding of foodstuffs for food security purposes, or to waive the application of such rules" (De Schutter 2011, 9). By proposing a legal waiver, the SRRTF endorsed developing countries' demands that public food stockholding be exempt from the WTO's agricultural subsidy rules but offered a different solution by calling on WTO members to adopt the legal waiver "for situations where trade commitments restrict a countries' [sic] ability to pursue national food security" (De Schutter 2011, 16–17). The SRRTF's proposal for a legal waiver for public food stockholding was a novel development in the agriculture negotiations; it sought to provide developing countries with a sweeping exemption from global trade rules rather than a narrower change to how agricultural subsidy were calculated. The SRRTF's proposal was purposely modeled after the 2001 WTO legal waiver on intellectual property rights that enabled developing countries to manufacture generic versions of essential medicines to protect public health (Sell 2001; Shadlen 2004), which the SRRTF argued provided a precedent for a similar legal waiver to protect food security.

The central message of the SRRTF's report and media campaign was that food security was being held "hostage to trade in WTO negotiations" (OHCHR 2011). Here, in contrast to his earlier 2008 report, the SRRTF took a much firmer stance in criticizing the lack of political support by developed countries for new global trade rules intended to create a more enabling environment for developing countries to fight hunger. In a press release published on the OHCHR website, the SRRTF expressed the problem with WTO rules: "The world is in the midst of a food crisis which requires a rapid policy response. But the World Trade Organization agenda has failed to adapt, and developing countries are rightly concerned that their hands will be tied by trade rules. . . . Current efforts to build humanitarian food reserves in Africa must tip-toe around the WTO rulebook. This is the world turned upside down. WTO rules should revolve around the human right to adequate food, not the other way around" (OHCHR 2011).

The SRRTF's report generated further international attention after the WTO director-general, Pascal Lamy, took the extraordinary step of criticizing the report in an open letter published on the WTO website (VanGrasstek 2013). In the letter, Lamy rebuked the SRRTF's claim that global trade rules were hindering progress on achieving food security (WTO 2011d). The WTO director-general was infuriated by the SRRTF's report, which he saw as creating bad press for the organization and stirring division among its members (Häberli 2012, 19). In addition, the director-general faced pressure from agricultural-exporting countries to denounce the SRRTF's report; these countries were highly dissatisfied with his earlier cooperation with the SRRTF, including participating in several public debates together, which they saw as providing the SRRTF with legitimacy and a platform to weigh in on debates about WTO trade rules.[59] In response, the WTO director-general's letter publicly expressed his disagreement with the SRRTF's analysis and recommendations. He warned that policies such as public food stockholding could be used improperly and could "introduce distortions and undermine economic efficiency, exacerbating the negative impacts on poor consumers of high food prices," thereby taking a position that sided with agricultural exporters (WTO 2011d). In addition, the WTO director-general posted a more technical seven-page document with comments prepared by experts in the WTO secretariat that challenged the SRRTF report's findings point by point. These comments had been shared earlier with the SRRTF, who had solicited feedback and comments from the WTO secretariat on a draft of the compatibility review.[60] That WTO secretariat officials disagreed with the SRRTF's report was unsurprising. As Daugbjerg, Farsund, and Langhelle (2015, 3,15) argue, the SRRTF's 2011 report articulated a significant intellectual challenge to the widely held assumptions of trade policy makers that agricultural markets were "basically stable and capable of providing society's desired outcomes."

Ironically, rather than working to discredit the SRRTF, as agricultural exporters had sought to do, the WTO director-general's letter had the opposite effect. The letter angered many developing-country WTO members, including G33 members, whose positions the SRRTF had endorsed in the report but which now were the subject of veiled criticism by the WTO's executive head, who was obligated to be neutral. In addition, the letter created an international uproar, with over five hundred international NGOs, labor unions, and social movements, organized under the umbrella of Our World Is Not for Sale, rallying to defend the SRRTF against the criticisms levied by the WTO director-general (Rajagopal 2005).[61] In an open latter, these groups stated, "[Our World Is Not for Sale] believes that WTO is violating the right to food. We fully agree with Professor De Schutter when he states that 'in the long term, poor net-food-importing countries will not be helped by being fed.' They will be helped by being able to feed themselves. There is increasing global consensus on this issue" (Our World Is Not for Sale 2011). The SRRTF's intervention to influence decision-making at the 2011 WTO Ministerial thus generated significant global attention and debate. Not only did the SRRTF's report attract major interest from states, policy makers, and the media, but the efforts by WTO members and the director-general to discredit the report, and the counter-response this stirred from global civil society, further increased the spotlight on the efforts by the SRRTF to influence decision-making in trade negotiations.

The 2011 WTO Ministerial ultimately failed to produce an outcome. There was no final ministerial communiqué or declaration, as WTO members were unable to reach consensus on any issue (Ismail 2012; Hufbauer and Cimino 2013). Despite this failure, the chair's concluding statement acknowledged that food security had become one of the "main challenges facing the WTO membership" and noted that food security had been a key topic of discussion among trade ministers during the meeting.

Trade ministers had, for example, "stressed the importance of addressing the root causes of food insecurity" and had "signaled their support
for a proposal to establish a work programme on trade-related responses
to mitigate the impact of food market prices and volatility, especially on
LDCs and NFIDCs" (WTO 2011b, 5–6). Despite the lack of a concrete
outcome at the 2011 Ministerial Meeting, there was a major uptake by
WTO members of the SRRTF's report. Developing-country trade ministers were seen carrying copies of it report at the ministerial and discussed
its contents and recommendations during negotiating sessions.[62] The SR-
RTF's report was also heavily discussed by trade experts and became a key
reference point for subsequent analysis on trade rules and food security.
NGOs, for example, identified the proposed waiver from existing WTO
rules to permit public food stockholding as a promising strategy for advancing developing countries' interests in the Doha Round (Dommen
and Finnegan 2013.

The SRRTF's Impacts on Global Trade Rulemaking

The SRRTF was not just a highly visible figure engaged in the politics
of agricultural trade liberalization—his interventions had an impact on
rulemaking at the WTO. Most notably, intervention by the SRRTF
helped put a legal waiver for public food stockholding on the negotiating agenda and shaped the resulting outcome. Following the failed 2011
Ministerial, WTO members increasingly focused on the issue of public
food stockholding. Developing countries redoubled their efforts to solve
the food-stockholding problem, in response to growing threats from the
the US and other major agricultural exporters that they could take legal
action against developing countries that exceeded their Uruguay Round
subsidy commitments (WTO 2013b). Agricultural exporters were especially critical of public food stockholding because of concerns over the
lost potential commercial opportunities resulting from developing countries encouraging greater domestic food production at the expense of imports. In addition, many agricultural trade exporters regarded public food
stockholding as indicative of a pendulum shift toward food self-sufficiency
in developing countries, which they saw as going against the WTO's project of trade liberalization (S. Murphy 2015; Clapp 2017).

The SRRTF's 2011 recommendation for a legal waiver for public
food stockholding resurfaced in advance of the 2013 Bali Ministerial in a

negotiating proposal tabled by the G33. WTO members had agreed to finalize a deal at Bali on trade facilitation and select issues pertaining to agriculture in the hope of restarting the stalled Doha negotiations (Narlikar and Tussie 2016). In the lead-up to the Bali Meeting, the G33 made protecting public food stockholding their top negotiating priority (ICTSD 2012). One reason for this was the very real risk that India's massive food stockholding program, which came into effect in 2013, would breach its agricultural subsidy limits. The G33's bargaining proposal demanded a peace clause—that is, a legal waiver—to ensure that developing countries could operate food stockholding free from the specter of a trade dispute.

The G33 proposal for a peace clause on public food stockholding proved to be the most controversial issue at the Bali Ministerial. North-South disagreement on the peace clause nearly derailed the ministerial (R. Wilkinson, Hannah, and Scott 2014). The US—the world's largest agricultural exporter—stated that it was "categorically against" exempting public food stockholding from the rules in the AoA, a proposal it viewed as effectively rewriting international trade law in a way that was overly generous to developing countries without any guarantee of a comprehensive deal on agriculture (ICTSD 2013). In response to the US refusal, the Indian minister of commerce and industry, Anand Sharma, threatened to veto the deal on trade facilitation unless WTO members reached an agreement on public food stockholding, stating:

> For India food security is non-negotiable. Governments of all developing nations have a legitimate obligation and moral commitment towards food and livelihood security of hundreds of millions of their hungry and poor. Public procurement at administered prices is often the only method of supporting farmers and building stocks for food security in developing countries. Need of public stockholding of food grains to ensure food security must be respected. (Sharma 2013)

Despite their opposing positions, the US and India eventually reached a hard-fought, last-minute compromise that paved the way for trade ministers to issue the Ministerial Decision on Public Stockholding for Food Security Purposes in Bali. In this decision, trade ministers agreed to an interim, temporary peace clause that would exempt spending on public food stockholding from counting toward developing countries' agricultural subsidy limits until 2017, by which time WTO members were expected to complete negotiations on a permanent solution (WTO 2013c).

A key reason for the breakthrough at Bali was that the decision on public food stockholding was written with sufficient ambiguity to allow both the US and India "to emerge as winners" (Narlikar and Tussie 2016, 225).

The US-India compromise on public food stockholding was hailed as a historic success by aiding to secure passage of the trade facilitation agreement, the first trade agreement completed since the creation of the WTO in 1994. Yet Bali was not decisive, as a few months later Indian prime minister Narendra Modi, who was unhappy with the pace of talks on a permanent solution for public food stockholding, refused to ratify the trade facilitation agreement. Modi's gambit forced the US into further bilateral negotiations; US firms, such as UPS, which were expected to be big winners from reducing the costs of trade under the Bali trade facilitation agreement pressured the US government to make a deal. High-level talks between President Obama and Prime Minister Modi in September 2014 eventually resulted in a further bilateral deal to abandon the 2017 deadline and secured India's and the G33's preferred outcome that the peace clause would remain in effect indefinitely until WTO members agreed to a permanent solution (R. Wilkinson 2015).

While scholars have paid significant attention to the India-US contests over public food stockholding at Bali and the events that followed, there has been far less consideration of the origins of this proposal. It can be particularly difficult to trace the origins of ideas in WTO negotiations, especially since many states and nonstate actors have been involved in the policy debates on public food stockholding. While it has been suggested that the peace clause was first suggested by China in 2013 (Singh and Gupta 2016, 321), the evidence supports the claim that the G33's position was prompted by the SRRTF's recommendation for a legal waiver in the 2011 report. In over a decade of negotiations on public food stockholding prior to the Bali Ministerial, including the tabling of fifteen different bargaining proposals, WTO members had not once proposed anything resembling a legal waiver. It was only after the idea of a legal waiver was advocated by the SRRTF in 2011 that this solution to the legal uncertainty surrounding public food stockholding was added to the G33's bargaining demands at the WTO. Indeed, all the pre-2011 proposals, including those produced by the G33, sought a "technical" solution for the public food stockholding problem; these proposals focused on different ways to change the formula in the AoA for calculating spending on agricultural subsidies (Das 2016). Similar solutions focused on the accounting of agricultural subsidies were also presented by experts affiliated with IOs such as the FAO (Konandreas and Mermigkas 2014) and the South Centre (Correa 2014), and NGOs such as IATP and ICTSD (Montemayor 2014). The SRRTF's 2011 proposal for a legal waiver, however, was substantively different from all of these proposals focused on the accounting of agricultural subsidy spending. Lacking claims to trade expertise, the SRRTF instead adopted a "systems of law" approach to argue that states had the right to opt out of their WTO commitments if such commitments clashed with their obligations to respect the human right to food of their citizens.

Two years after the idea was introduced by the SRRTF, the legal waiver had become the centerpiece of the G33's bargaining strategy on public food stockholding at the WTO. This was not a coincidence, as strong ties had been established between the SRRTF and G33 countries. Multiple face-to-face exchanges took place between the SRRTF and the G33 negotiators prior to Bali, including an extensive discussion of the SRRTF's proposal for a legal waiver in a special meeting held in March 2012 in Geneva.[63] G33 members were receptive to the SRRTF's proposals for a legal waiver, regarding the SRRTF as a key UN ally that endorsed their positions in the agriculture negotiations (Raja 2013). The SRRTF also discussed the legal waiver proposal with experts from the South Centre, a Southern intergovernmental think tank that works closely with the G33 governments on their bargaining strategy (Eagleton-Pierce 2013, 145–47; Hannah, Ryan, and Scott 2017). Senior officials from the South Centre had reviewed a draft of the SRRTF's 2011 compatibility review and indicated their support for the recommendation of a legal waiver as a novel approach to advance the G33's interests on public food stockholding.

Timing was also an important factor behind the G33's decision to focus on a peace clause at the Bali Ministerial Meeting. By 2013, the G33 desperately needed an immediate solution to address the very real risk to India of a WTO trade dispute over its public food-stockholding program, with the US threatening to take legal action. In this context, the SRRTF's proposal for a legal waiver was a ready-made and relatively simple solution to ensure that India, and other developing countries, were not held over a barrel in trade negotiations. A legal waiver was seen as providing the G33 with the space to continue negotiating at the WTO without the threat of a trade dispute. Indeed, Indian minister of commerce and industry Sharma referred to the work of the SRRTF in publicly defending his government's position in proposing the peace clause to protect public food stockholding (Raja 2013). The evidence is compelling that the G33 chose to pursue a legal waiver after they were introduced to the proposal by the SRRTF as a solution to overcome resistance by agricultural exporters and address the risks of being in violation of their WTO commitments on agricultural subsidy spending.

Conclusion

The SRRTF chose to intervene multiple times at the WTO by taking the side of food-insecure developing countries in the agriculture negotiations. He was motivated to intervene out of a belief that supporting food-insecure countries in trade negotiations was necessary to achieve world food security. In taking sides, the SRRTF invoked his moral and legal authority as a UN-appointed human rights expert to claim that pro–food security proposals by developing countries, such as the SSM and public food stockholding, supported the realization of the human right to food; he thereby sought to add legitimacy to the bargaining position of food-insecure WTO members in the hope of tilting the balance of negotiations in their favor. The SRRTF expressed public disagreement with the bargaining position of major agricultural exporters by asserting that developing countries should increase their domestic food production and become less dependent on food imports. Agricultural exporters saw the SRRTF's interventions in the agriculture negotiations as a threat to their economic interests and responded by seeking to discredit the SRRTF and limit its right to work on trade issues. Thus, by taking sides at the WTO, the SRRTF discarded any pretense of being a neutral, third-party observer. The SRRTF's interventions altered the negotiating dynamics and outcomes of WTO negotiations by proposing the legal waiver as a means to end uncertainty over the legality of public food stockholding. Though the SRRTF had no formal access to the negotiations and lacked trade expertise, WTO members were persuaded to take up his proposal for a legal waiver. Following the resolution of a high-stakes political fight between India and the US, two of the WTO's most powerful players, the SRRTF's proposal for a legal waiver for food stockholding became part of new global trade rules.

CONCLUSION

THIS BOOK HAS SHOWN that UN actors have intervened to shape WTO rules governing trade in agriculture. Although lacking a formal seat at the bargaining table in the trade regime, which is exclusive to states, the FAO, WFP, OHCHR, and SRRTF all made the choice to insert themselves directly into the politics of multilateral trade negotiations with the aim of altering the trajectory and results of global trade rulemaking. While the FAO, WFP, OHCHR, and SRRTF intervened on different issues and at different points in time, they each acted out of concern that proposed trade rules could have negative consequences for world food security, undermining efforts by the international community to reduce hunger and protect the human right to food.

This study has identified four distinct cross-institutional political strategies utilized by UN actors to influence global trade rulemaking at the GATT/WTO: mobilizing states, public shaming, invoking alternative legal frameworks, and taking sides. The analysis has shown that, by employing these strategies, UN actors were able to exert influence over the discourse, agenda, and/or outcomes of multilateral trade negotiations. Though the FAO, WFP, OHCHR, and SRRTF are nontrade institutions—they do not have mandates to make or enforce global trade rules—and though each faced resistance from powerful states, these UN actors nonetheless intervened in an effort to shape the rules of the WTO.

By demonstrating the previously unrecognized role of the FAO, WFP, OHCHR, and SRRTF in contesting global trade rulemaking at the GATT/WTO, this book has contributed to our understanding of IOs as actors in global trade politics. First, this book has shown that IOs are not passive to potential "trade-and" conflicts generated by the expanded authority of the multilateral trade regime and its binding, powerful rules but may respond by seeking to shape the substantive content of those rules. As demonstrated in the case studies, to the extent that their interventions were successful, UN actors contributed to ameliorating potential conflicts between the goal of agricultural trade liberalization and the goals of fighting world hunger and protecting the human right to food. In the case of the WFP, for instance, its intervention served to block new WTO rules that would have restricted the global supply of food aid and risked leading to preventable deaths from starvation and malnutrition. Second, the book has contributed to our understanding of who makes the rules governing global trade. In contrast to existing scholarship that has assumed the role of IOs in multilateral trade negotiations to be limited largely to providing demand-driven technical assistance and other supporting functions (Prowse 2002; Smeets 2013), this analysis has shown that IOs are playing a far more agentic and consequential role in GATT/WTO negotiations. By inserting themselves into the politics of interstate negotiations, UN organizations have contributed to shaping discourse, agenda setting, and outcomes at the WTO and therefore need to be considered as actors in global trade rulemaking alongside states, private actors, and global civil society. Third, the analysis has shown that UN actors are playing a more significant role in global economic governance than previously recognized—not, however, by being delegated authority for governing international trade directly but by intervening in the trade regime to shape the rules governing global trade relations.

Beyond contributing to scholarship on global trade politics, this book, by developing the concept of *intervention*, also advances our understanding of IOs as actors in complex global governance. The analysis has shown that IOs may engage in intervention behavior with the purpose of altering the course of decision-making at other overlapping organizations over which they have no formal control. IOs may be motivated to intervene at another organization in a regime complex by their sense of social purpose, seeking to alter prospective decisions that they expect will have negative consequences for their own goals and those of the international community that they have been charged to uphold. Intervention is thus a type of unsolicited and self-directed political behavior by IOs, rather than an action undertaken on the formal or informal orders of their member states or those of the target organization. In choosing to intervene in decision-making at an overlapping organization, IOs may confront and challenge the interests of states. As a result, an intervening IO risks potential backlash from dissatisfied states that view its actions as unwelcome meddling in the business of states. Since, in a regime complex, one IO does not have control over the decision-making process of an overlapping organization, in order to exert influence, IOs develop distinct new externally oriented political strategies to exercise influence beyond their own organizational boundaries.

The FAO, WFP, OHCHR, and SRRTF:
Shadow Negotiators in the Trade Regime

The four case studies presented in this book demonstrate that UN actors did not sit idly by in the face of decisions taken by states at the GATT/WTO that they feared could worsen world food security. In the absence of formal channels or procedures to prevent states from creating global trade rules that could have negative implications for global hunger and the human right to food, these IOs took extraordinary actions to transform themselves into players in multilateral trade negotiations. Seeking to affect change in global trade rulemaking and prevent undesirable outcomes, the FAO, WFP, OHCHR, and SRRTF chose to intervene in an effort to steer multilateral trade negotiations toward outcomes to protect food security. UN actors thus transformed themselves into protagonists in global trade rulemaking, despite not having formal control over the negotiation process at the GATT/WTO or, indeed, permission to actively participate as a party to the negotiations. While lacking a seat at the bargaining table, UN actors behaved effectively as shadow negotiators, engaging in activities—such as framing debate, drafting bargaining proposals, organizing and steering coalitions, and blocking agreements they disagreed with—that are common behavior for trade negotiators seeking to shape the outcome of multilateral trade negotiations at the GATT/WTO.

As this analysis has shown, the FAO intervened during both the Uruguay Round and Doha Round negotiations on agriculture. While the FAO supported the WTO's agenda of agricultural trade liberalization, its senior leadership, given their organization's mission to reduce world hunger, chose to intervene in multilateral trade negotiations out of concern that prospective global trade rules could increase world food prices and thereby reduce access to food among the world's poorest households. The FAO developed an intervention strategy of mobilizing states, where it enrolled GATT/WTO members and took on an informal leadership role in the negotiation process. In the Uruguay Round negotiations, FAO officials coordinated and steered a bargaining coalition of food import–dependent GATT members, including devising negotiation strategy and drafting bargaining proposals that were tabled by states. Subsequently, in the Doha Round, the FAO led talks among WTO members to establish a food-financing facility intended to assist countries experiencing difficulties with financing adequate levels of commercial food imports. In intervening at the GATT during the Uruguay Round, FAO officials opted to work behind the scenes rather than in the public spotlight, so that their efforts to alter global trade rules would not antagonize powerful states whose interests their interventions challenged. The FAO utilized its expert authority on agricultural policy and its credibility as an advocate for developing countries to mobilize like-minded states at the GATT/WTO. Its interventions had meaningful impacts on global trade rulemaking. FAO officials were pivotal in framing world food prices as a trade policy issue and in putting the issue of how WTO-mandated reductions in agricultural subsidies could lead to higher food prices on the agenda of the GATT/WTO agriculture negotiations. FAO officials played a central role in writing the text of a new WTO agreement designed to protect food-insecure countries and driving its adoption as part of the Uruguay Round agreements (the 1994 Decision on Measures Concerning the Possible Negative Effects of the Reform Programme on Least-Developed and Net Food-Importing Developing Countries).

The WFP intervened in the WTO Doha Round agriculture negotiations out of concern that proposed rules to ban certain types of international food aid would result in additional vulnerable people, such as refugees and victims of natural disasters, suffering from malnutrition and starvation—an outcome that was antithetical to its mission as the world's largest humanitarian agency. Initially, the WFP used formal channels to directly communicate its concerns to WTO members; however, it failed in its attempts to persuade states to change course, even after numerous high-level face-to-face consultations. In response, and out of a sense of growing desperation, WFP officials chose an extraordinary strategy to exert influence on global trade rulemaking: using the international media as a platform from which to publicly shame WTO members. The WFP utilized the media to portray the proposed food aid disciplines as a threat to the food security and lives of vulnerable populations and to claim that WTO members were acting contrary to the interests and values of the international community. In intervening at the WTO, the WFP traded on its moral authority as the UN agency responsible for feeding the world's hungriest people, in the hope that its actions would prompt a global outcry and thus pressure WTO members to alter the proposed rules. In the end, its intervention had a significant impact on the negotiating agenda and outcome of the WTO agriculture negotiations. The WFP's use of public shaming led WTO members to backpedal and discard the proposed food aid rules. Furthermore, WTO members subsequently incorporated demands made by the WFP, such as rules explicitly permitting the continued use of in-kind food aid in humanitarian emergencies and a commitment by states to maintain adequate levels of international food aid, into a new WTO agreement governing agricultural exports (the 2015 WTO Ministerial Decision on Export Competition).

The OHCHR chose to intervene at the WTO with the goal of constructing new food security safeguards for vulnerable groups in global trade rules. While the OHCHR has no mandate related to governing international trade, it is the world's watchdog for human rights, and its officials were concerned that WTO rules lacked adequate protections for vulnerable groups adversely affected by agricultural trade liberalization. The OHCHR used the strategy of invoking an alternative legal framework to influence global trade rulemaking, seeking to persuade WTO members that the agriculture negotiations could result in potential inconsistencies between WTO rules and international human rights law. The OHCHR sought to inform trade negotiators that their bargaining positions at the WTO could inadvertently violate their government's legal obligations as parties to human rights treaties. The OHCHR also invoked its authority as the world's protector of human rights to call on WTO members to create new trade rules that would protect the human rights of specific categories of persons. Though the OHCHR lacked formal channels of access at the WTO, its interventions had a meaningful impact on the global trade rulemaking process. In addition to contributing to reframing how human rights were understood at the WTO, the OHCHR's own proposals for new food security safeguards targeted at specific vulnerable groups, such as poor farmers and agricultural laborers, were incorporated into the final draft text of the Doha Round agriculture agreement (the 2008 Revised Draft Modalities for Agriculture, or "Rev. 4"), which remains the basis for negotiations in the post-Doha agriculture negotiations.

The SRRTF intervened at the WTO in the period following the collapse of the Doha Round in 2008, out of concern that WTO rules constrained the policy space of governments to introduce food security programs intended to respond to global food crises and thereby generated conflicts between the trade regime and global efforts to fight hunger. Lacking a seat at the bargaining table and any power to compel WTO members to change trade rules, the SRRTF adopted the intervention strategy of taking sides with a group of WTO members, the G33, with food security sensitivities in the agriculture negotiations. By taking sides, the SRRTF openly endorsed bargaining proposals tabled by the G33 in the negotiations, including proposals intended to loosen WTO rules to increase states' policy space to pursue food security objectives. In choosing to take sides, the SRRTF did more than simply lend some WTO members public support. As a prominent UN voice for food security, the SRRTF, through this intervention, enhanced the legitimacy of the G33's bargaining demands by painting the measures it proposed not just as a matter of these countries' individual trade interests but as supportive of the international community's goal to end hunger. Furthermore, the SRRTF sought to influence global trade rulemaking by calling on WTO members to adopt a legal waiver to end uncertainty surrounding the legality of public food-stockholding programs under international trade law. The SRRTF's innovative proposal for a legal waiver was ultimately taken up by trade ministers and formed the basis of a new WTO agreement on public food stockholding (the 2013 WTO Ministerial Decision on Public Food Stockholding for Food Security Purposes). These latter two cases of the OHCHR and SRRTF also demonstrate the evolution of debates about food security at the WTO and the growing prominence of human rights in contestation over global trade rules.

Analysis of the interventions by the FAO, WFP, OHCHR, and SRRTF at the GATT/WTO reveals a number of important insights regarding how IOs are responding to institutional proliferation and increasing complexity in global governance. Intervention by UN actors at the GATT/WTO is not indicative of a power struggle between the UN system and the trade regime, with the former seeking to curb the latter's expanded authority into agriculture and food security. While UN actors sought to alter global trade rules, their actions were not intended to challenge or supplant the trade regime as the principal forum for negotiating multilateral trade treaties and settling trade disputes. On the contrary, the FAO, WFP, OHCHR, and SRRTF all expressed their support for the WTO's mission to establish a rules-based international trading system. Nor were their actions motivated by ideological or principled opposition to the WTO's goal of agricultural trade liberalization. None of the UN actors analyzed in this study took an antitrade stance when intervening at the WTO; instead, each affirmed the potential benefits that freer and fairer agricultural trade could have for economic development in the global South. Nor were UN actors seeking to act as "spoilers," preventing states from reaching agreement or preventing new trade agreements from being created. Instead, as this analysis has shown, interventions by UN actors in multilateral trade negotiations were narrowly targeted and intended only to alter certain specific provisions of prospective trade agreements. These UN actors intervened with the goal of modifying the content of prospective trade agreements, seeking to insert provisions that they believed would lessen potential negative effects for world food security.

This book has identified four intervention strategies utilized by IOs seeking to influence decision-making at other organizations: mobilizing states, public shaming, invoking alternative legal frameworks, and taking sides. These four strategies show that intervention by IOs can manifest in multiple forms. In addition, they indicate that IOs are innovative in developing actions intended to alter decision-making at an overlapping organization over which they have no formal control. The strategies emerged as part of a fluid and adaptive response to the opportunities and constraints each organization faced in seeking to influence multilateral trade negotiations at the GATT/WTO. The case studies presented in this book focused on one intervention strategy used by each IO in order to fully demonstrate how each strategy was executed and assess its effects. However, this is not to suggest that an IO is limited to using only one intervention strategy. Intervention strategies are not necessarily mutually exclusive: there could be situations when one intervention strategy does not work and an IO attempts another or potentially employs a combination of strategies at the same time. Finally, while this book has identified four distinct intervention strategies, these are not necessarily exhaustive, and it is reasonable to expect that IOs may develop other intervention strategies in response to the distinct opportunities and challenges they face in seeking to influence decision-making at overlapping organizations.

UN actors drew on various forms of authority in seeking to influence global trade rulemaking. The FAO, for example, relied on its expert authority, attracting states by deploying its specialized knowledge about agricultural trade, which it used to frame issues, run econometric analyses, and formulate technically sophisticated bargaining proposals for like-minded GATT/WTO members. Given that global trade rules have become ever more technical and complex, trade expertise can be an important resource for IOs seeking to exert influence in multilateral trade negotiations. In other cases, however, intervention by UN actors drew primarily on other forms of authority. For example, the WFP, which specializes in the delivery of humanitarian assistance and has no claim to technical trade expertise (a fact it repeatedly acknowledged to WTO members), made normative claims of right and wrong, publicly asserting that WTO members were behaving irresponsibly by proposing a rule that risked increasing starvation. In doing so, the WFP relied on its moral authority, that is, its standing as the UN body that feeds the world's hungry, to claim that its actions, by preventing unnecessary deaths, were in the universal interest of humanity. The OHCHR and SRRTF drew on a combination of delegated, moral, and expert authority. These actors used their status as international authorities to make normative claims—that international human rights law obligated WTO members to protect the human rights of vulnerable groups—based on their expertise in international human rights law and justified their actions in reference to the responsibility assigned to them by states to speak on behalf of the world's marginalized peoples. These cases thus demonstrate that UN actors were not solely reliant on expert authority in the form of technical trade knowledge but also drew on other sources of expertise, such as knowledge of international human rights law, as well as moral authority, to exert influence over the course and outcomes of multilateral trade negotiations.

An important insight from the cases is that the intervention strategies employed by UN actors at the GATT/WTO varied significantly in terms of their publicness and visibility. Some intervention strategies were highly visible and took place in the public sphere, where others were executed behind closed doors and hidden from public view. The intervention strategies used by the WFP and FAO highlight the two opposite ends of this spectrum. The WFP's intervention into global trade rulemaking, publicly shaming WTO members at the Hong Kong Ministerial, was a highly public and intentionally attention-grabbing act that played out in the global media spotlight and was thus visible to the entire world. In sharp contrast, the FAO's strategy of mobilizing states in the agriculture negotiations during the Uruguay Round took place behind closed doors and was invisible to the outside world. Indeed, even some GATT/WTO members were unaware that FAO officials were steering the negotiating strategy of, and drafting bargaining proposals for, food import–dependent developing countries. The intervention strategies deployed by the OHCHR and SRRTF fell somewhere in between these two extremes: their interventions were also visible and public, and attracted attention, but to a lesser degree than the WFP's strategy of public shaming. That UN actors' intervention strategies differed in terms of their publicness and visibility suggests that IOs may choose different arenas—ranging from closed-door bargaining sessions at the WTO headquarters in Geneva to the court of global public opinion—in seeking to affect change.

Through their interventions at the WTO, UN actors actively challenged the interests of powerful states. The FAO, by seeking to insert protections for food import–dependent developing countries against higher world food prices, directly challenged the economic interests of the major agricultural exporters, such as the US and EU, who are among the most powerful states in the trade regime. Similarly, the WFP's actions directly opposed the bargaining position and interests of the EU, Canada, and Australia and had the effect of weakening their positions in the agriculture negotiations. The OHCHR defied the preferences of most WTO members by working to bring human rights issues into WTO negotiations, something that states had historically resisted and sought to prevent. In the case of the SRRTF, it chose to openly oppose, and attempted to tilt the political balance against, the US and other powerful agricultural-exporting countries. The cases show that UN actors knowingly sought to influence global trade rules in ways that directly challenged the economic interests of powerful states and weakened their hands in the context of multilateral trade negotiations. Interventions by UN actors should thus not be confused with simply "technical" engagement in trade matters; this was purposeful political action intended to influence the international distribution of the benefits and costs of global trade rules.

Indeed, it is precisely because UN actors challenged the interests of powerful states that their interventions risked generating potentially costly backlash for their organizations. As these cases show, UN actors experienced varying degrees of backlash from states in response to their efforts to influence the trajectory of multilateral trade negotiations at the GATT/WTO. The backlash experienced by the WFP provides the most severe example: the WFP received a strong public rebuke from EU member states and other WTO members to its intervention at the Hong Kong Ministerial Meeting, and the heaviest price was paid by the WFP executive director when the EU blocked his reappointment to a second term, though reappointment was then standard practice. The OHCHR, SRRTF, and FAO all experienced various forms of pushback from states. In the case of the OHCHR, powerful states signaled their displeasure with the High Commissioner's report on agricultural trade liberalization by voting against endorsement of the report at the CHR and also communicated their disapproval directly to the High Commissioner for trying to interfere in trade negotiations. The SRRTF was subject to coordinated political attacks by major agricultural-exporting countries at the HRC and at the WTO, where powerful states sought to weaken his credibility and disputed his right to weigh in on multilateral trade negotiations. In the FAO's case, powerful states—including the US, the EU, and other major agricultural exporters—sought to curtail the organization's involvement in the agriculture negotiations by seeking to prevent the FAO from holding observer status in the Uruguay Round and later attempting to exclude FAO officials from having a seat on the interagency panel for a food-financing facility in the Doha Round.

While intervention by UN actors in multilateral trade negotiations dissatisfied many powerful states, it did not elicit the most potentially extreme forms of backlash, such as cuts to IOs' budgets or changes to their mandates. In the cases analyzed in this study, states would have been understandably reluctant, and therefore unlikely, to have pursued such drastic measures against intervening IOs. First, none of these IOs took actions that were clearly inconsistent with or contradictory to their official mandates and functions. For states to sanction an IO and/or its officials for behaving in ways that arguably comply with their missions may prove difficult if there is no clear violation of the terms of its official mandate or organizational rules. Second, if dissatisfied states had pursued drastic backlash measures against IOs, such as proposing cuts to their budgets, for speaking out or taking a position on global trade rules, this would very likely have generated significant public outcry as well as resistance to such measures from other states, global civil society, and other stakeholders (including other IOs). Dissatisfied states would have to carefully weigh their desire to punish an intervening IO against the potential harm to their reputation for appearing to seek retribution: for example, had the EU proposed cutting the WFP's budget to feed vulnerable people in retaliation for its advertisement in the *Financial Times*, there is no doubt that this would have been an unmitigated public relations disaster for the EU, in addition to undermining its bargaining position at the WTO. Third, dissatisfied states may be unwilling to take punitive measures out of a reasonable concern that doing so would bring unwanted further international attention and public scrutiny to already complicated and highly politicized trade negotiations. This is not to suggest, however, that in other cases states will always choose not to pursue more punitive measures against IOs that they deem to be engaged in unwanted interference in their business. This remains an option for states, and one could foresee situations where states might choose to drastically punish an intervening IO, especially if the IO took action that dissatisfied the majority of its member states and/or took a position that was widely seen as egregiously violating the interests or values of the international community.

IOs Navigating Complex Global Governance

This book has challenged existing conceptions of IOs in regime complexes as merely the arenas in which states pursue cross-institutional political strategies. As I have shown, rising institutional density and overlapping authority in global governance are driving IOs to behave in new ways. Just as we would expect IOs not to be indifferent to objectionable decisions taken by states within their own institutions, this book has shown that IOs are also not passive to decisions taken at overlapping institutions that they expect will result in negative spillover effects for their goals and values or those of the international community they are charged with upholding. As I have argued in this book, such situations may prompt IOs to take externally oriented political action that seeks to alter decision-making at other institutions within their regime complex.

The analysis presented in this book contributes to our understanding of IOs as actors in world politics by demonstrating a novel form of IO agency—intervention—in which IOs insert themselves into the politics of decision-making at other IOs. While it is widely accepted among scholars that IOs have their own interests and capabilities for political action, existing research has largely focused on how IOs exercise influence within their organizational boundaries and in areas where they have official, formal roles. By contrast, this study has focused on the ways IOs are seeking to exercise influence outside their organizational boundaries at other organizations and in situations where they do not formally participate in the decision-making process of the overlapping organization. The analysis has thus indicated a much wider scope of IOs' agency in global governance than conceptualized by existing constructivist and principal-agent approaches. As I have shown, the agency of IOs is not restricted to the strict confines of their delegation contract with their principals or bound to issue areas where they enjoy exclusive competence and expertise, but instead can be used to influence the decision-making process of other international institutions over which they have no formal authority.

As this analysis has shown, intervention is a distinct form of interaction among IOs that differs from cooperation and competition. Intervention is not a situation where two or more IOs collaborate to achieve a joint policy or regulatory goal. The interventions undertaken by UN actors did not involve them working in tandem or partnership with the GATT/WTO secretariat. Intervention should also not be confused with competition among IOs, where they engage in a battle for turf, members, resources, or policy influence at the other's expense. UN actors were dissatisfied with certain trade rules, but they did not contest the WTO's role as an institution. In none of the cases did the intervening IO view or treat the WTO as a threat to their own institutional authority, and these IOs were certainly not behaving with the aim of seeking to obtain mandates and/ or expanded power to enforce global trade rules. Their purpose in choosing to intervene was solely focused on altering an anticipated decision by states in multilateral trade negotiations; intervention was never directed toward changing the behavior of the GATT/WTO secretariat.

The cases also demonstrate that a diverse range of IOs have engaged in intervention and sought to influence global trade rulemaking at the GATT/WTO. While the four intervening IOs examined in this study are all part of the UN system, they differ from one another in important ways. First, they have distinct missions and operate in different issue areas related to the global governance of food security, including reducing hunger and improving agricultural production (FAO); delivering humanitarian assistance in emergency situations (WFP); monitoring and implementing international human rights treaties (OHCHR); and promoting the human right to food (SRRTF). Second, these IOs vary significantly in the material and human resources at their disposal. As the case studies have shown, intervention was undertaken by large IOs with significant material resources, such as the WFP with its $8.4 billion budget and seventeen thousand staff located around the world, as well as those with minimal resources like the SRRTF, whose team consists of just a handful of individuals and operates on a shoestring budget. Third, the four intervening IOs also vary in their relationship to the trade regime. While the FAO and WFP hold official observer status at the WTO, which provides them with formal access to privileged information and enables frequent interaction with trade negotiators, the OHCHR and SRRTF lack such status to the WTO and therefore lack equivalent access to information or access to trade negotiators. Intervention was thus pursued by IOs with diverging missions and from different elemental regimes within the regime complex for food security (including agriculture and food, humanitarian aid, and human rights), by IOs with abundant or limited financial and human resources, and by IOs with or without formal access to the trade regime. This suggests that intervention is not limited to a single type of IO but can be undertaken by a wide variety of IOs.

In all of the cases analyzed, intervention was solely unidirectional: the FAO, WFP, OHCHR, and SRRTF each intervened in the decision-making process of the GATT/WTO, but there is no evidence that the GATT/WTO ever sought to intervene in decision-making at those other institutions. It was the potential for global trade rules to have negative spillover effects for food security that prompted UN actors to seek to influence decision-making at the GATT/WTO. There was no reciprocal or equivalent action by the GATT/WTO to alter decision-making at the FAO, WFP, OHCHR, or SRRTF, since no decisions taken at these IOs would have had negative spillover effects for the ability of the GATT/WTO secretariat to fulfil its mission and goals.

Intervention is thus a distinct form of interaction among IOs. It does not necessarily involve or require any direct interaction between secretariats. Indeed, as the cases have shown, the GATT/WTO secretariat was often bypassed or irrelevant to the actions taken by UN actors to alter the course of global trade rulemaking by states. This is not to suggest that the GATT/WTO secretariat was unaware or indifferent to the efforts of UN actors to shape global trade rules. On the contrary, GATT/WTO secretariat officials had front-row seats to observe these events and, in some instances, voiced displeasure about the efforts of other IOs to influence trade negotiations. However, since the actions by intervening IOs were not targeted at the GATT/WTO secretariat and did not require it to respond, GATT/WTO secretariat officials generally remained neutral and did not become directly involved. The only notable exception was in the case of the SRRTF's intervention at the 2011 Ministerial, where, under pressure from powerful WTO members, the WTO director-general publicly disagreed with the recommendations put forward by the SRRTF by posting an official letter of response on the WTO website.

While intervention is distinct from cooperation and competition among IOs, these multiple forms of IO interaction can coexist. The cases in this study suggest that intervention can take place alongside and in parallel to cooperation between an intervening and target IO. The FAO and WFP both have formal cooperation arrangements with the WTO and work closely with the WTO secretariat by, for example, sharing information and providing technical assistance. Yet both the FAO and WFP intervened in interstate bargaining at the WTO and did so while continuing to formally cooperate with the WTO secretariat. None of the cases analyzed in this study included an IO in overt competition with the WTO; however, there is no reason why an IO competing with the WTO secretariat for turf or resources could not also concurrently seek to intervene if it had serious concerns that prospective trade rules proposed by WTO members would have harmful consequences. This suggests that IO interaction can be multilayered, with forms of cooperation, competition, and intervention potentially occurring simultaneously between IOs in a regime complex.

Generalizability and Directions for Future Research

This book has focused on intervention by multiple IOs in the agriculture negotiations at the GATT/WTO. There is reason to believe, however, that IO intervention is not limited to the agriculture negotiations but likely a broader phenomenon in multilateral trade negotiations. Many areas of WTO negotiations similarly have consequences for issues beyond trade, creating conditions where multiple IOs may be concerned with the implications of global trade rules and have an interest and stake in negotiation outcomes. We might expect IOs such as the WHO to have a stake in global trade rules that determine access to essential medicines and vaccines needed to combat global health crises, for instance, or the UNEP to have a stake in the WTO negotiations to reduce fisheries subsidies that contribute to the depletion of global fish stocks, which could prompt them to seek to intervene in rulemaking at the WTO. Intervention could thus be expected in other areas of the trade regime beyond agriculture and food security. In addition, there is no reason why intervention would be limited to IOs that are part of the UN system. Many other IOs, such as the World Bank, the OECD, and the International Organization for Standardization, have a significant interest in ensuring coherence between their policies and those of the WTO. Further research is therefore needed to more fully map the landscape of IO intervention in the trade regime to determine the extent and frequency of this phenomenon across multiple negotiating areas. By unearthing the role of IOs in influencing trade negotiations, this study opens up a new research agenda for trade scholarship that calls for taking seriously the agentic role of IOs in multilateral trade negotiations. Doing so is crucial to building a more complete understanding of who shapes the rules of global trade.

At the same time, it is also reasonable to expect intervention to be a more widespread phenomenon beyond the regime complex for food security or the multilateral trading system. Many regime complexes exhibit the basic features necessary to produce potential situations of intervention: (1) partially overlapping authority among two or more IOs with different goals; (2) IOs with their own preferences and capabilities for political action; and (3) instances where decisions taken at one IO have significant consequences for other IOs in the regime complex. This book therefore opens up space for a new research agenda on how IOs are navigating complexity in global governance that focuses on how IOs are exercising influence beyond their own organizational boundaries and in other institutions over which they have no formal control.

Notes

Introduction

1. For example, Egypt, Jamaica, and many other food import–dependent developing countries threatened to exit and/or block the agriculture negotiations during the Uruguay Round (Margulis 2017). Similarly, the Indian government threatened to block the WTO agreement on trade facilitation in 2014 because of concerns about the lack of progress on negotiating new rules on public food stockholding and the implications for national food security.

2. This study focuses explicitly on IOs that are external to the multilateral trade system, which excludes the GATT/WTO secretariats. Several studies, such as Elsig (2011), Jinnah (2014), and Xu and Weller (2018), that examine the role of the GATT/WTO secretariats show that they tend to exercise influence primarily in the agreement implementation phase, rather than in the negotiation of trade agreements.

3. WTO trade ministers declared the Doha Round of multilateral trade negotiations to have reached an impasse in December 2011.

Chapter 1

1. Exceptions are Betts (2013) and Gómez-Mera (2016).

2. In some cases, states may choose to delegate decision-making authority (e.g., International Criminal Court, WTO dispute panels), but states retain control over key decision-making in the most IOs.

Chapter 2

1. Other IOs in the international regime for food security included the International Fund for Agriculture Development (IFAD), the UN Development Programme (UNDP), UNCTAD, and the World Bank (Shaw and Clay 1998).

2. The GATT primarily covered tariff reductions on industrial goods and included few rules on agriculture. Even the few trade rules on the books that applied to agriculture were not enforced because of US demands for exemptions (Josling, Tangermann, and Warley 1996; Trebilcock and Howse 2005).

3. Nontrade concerns refer to areas of economic activity that have commercial aspects while also providing public goods. The idea of food security as a nontrade concern emerged during the Uruguay Round agriculture negotiations when Japan, South Korea, and India—all countries that experienced major food insecurity crises in the twentieth century—demanded lesser liberalization commitments in agriculture to ensure that states had the flexibility to achieve food security (GATT 1989c). This demand, however, was vehemently rejected by major net food exporters such as the US and the Cairns Group, which viewed it as too wide a deviation from the goal of liberalizing agricultural trade (Margulis 2017). As a result, while GATT members agreed to recognize nontrade concerns as a principle in the preamble of the AoA, the text of the AoA did not include any specific rules on food security as a nontrade concern. Instead, in recognition that this remained a contentious issue, Article 20 of the AoA established that nontrade concerns would be on the agenda of future agricultural negotiations (GATT 1994a).

Chapter 3

1. For example, the projected increase in net food import costs was 29 percent for Egypt, 30 percent for Jamaica, 24 percent for Mexico, 28 percent for Morocco, and 33 percent for Peru (GATT 1989d, 8).

2. Interviews with FAO assistant director-general and division director, February 2009.

3. Interview with FAO division director, February 2009.

4. Ibid.

5. Interviews with developing-country trade negotiators, December 2008, February, April, and June 2009, and September 2019.

6. Interview with FAO division director, February 2009.

7. Ibid.

8. Ibid.

9. Interviews with developing-country trade negotiators and FAO division director, December 2008, February, April, and June 2009, and September 2019.

10. Interview with FAO division director, February 2009.

11. Ibid.

12. Ibid.

13. The full title is "Decision on Measures Concerning the Possible Negative Effects of the Reform Programme on Least-Developed and Net Food-Importing Developing Countries."

14. Statement by Dr. Kirit S. Parikh, director of the Indira Gandhi Institute of Development Research at the FAO Workshop on Agriculture, Trade and Food Security, September 1999.

15. Food imports in many NFIDCs and LDCs in the 1980s were often the responsibility of state-owned enterprises or marketing boards, such as Egypt's General Authority for Supply Commodities, and were then redistributed to the commercial market and citizens.

16. NFIDCs and LDCs had different agricultural interests at the WTO. The main concern for LDCs at the time was preference erosion for their agricultural and tropical product exports to their former colonizing states. NFIDCs, who as a group have larger and more diverse economies than LDCs, and include many oil exporters, had interests beyond agriculture that included tariff and nontariff barriers on manufactured goods, textiles, and services (FAO 2002c, 263; Ng and Aksoy 2008).

17. Interviews with FAO director and senior economists, November 2008 and February 2009.

18. Interview with developing-country trade negotiator, November 2019.

19. Interviews with FAO senior economists, November 2008.

20. Interviews with developing-country ambassadors to WTO, April 2009.

21. Interview with former FAO deputy director-general, May 2009.

22. Interview with FAO director, October 2008.

23. Paragraph 5 of the Marrakesh Decision (GATT 1994b) stated: "Ministers recognize that as a result of the Uruguay Round certain developing countries may experience short-term difficulties in financing normal levels of commercial imports and that these countries may be eligible to draw on the resources of international financial institutions under existing facilities, *or such facilities as may be established*, in the context of adjustment programmes, in order to address such financing difficulties" (italics added).

24. There was not a straightforward private sector solution at the time. Unlike in developed countries, commercial banking was still an immature sector in NFIDCs and LDCs, meaning that governments could not simply turn to national private banks and use domestic savings as an alternative source of capital to finance food imports.

25. FAO workshop held in March 2001 at the Palais des Nations, Geneva.

26. Interview with developing-country trade negotiator, November 2019.

27. Interview with developing-country trade negotiator, November 2019.

28. The proposal was jointly tabled by Côte d'Ivoire, Cuba, Dominican Republic, Egypt, Honduras, Jamaica, Kenya, Mauritius, Morocco, Pakistan, Peru, Senegal, Sri Lanka, St. Lucia, Trinidad and Tobago, Tunisia, and Venezuela.

29. Statement by the representative of Honduras at the Committee on Agriculture, March 2001 (WTO 2001e, 5).

30. Interviews with developing-country trade negotiator, WTO director, and World Bank senior economist, September and November 2008.

31. Interviews with FAO officials, October 2008 and March 2009.

32. Interview with developing-country trade negotiator, November 2019.

33. Interviews with World Bank senior economist, September 2008.

34. Interviews with FAO director and senior economist, October 2008.

Chapter 4

1. The cause of growing wheat surpluses in North America was a combination of technological advances in production, government policies incentivizing overproduction by farmers, and a quicker-than-expected recovery of wheat production in postwar Europe (Friedmann 1982).

2. The AoA committed developed countries to cut budgetary spending on agricultural export subsidies by 36 percent and the quantities of subsidized exports by 21 percent over five years (i.e., 1995–2000). Developing countries committed to cut budgetary spending by 24 percent and quantities of subsidized exports by 14 percent over ten years (1995–2005). These commitments applied only to the sixteen GATT members that had agricultural export subsidy programs at the time of the Uruguay Round negotiations (Australia, Brazil, Canada, Colombia, EU, Iceland, Indonesia, Israel, Mexico, Norway, South Africa, Switzerland-Liechtenstein, Turkey, United States, Uruguay, and Venezuela). WTO members without scheduled agricultural export subsidy commitments are not permitted to subsidize exports (GATT 1994a).

3. Article 9.1 of the AoA defines an agricultural export subsidy as follows: "1) the provision by governments or their agencies of direct payments-in-kind, to a firm, to an industry, to producers of an agricultural product, to a co-operative or other association of such producers, or to a marketing board, contingent on export performance; 2) the sale or disposal for export by governments or their agencies of non-commercial stocks of agricultural products at a price lower than the comparable price charged for a like product to buyers in the domestic market; 3) payments on the export of an agricultural product that are financed by virtue of governmental action, whether or not a charge on the public account is involved, including payments that are financed from the proceeds of a levy imposed on the agricultural product concerned, or on an agricultural product from

which the exported product is derived; 4) the provision of subsidies to reduce the costs of marketing exports of agricultural products (other than widely available export promotion and advisory services) including handling, upgrading and other processing costs, and the costs of international transport and freight; 5) internal transport and freight charges on export shipments, provided or mandated by governments, on terms more favourable than for domestic shipments; and 6) subsidies on agricultural products contingent on their incorporation in exported products" (GATT 1994a, 8).

4. The other two pillars of the agriculture negotiations are "domestic support," which covers subsidies and other payments to producers, and "market access," which covers tariff and nontariff barriers to trade.

5. The Cairns Group is a bargaining coalition of major agricultural exporters seeking aggressive agricultural trade liberalization. It was established in 1986 at the launch of the GATT Uruguay Round, and current members include Argentina, Australia, Brazil, Canada, Chile, Colombia, Costa Rica, Guatemala, Indonesia, Malaysia, New Zealand, Pakistan, Paraguay, Peru, Philippines, South Africa, Thailand, Uruguay, and Viet Nam.

6. Interviews with developed- and developing-country WTO ambassadors and trade negotiators and WFP director, 2008 and 2009.

7. Interview with WFP director, May 2008.

8. Interviews with developed- and developing-country trade negotiators, 2008 and 2009.

9. Interview with WFP director, December 2008.

10. Interviews with WFP directors, deputy directors, and executive board members, October 2008 and February 2009.

11. Interview with WFP senior economist, March 2009.

12. Interviews with WFP director and developed-country negotiators, 2008–9.

13. Interviews with developed- and developing-country trade negotiators, 2008 and 2009.

14. Interviews with developed-country negotiators and WFP director, 2008–9.

15. Interview with WFP director, May 2009.

16. Interviews with WFP directors and deputy director, December 2008 and May 2009.

17. Interviews with WFP senior economist and developed-country negotiators, 2008–9.

18. Interviews with developed- and developing-country trade negotiators, 2008–9.

19. Ibid.

20. Ibid.

21. Interview with WFP director, March 2009.

22. Interviews with WFP directors and deputy director, December 2008 and May 2009.

23. Ibid.

24. Interview with WFP director, March 2009.

25. Interviews with WFP country director and senior economists, March 2009.

26. Interview with developed-country negotiator, February 2009.

27. Interview with developed-country trade negotiator, February 2009.

28. Interviews with developed- and developing-country trade negotiators, 2008 and 2009.

29. Interview with WFP director, March 2009.

30. Ibid.

31. Interviews with senior WFP and UN officials, October 2008 and February 2009.

32. Interview with WFP director, February 2009.

Chapter 5

1. In this chapter, reference to the OHCHR includes both its executive head, the UN High Commissioner for Human Rights, and the OHCHR secretariat, unless specified otherwise.

2. The nine core UN human rights treaties are the International Convention on the Elimination of All Forms of Racial Discrimination (ICERD); the International Covenant on Civil and Political Rights (ICCPR); the International Covenant on Economic, Social and Cultural Rights (CESCR); the Convention on the Elimination of All Forms of Discrimination against Women (CEDAW); the Convention against Torture and Other Cruel, Inhuman or Degrading Treatment or Punishment (CAT); the Convention on the Rights of the Child (CRC); the International Convention on the Protection of the Rights of All Migrant Workers and Members of Their Families (CMW); the International Convention for the Protection of All Persons from Enforced Disappearance (CPED); and, the Convention on the Rights of Persons with Disabilities (CRPD). Each human rights treaty has a mechanism, typically an expert committee of international jurists, that is responsible for monitoring states' implementation of the treaty and reporting to various intergovernmental bodies.

3. The Human Rights Council (HRC) is a standing body composed of forty-seven UN member states that are elected on a rotating basis by the UN General Assembly. The HRC has the authority to investigate allegations of breaches of human rights in UN member states. The HRC replaced the Commission on Human Rights in 2006.

4. The Special Procedures of the HRC are independent human rights experts appointed by UN members with mandates to report and advise on specific human rights issues or the human rights situations in particular countries.

5. This includes the 1999 General Comment No. 12 by the Committee on Economic, Social and Cultural Rights (CESCR) and the 2004 Voluntary Guidelines to Support the Progressive Realization of the Right to Adequate Food in the Context of National Food Security (VGRTF).

6. NGOs with consultative status at the CHR/HRC are permitted to attend and observe nearly all proceedings, submit written statements, make oral interventions, participate in debates and informal meetings, and organize side events during official meetings.

7. Interview with OHCHR human rights officer, March 2009.

8. Interviews with WTO counselors in the Director-General's Office and OHCHR human rights officers, March and April 2009.

9. World Bank data, 2001.

10. Personal communication with Mary Robinson, June 2009.

11. Interview with OHCHR senior human rights officer, March 2009.

12. Interview with OHCHR human rights officer, March 2009.

13. The report was released in January 2002 but not tabled for debate by UN members until the Fifty-Eighth Session of the Commission on Human Rights in April 2002.

14. Interview with OHCHR senior human rights officer, March 2009.

15. Ibid.

16. Multiple interviews with developed- and developing-country trade negotiators, 2008 and 2009.

17. Interviews with WTO senior legal counselors and deputy director, October 2008.

18. Interviews with developed- and developing-country negotiators, OHCHR human rights officers, and WTO deputy director, 2008–9.

19. Interviews with developed-country negotiators, OHCHR senior human rights officers, and executive senior adviser to the UN High Commissioner for Human Rights, 2008–9.

20. In addition to the agriculture negotiations, the OHCHR closely followed the negotiations on intellectual property rights and the potential launch of additional negotiations on trade and investment at the WTO.

21. Interview with OHCHR human rights officer, March 2009.

22. Ibid.

23. The Sub-Commission on the Promotion and Protection of Human Rights was replaced by the Advisory Committee in 2006 when the CHR was reconstituted as the UN Human Rights Council.

24. Interviews with OHCHR human rights officers, March and April 2009.

25. The G20 bargaining coalition at the WTO is distinct from the G20 club of the world's largest economies. From here onward, *G20* refers to the former.

26. In addition, there is evidence that the OHCHR's interventions at the WTO changed the trade policy formulation practices of several WTO members. One of the key recommendations by the High Commissioner was for WTO members to undertake human rights impact assessments when negotiating trade agreements. The OHCHR was the first UN agency to call for this practice and subsequently has become a global leader in the design of methodologies and dissemination of best practices for implementing human rights impact assessments of trade agreements (Forman and MacNaughton 2015). Many WTO members have adopted the OHCHR's recommendations to undertake human rights impact assessments of trade agreements. The EU, Thailand, and Costa Rica were among the first WTO members to undertake human rights impacts assessments for trade (Bürgi Bonanomi 2017). Interest in human rights impact assessments has grown considerably. In 2018, the HRC established an expert committee to further develop international guidelines for human rights impact assessments .

27. Interviews with trade negotiators, OHCHR human rights advisers, and WTO legal counselors, 2008–9.

28. Interview with Gabrielle Marceau, counselor in the Legal Affairs Division of the WTO, October 2008.

29. The WTO Public Forum is the main outreach event that promotes policy dialogue and exchange between the WTO (both members and the secretariat) and NGOs, parliamentarians, academics, and business.

30. The report of the chairperson of the agriculture negotiations concluded with regard to Special Products that WTO members should "be able to go with what is in the text at a pinch" (WTO 2008c, 1).

Chapter 6

1. In this chapter the acronym SRRTF refers both to the office and to the individual mandate holder.

2. The latter task was taken up by the Committee on Economic, Social, and Cultural Rights (CESCR), a human rights treaty body, which in 1999 published General Comment 12, a document considered by states and experts as the "authoritative interpretation" of states' obligation to realize the right to food (Mechlem 2004, 638). General Comment 12 defines the right to food as "the right of everyone to have physical and economic access at all times to food in adequate quantity and quality or to means of its procurement" and the duty of states to respect, protect, and fulfill the right to food (CESCR 1999, 3).

3. Several reports and official communications issued by Ziegler and De Schutter during their terms as SRRTF explicitly addressed the WTO and agricultural trade liberalization. Hilal Elver, who served as the third SRRTF (2014–20),

similarly identified the WTO as a top priority for her mandate (Elver 2016, 18, 20). Michael Fakhri, who was appointed in 2020, has also focused on the WTO.

4. Jean Ziegler made several requests to the WTO director-general to arrange a meeting with WTO members, but his requests never received an official reply (personal communication with OHCHR human rights officer, March 2008).

5. For an overview of Jean Ziegler's work as SRRTF between 2000 and 2008, see Ziegler et al. (2011).

6. A key part of the work of UN human rights experts is undertaking fact-finding country missions in order to investigate human rights situations and meet with governments and other stakeholders (Nifosi 2005; Naples-Mitchell 2011; Piccone 2012; Subedi 2016). Fact-finding missions by UN human experts to other IOs are comparatively rare.

7. Interview with Olivier De Schutter, April 2009.

8. The WTO director-general, Pascal Lamy, organized the 2008 July Mini-ministerial in the hope of spurring the WTO's most powerful members—the US, the EU, India, Brazil, and China—to break the impasse in the agriculture negotiations and arrive at a political compromise to salvage the Doha Round.

9. Interview with Olivier De Schutter, April 2009.

10. Ibid.

11. Interview with IATP policy adviser, March 2009.

12. NGOs that were part of the trade policy community in Geneva, such as Oxfam, ICTSD, and IATP, welcomed the SRRTF's outreach to them and would become important allies of the SRRTF as well as a source of key information and expertise about developments in the WTO negotiations.

13. Interviews with officials from the OHCHR Special Procedures Division, March and April 2009.

14. Interviews with developed- and developing-country WTO member state representatives, April and June 2009.

15. Interviews with OHCHR human rights advisers and developed- and developing-country WTO member state representatives, March and July 2009.

16. The report was officially released on February 4, 2009, and was thus available in the public domain for over a month prior being formally presented.

17. Since the SRRTF's report had been publicly available for over a month prior, and since it addressed such a controversial topic—global trade rules—many states were eager to make their views known on it, even if the report was not slated for discussion until the afternoon plenary session.

18. Statement by Alexandre Guido Lopes Parola, representative of Brazil to the WTO at the Tenth Session of the Human Rights Council, March 9, 2009.

19. Statement by Maria Nazareth Farani Azevedo, representative of Brazil to the HRC, March 9, 2009.

20. Ibid.

21. Statement by Maria Lourdes Bone, representative of Uruguay to the HRC, March 9, 2009.

22. Statement by Jonathan Kenna, representative of Australia to the HRC, March 9, 2009.

23. Interviews with developing- and developed-country representatives to the HRC and WTO, 2008–9.

24. Interview with Olivier De Schutter, April 2009.

25. Interview with Brazilian trade negotiator, April 2009.

26. Ibid.

27. Ibid.

28. Ibid.

29. The standard practice of the HRC is to issue a thematic resolution in which states express their views on the findings and conclusions of UN human rights experts. These resolutions are not legally binding. Resolutions of the HRC, like other UN bodies, involve text-based negotiations. The negotiation process is as follows: one or several states (i.e., "sponsors" and "co-sponsors") lead the drafting of the resolution, which is circulated to other HRC members for comments and negotiated changes in "informal meeting"; a final meeting is held, known as "open-ended informal," that includes HRC members, observer states, and accredited civil society organizations, where final changes are made to the resolution before adoption by the HRC by consensus or two-thirds majority vote. The open-ended informal consultation on the draft resolution on the right to food was held on the afternoon of March 10, 2009, at the UN office in Geneva and was attended in person by the author.

30. Field notes from direct observation of the open-ended informal consultations on the draft resolution on the right to food, March 2009.

31. Ibid.

32. Ibid.

33. Ibid.

34. Interview with Juan Antonio Fernandez Palacios, Cuba's ambassador to the UN, Geneva, March 2009.

35. Confidential interviews with developed- and developing-country representatives to the HRC, March 2009.

36. Paragraph 21 of HRC Resolution A/HRC/10/12 "took note" of the SR-RTF's report and encouraged the SRRTF to "to continue to engage with the World Trade Organization to follow up on the issues of concern identified in his report" (HRC 2009).

37. Interviews with developed- and developing-country representatives to the HRC, April and May 2009.

38. Interview with Canadian representative to the HRC, April 2009.

39. Interview with Olivier De Schutter, April 2009.

40. Ibid.

41. Interviews with officials from the OHCHR Special Procedures Division, Geneva, April 2019.

42. Communication from Priscilla Claeys, adviser to Olivier De Schutter. August 2009.

43. Interviews with representatives to the WTO of Brazil, Canada, New Zealand, and Uruguay, Geneva, April, May, and June 2009.

44. Ibid.

45. Ibid.

46. Interviews with representatives to the WTO of Brazil, Canada, New Zealand, and Uruguay, April, May, and June 2009.

47. Interviews with former chairperson of the WTO Committee on Agriculture, April 2009.

48. Interviews with the trade representatives of Uruguay and New Zealand, July 2009.

49. Interviews with WTO secretariat officials and trade representatives from developed and developing countries, 2008–9.

50. Interview with developed- and developing-country representatives to the WTO, July and August 2009.

51. Ibid.

52. Interview with Brazilian and Uruguayan representatives to the WTO, July 2009.

53. Communication with senior adviser to Olivier De Schutter, August 2009.

54. Interview with Olivier De Schutter, July 2009; personal correspondence with Olivier De Schutter by email, November 2009.

55. Interview with Cairns Group member representatives to the WTO, July and August 2009.

56. *Public food stockholding* refers to state-managed programs of purchasing, storing, and distributing agricultural commodities. Sometimes referred to as "food reserves" or "domestic food aid," public food stockholding is used by governments to achieve a mix of policy goals, including stabilizing domestic food prices and supplies, providing subsidized food to targeted populations, and supporting rural livelihoods.

57. Personal communication with Olivier De Schutter, August 2011.

58. Personal communications with media officer for the SRRTF, January 2012.

59. Confidential interview with Cairns Group member representatives to the WTO, July and August 2009.

60. Personal communications with media officer for the SRRTF, January 2012.

61. OWINFS members include several NGOs active in the WTO agriculture negotiations, including the Third World Network, the IATP, and Action Aid. A full list of the members of OWINFS can be found on the organization's website: https://ourworldisnotforsale.net/members.

62. Communications with participants, December 2011.

63. Personal communications with Olivier De Schutter, March 2012.

References

Aaronson, Susan Ariel. 2007. "Seeping in Slowly: How Human Rights Concerns Are Penetrating the WTO." *World Trade Review* 6 (3): 413–49.

Aaronson, Susan Ariel, and M. Rodwan Abouharb. 2011. "Unexpected Bedfellows: The GATT, the WTO and Some Democratic Rights." *International Studies Quarterly* 55 (2): 379–408.

Aaronson, Susan Ariel, and Jamie M. Zimmerman. 2007. "Fair Trade? How Oxfam Presented a Systemic Approach to Poverty, Development, Human Rights, and Trade." *Human Rights Quarterly* 28 (4): 998–1030.

Abbott, Frederick M., Christine Kaufmann, and Thomas Cottier, eds. 2006. *International Trade and Human Rights: Foundations and Conceptual Issues.* World Trade Forum, vol. 5. Ann Arbor: University of Michigan Press.

Abbott, Kenneth W. 2012. "The Transnational Regime Complex for Climate Change." *Environment and Planning C: Government and Policy* 30 (4): 571–90.

Abbott, Kenneth W., Philipp Genschel, Duncan Snidal, and Bernhard Zangl. 2015a. *International Organizations as Orchestrators.* Cambridge: Cambridge University Press.

———. 2015b. "Two Logics of Indirect Governance: Delegation and Orchestration." *British Journal of Political Science* 46 (4): 719–29. https://doi.org/10.1017/S0007123414000593.

Abbott, Kenneth W., Jessica F. Green, and Robert O. Keohane. 2016. "Organizational Ecology and Institutional Change in Global Governance." *Inter-*

national Organization 70 (2): 247–77. https://doi.org/10.1017/S002081831
5000338.

Abbott, Kenneth W., and Duncan Snidal. 1998. "Why States Act through Formal International Organizations." *Journal of Conflict Resolution* 42 (1): 3–32.

———. 2000. "Hard and Soft Law in International Governance." *International Organization* 54 (3): 421–56.

———. 2010. "International Regulation without International Government: Improving IO Performance through Orchestration." *Review of International Organizations* 5 (3): 315–44.

Abbott, Philip C. 2012. "Export Restrictions as Stabilization Responses to Food Crisis." *American Journal of Agricultural Economics* 94 (2): 428–34. https://doi.org/10.1093/ajae/aar092.

Adams, Richard H. 1983. "The Role of Research in Policy Development: The Creation of the IMF Cereal Import Facility." *World Development* 11 (7): 549–63. https://doi.org/10.1016/0305-750X(83)90001-3.

Adler-Nissen, Rebecca. 2014. "Stigma Management in International Relations: Transgressive Identities, Norms, and Order in International Society." *International Organization* 68 (1): 143–76. https://doi.org/10.1017/S0020818313000337.

Ala'i, Padideh. 2001. "A Human Rights Critique of the WTO: Some Preliminary Observations." *George Washington International Law Review* 33 (3–4): 537–54.

Albin, Cecilia, and Ariel Young. 2012. "Setting the Table for Success—or Failure? Agenda Management in the WTO." *International Negotiation* 17 (1): 37–64. https://doi.org/10.1163/157180612X630929.

Alons, Gerry. 2014. "Farmers versus Ideas: Explaining the Continuity in French Agricultural Trade Policy during the GATT Uruguay Round." *Journal of European Public Policy* 21 (2): 286–302. https://doi.org/10.1080/13501763.2013.836055.

Alston, Philip. 1992. *The United Nations and Human Rights: A Critical Appraisal.* Oxford: Oxford University Press.

———. 1997. "Neither Fish nor Fowl: The Quest to Define the Role of the UN High Commissioner for Human Rights." *European Journal of International Law* 8 (2): 321–35.

———. 2011. "Hobbling the Monitors: Should UN Human Rights Monitors Be Accountable." *Harvard International Law Journal* 52:561–648.

Alter, Karen J., and Sophie Meunier. 2009. "The Politics of International Regime Complexity." *Perspectives on Politics* 7 (1): 13–24.

Alter, Karen J., and Kal Raustiala. 2018. "The Rise of International Regime Complexity." *Annual Review of Law and Social Science* 14:329–49. https://doi.org/10.1146/annurev-lawsocsci-101317-030830.

Alvarez, José E. 2002. "The WTO as Linkage Machine." *American Journal of International Law* 96 (1): 146–58. https://doi.org/10.2307/2686131.

Andersen, Henrik. 2015. "Protection of Non-trade Values in WTO Appellate Body Jurisprudence: Exceptions, Economic Arguments, and Eluding Questions." *Journal of International Economic Law* 18 (2): 383–405. https://doi.org/10.1093/jiel/jgv020.

Andersen, Regine. 2003. "FAO and the Management of Plant Genetic Resources." In *Yearbook of International Co-operation on Environment and Development 2003/2004*, 43–53. London: Earthscan Publications.

Andrée, Peter, Jeffrey Ayres, Michael Bosia, and Marie-Josée Massicotte, eds. 2014. *Globalization and Food Sovereignty: Global and Local Change in the New Politics of Food.* Toronto: University of Toronto Press.

Avant, Deborah D., Martha Finnemore, and Susan K. Sell. 2010. *Who Governs the Globe?* Cambridge: Cambridge University Press.

Baer-Nawrocka, Agnieszka, and Arkadiusz Sadowski. 2019. "Food Security and Food Self-Sufficiency around the World: A Typology of Countries." *PloS One* 14 (3): e0213448-e0213448. https://doi.org/10.1371/journal.pone.0213448.

Baker, Andrew. 2012. "The 'Public Interest' Agency of International Organizations? The Case of the OECD Principles of Corporate Governance." *Review of International Political Economy* 19 (3): 389–414. https://doi.org/10.1080/09692290.2011.552789.

Ball, Richard, and Christopher Johnson. 1996. "Political, Economic, and Humanitarian Motivations for PL 480 Food Aid: Evidence from Africa." *Economic Development and Cultural Change* 44 (3): 515–37. https://doi.org/10.1086/452230.

Ballenger, Nicole, and Carl Mabbs-Zeno. 1992. "Treating Food Security and Food Aid Issues at the GATT." *Food Policy* 17 (4): 264–76.

Ban, Cornel, Leonard Seabrooke, and Sarah Freitas. 2016. "Grey Matter in Shadow Banking: International Organizations and Expert Strategies in Global Financial Governance." *Review of International Political Economy* 23 (6): 1001–33. https://doi.org/10.1080/09692290.2016.1235599.

Barnett, Michael N., and Raymond Duvall. 2005. "Power in International Politics." *International Organization* 59 (1): 39–75. https://doi.org/10.1017/S0020818305050010.

Barnett, Michael N., and Martha Finnemore. 1999. "The Politics, Power, and Pathologies of International Organizations." *International Organization* 53 (4): 699–732. https://doi.org/10.1162/002081899551048.

———. 2004. *Rules for the World: International Organizations in Global Politics.* Ithaca, NY: Cornell University Press.

Barrett, Christopher B. 1998. "Food Aid: Is It Development Assistance, Trade

Promotion, Both, or Neither?" *American Journal of Agricultural Economics* 80 (3): 566–71. https://doi.org/10.2307/1244559.

Barrett, Christopher B., and Daniel G. Maxwell. 2005. *Food Aid after Fifty Years: Recasting Its Role.* New York: Routledge.

Barton, John H., Judith L. Goldstein, Timothy E. Josling, and Richard H. Steinberg. 2008. *The Evolution of the Trade Regime: Politics, Law, and Economics of the GATT and the WTO.* Princeton, NJ: Princeton University Press.

Bauer, Michael W., and Jörn Ege. 2016. "Bureaucratic Autonomy of International Organizations' Secretariats." *Journal of European Public Policy* 23 (7): 1019–37. https://doi.org/10.1080/13501763.2016.1162833.

Bauer, Michael W., Christoph Knill, and Steffen Eckhard, eds. 2017. *International Bureaucracy: Challenges and Lessons for Public Administration Research.* Basingstoke: Palgrave Macmillan.

Bayram, A. Burcu, and Erin R. Graham. 2017. "Financing the United Nations: Explaining Variation in How Donors Provide Funding to the UN." *Review of International Organizations* 12 (3): 421–59. https://doi.org/10.1007/s11558-016-9261-0.

Belgasmi, Daly. 2006. "International Obligations for Providing Food Aid." *Refugee Survey Quarterly* 25 (4): 179–90.

Bernal, Luisa E. 2005. *Methodology for the Identification of Special Products (SP) and Products for Eligibility under the Special Safeguard Mechanism (SSM) by Developing Countries.* Geneva: International Centre for Trade and Sustainable Development.

Bernal, Richard L. 1999. "Sleepless in Seattle: The WTO Ministerial of November 1999." *Social and Economic Studies* 48 (3): 61–84.

Bernstein, Henry. 2014. "Food Sovereignty via the 'Peasant Way': A Sceptical View." *Journal of Peasant Studies* 41 (6): 1031–63.

Bernstein, Steven, and Erin Hannah. 2012. "The WTO and Institutional (In)coherence in Global Economic Governance." In *The Oxford Handbook on the World Trade Organization,* edited by Martin Daunton, Amrita Narlikar, and Robert M. Stern, 776–808. Oxford: Oxford University Press.

Betts, Alexander. 2013. "Regime Complexity and International Organizations: UNHCR as a Challenged Institution." *Global Governance: A Review of Multilateralism and International Organizations* 19 (1): 69–81.

Bexell, Magdalena. 2014. "Global Governance, Legitimacy and (De)legitimation." *Globalizations* 11 (3): 289–99. https://doi.org/10.1080/14747731.2014.919744.

Biermann, Frank, Philipp Pattberg, Harro van Asselt, and Fariborz Zelli. 2009. "The Fragmentation of Global Governance Architectures: A Framework for Analysis." *Global Environmental Politics* 9 (4): 14–40.

Biermann, Frank, and Bernd Siebenhüner, eds. 2009. *Managers of Global Change: The Influence of International Environmental Bureaucracies.* Cambridge, MA: MIT Press.

Biermann, Rafael, and Michael Harsch. 2017. "Resource Dependence Theory." In *Palgrave Handbook of Inter-organizational Relations in World Politics*, edited by Joachim A. Koops and Rafael Biermann, 135–55. London: Palgrave Macmillan UK.

Biermann, Rafael, and Joachim A. Koops. 2017. "Studying Relations among International Organizations in World Politics: Core Concepts and Challenges." In *Palgrave Handbook of Inter-organizational Relations in World Politics*, edited by Joachim A. Koops and Rafael Biermann, 1–46. London: Palgrave Macmillan.

Blanchard, Emily J. 2015. "A Shifting Mandate: International Ownership, Global Fragmentation, and a Case for Deeper Integration under the WTO." *World Trade Review* 14 (1): 87–99.

Block-Lieb, Susan, and Terence C. Halliday. 2017. *Global Lawmakers: International Organizations in the Crafting of World Markets.* Cambridge: Cambridge University Press.

Blustein, Paul. 2008. *The Nine-Day Misadventure of the Most Favored Nations: How the WTO's Doha Round Negotiations Went Awry in July 2008.* Washington, DC: Brookings Institution.

Bode, Ingvild. 2018. "Expertise as Social Practice: The Special Procedures at the UN Human Rights Council and the Individual Construction of Experts." In *Transnational Expertise: Internal Cohesion and External Recognition of Expert Groups*, edited by Andrea Schneiker, Christian Henrich-Franke, Robert Kaiser, and Christian Lahusen, 101–26. Baden-Baden: Nomos.

Boughton, James M. 2001. *Silent Revolution: The International Monetary Fund, 1979–1989.* Washington, DC: International Monetary Fund.

Boyle, Kevin. 2004. "Marking Another Birthday: Ten Years of the United Nations High Commissioner for Human Rights." *Netherlands Quarterly of Human Rights* 22 (2): 301–11.

Breitmeier, Helmut, Sandra Schwindenhammer, Andrés Checa, Jacob Manderbach, and Magdalena Tanzer. 2020. "Politicized Sustainability and Agricultural Policy: Comparing Norm Understandings of International Organizations." *Journal of Comparative Policy Analysis: Research and Practice* 23 (5–6): 625–43. https://doi.org/10.1080/13876988.2020.1769480.

Brooks, Jonathan. 2014. "Policy Coherence and Food Security: The Effects of OECD Countries' Agricultural Policies." *Food Policy* 44:88–94.

Brooks, Jonathan, and Alan Matthews. 2015. *Trade Dimensions of Food Security.* OECD Food, Agriculture and Fisheries Paper No. 77. Paris: Organisation for

Economic Co-operation and Development. https://doi.org/10.1787/5js65xn 79onv-en.

Broome, André. 2008. "The Importance of Being Earnest: The IMF as a Reputational Intermediary." *New Political Economy* 13 (2): 125–51. https://doi.org/10.1080/13563460802018216.

Broome, André, and Leonard Seabrooke. 2012. "Seeing Like an International Organisation." *New Political Economy* 17 (1): 1–16.

Brosig, Malte. 2013. "Introduction: The African Security Regime Complex—Exploring Converging Actors and Policies." *African Security* 6 (3–4): 171–90. https://doi.org/10.1080/19392206.2013.854088.

Bukovansky, Mlada. 2010. "Institutionalized Hypocrisy and the Politics of Agricultural Trade." In *Constructing the International Economy*, edited by Rawi Abdelal, Mark Blyth, and Craig Parsons, 68–90. Ithaca, NY: Cornell University Press.

Bürgi Bonanomi, Elisabeth. 2017. "Measuring Human Rights Impacts of Trade Agreements—Ideas for Improving the Methodology: Comparing the European Union's Sustainability Impact Assessment Practice and Methodology with Human Rights Impact Assessment Methodology." *Journal of Human Rights Practice* 9 (3): 481–503.

Burnett, Kim, and Sophia Murphy. 2014. "What Place for International Trade in Food Sovereignty?" *Journal of Peasant Studies* 41 (6): 1065–84. https://doi.org/10.1080/03066150.2013.876995.

Busch, Per-Olof, and Andrea Liese. 2017. "The Authority of International Public Administrations." In *International Bureaucracy: Challenges and Lessons for Public Administration Research*, edited by Michael W. Bauer, Christoph Knill, and Steffen Eckhard, 97–122. London: Palgrave Macmillan UK.

Bush, Ray. 2010. "Food Riots: Poverty, Power and Protest." *Journal of Agrarian Change* 10 (1): 119–29. https://doi.org/10.1111/j.1471-0366.2009.00253.x.

Byerlee, Derek. 1987. "The Political Economy of Third World Food Imports: The Case of Wheat." *Economic Development and Cultural Change* 35 (2): 307–28. https://doi.org/10.1086/451587.

Cathie, John. 1982. *The Political Economy of Food Aid*. Farnborough: Gower.

Cépède, Michel. 1984. "The Fight against Hunger: Its History on the International Agenda." *Food Policy* 9 (4): 282–90. https://doi.org/10.1016/0306-9192(84)90064-2.

CESCR (Committee on Economic, Social and Cultural Rights). 1999. *Substantive Issues Arising in the Implementation of the International Covenant on Economic, Social and Cultural Rights: General Comment 12, The Right to Adequate Food (Art. 11)*. Geneva: Office of the High Commissioner for Human Rights.

Chan, Anita. 2003. "Racing to the Bottom: International Trade without a Social

Clause." *Third World Quarterly* 24 (6): 1011–28. https://doi.org/10.1080/01436590310001630044.

Chang, Ha-Joon. 2006. "Policy Space in Historical Perspective with Special Reference to Trade and Industrial Policies." *Economic and Political Weekly* 41 (7): 627–33.

Cho, Sungjoon. 2014. *The Social Foundations of World Trade.* Cambridge: Cambridge University Press.

Chorev, Nitsan. 2005. "The Institutional Project of Neo-liberal Globalism: The Case of the WTO." *Theory and Society* 34 (3): 317–55.

———. 2012a. "Restructuring Neoliberalism at the World Health Organization." *Review of International Political Economy* 20 (4): 627–66. https://doi.org/10.1080/09692290.2012.690774.

———. 2012b. *The World Health Organization between North and South.* Ithaca, NY: Cornell University Press.

CHR (Commission on Human Rights). 2000. *The Right to Food: Commission on Human Rights Resolution 2000/10.* Geneva: Office of the High Commissioner for Human Rights.

Christoffersen, Leif E., Keith Bezanson, Keith Lele, Michael Davies, Carlos Perez del Castillo, and Thelma Awori. 2008. *FAO: The Challenge of Renewal. An Independent External Evaluation of the Food and Agriculture Organization.* Rome: Food and Agriculture Organization.

Chwieroth, Jeffrey M. 2009. *Capital Ideas: The IMF and the Rise of Financial Liberalization.* Princeton, NJ: Princeton University Press.

———. 2013. "'The Silent Revolution': How the Staff Exercise Informal Governance over IMF Lending." *Review of International Organizations* 8 (2): 265–90. https://doi.org/10.1007/s11558-012-9154-9.

Cismas, Ioana. 2015. "The Role of the UN Special Rapporteur in the Development of the Right to Food: Legitimation through Clarification." In *Cibo e diritto: Dalla Dichiarazione Universale alla Carta di Milano,* edited by Marco Gestri, 45–55. Modena: Muchi editore.

Claeys, Priscilla. 2015. *Human Rights and the Food Sovereignty Movement: Reclaiming Control.* Abingdon: Routledge.

Clapham, Andrew. 1994. "Creating the High Commissioner for Human Rights: The Outside Story." *European Journal of International Law* 5 (4): 556–68. https://doi.org/10.1093/oxfordjournals.ejil.a035895.

Clapp, Jennifer. 2004. "WTO Agricultural Trade Battles and Food Aid." *Third World Quarterly* 25 (8): 1439–52.

———. 2006. "WTO Agriculture Negotiations: Implications for the Global South." *Third World Quarterly* 27 (4): 563–77. https://doi.org/10.1080/01436590600720728.

———. 2009a. "Food Price Volatility and Vulnerability in the Global South: Considering the Global Economic Context." *Third World Quarterly* 30 (6): 1183–96. https://doi.org/10.1080/01436590903037481.

———. 2009b. "The Global Food Crisis and International Agricultural Policy: Which Way Forward?" *Global Governance: A Review of Multilateralism and International Organizations* 15 (2): 299–312.

———. 2012. *Hunger in the Balance: The New Politics of International Food Aid.* Ithaca, NY: Cornell University Press.

———. 2015. "Food Security and Contested Agricultural Trade Norms." *Journal of International Law and International Relations* 11:105–15.

———. 2017. "Food Self-Sufficiency: Making Sense of It, and When It Makes Sense." *Food Policy* 66:88–96.

Clapp, Jennifer, and Sophia Murphy. 2013. "The G20 and Food Security: A Mismatch in Global Governance?" *Global Policy* 4 (2): 129–38. https://doi.org/10.1111/1758-5899.12039.

Clapp, Jennifer, and Caitlin Scott. 2018. "The Global Environmental Politics of Food." *Global Environmental Politics* 18 (2): 1–11. https://doi.org/10.1162/glep_a_00464.

Clarke, Warren. 2019. "Institutional Density Reconsidered: States, International Organisations, and the Governance Space." *Journal of International Relations and Development* 22 (3): 698–721. https://doi.org/10.1057/s41268-017-0113-1.

Clay, Edward J. 2003. "Responding to Change: WFP and the Global Food Aid System." *Development Policy Review* 21 (5–6): 697–709.

Clay, Edward J., and Olav Stokke, eds. 2000. *Food Aid and Human Security.* Portland, OR: Frank Cass.

Cohn, Theodore. 1979. "The 1978–9 Negotiations for an International Wheat Agreement: An Opportunity Lost?" *International Journal* 35 (1): 132–49.

Coleman, William D. 1998. "From Protected Development to Market Liberalism: Paradigm Change in Agriculture." *Journal of European Public Policy* 5 (4): 632–51. https://doi.org/10.1080/135017698000061.

Coleman, William D., and Stefan Tangermann. 1999. "The 1992 CAP Reform, the Uruguay Round and the Commission: Conceptualizing Linked Policy Games." *JCMS: Journal of Common Market Studies* 37 (3): 385–405.

Colgan, Jeff D., Robert O. Keohane, and Thijs Van de Graaf. 2012. "Punctuated Equilibrium in the Energy Regime Complex." *Review of International Organizations* 7 (2): 117–43.

Conca, Ken. 2000. "The WTO and the Undermining of Global Environmental Governance." *Review of International Political Economy* 7 (3): 484–94.

Conceição, Pedro, and Ronald U. Mendoza. 2009. "Anatomy of the Global Food Crisis." *Third World Quarterly* 30 (6): 1159–82.

Conti, Joseph A. 2009. "Producing Legitimacy at the World Trade Organization: The Role of Expertise and Legal Capacity." *Socio-Economic Review* 8 (1): 131–55. https://doi.org/10.1093/ser/mwp023.

Correa, Carlos M. 2002. *Implications of the Doha Declaration on the TRIPS Agreement and Public Health.* Geneva: World Health Organization.

———. 2014. *Subsidies and Food Security at WTO: A Permanent Solution Is Still Pending.* Geneva: South Centre.

Cortell, Andrew P., and Susan Peterson. 2006. "Dutiful Agents, Rogue Actors, or Both? Staffing, Voting Rules, and Slack in the WHO and WTO." In *Delegation and Agency in International Organizations,* edited by Daniel L. Nielson, Darren G. Hawkins, David A. Lake, and Michael J. Tierney, 255–80. Cambridge: Cambridge University Press.

———. 2021. "Autonomy and International Organisations." *Journal of International Relations and Development,* October 5. https://doi.org/10.1057/s41268-021-00243-x.

Cottier, Thomas. 2002. "Trade and Human Rights: A Relationship to Discover." *Journal of International Economic Law* 5 (1): 111–32.

Cottier, Thomas, and Panagiotis Delimatsis, eds. 2011. *The Prospects of International Trade Regulation: From Fragmentation to Coherence.* Cambridge: Cambridge University Press.

Cox, Robert W. 1969. "The Executive Head: An Essay on Leadership in International Organization." *International Organization* 23 (2): 205–30. https://doi.org/10.1017/S002081830003157X.

Cullather, Nick. 2004. "Miracles of Modernization: The Green Revolution and the Apotheosis of Technology." *Diplomatic History* 28 (2): 227–54.

———. 2007. "The Foreign Policy of the Calorie." *American Historical Review* 112 (2): 337–64. https://doi.org/10.1086/ahr.112.2.337.

Curran, Louise, and Jappe Eckhardt. 2017. "Smoke Screen? The Globalization of Production, Transnational Lobbying and the International Political Economy of Plain Tobacco Packaging." *Review of International Political Economy* 24 (1): 87–118. https://doi.org/10.1080/09692290.2016.1269658.

Das, Sannoy. 2016. "Food Security Amendments to the WTO Green Box: A Critical Re-examination." *Journal of World Trade* 50 (6): 1111–32.

Daugbjerg, Carsten. 2017. "Responding to Non-linear Internationalisation of Public Policy: The World Trade Organization and Reform of the CAP, 1992–2013." *JCMS: Journal of Common Market Studies* 55 (3): 486–501. https://doi.org/10.1111/jcms.12476.

Daugbjerg, Carsten, Arild Aurvåg Farsund, and Oluf Langhelle. 2015. "Challenging Agricultural Normalism in the Global Food Security Debate?" Paper presented at the International Conference on Public Policy, Milan, July 1–4. https://www.ippapublicpolicy.org/file/paper/1433895322.pdf.

Daugbjerg, Carsten, and Alan Swinbank. 2009. *Ideas, Institutions, and Trade:*

The WTO and the Curious Role of EU Farm Policy in Trade Liberalization. Oxford: Oxford University Press.

Daugirdas, Kristina. 2019. "Reputation as a Disciplinarian of International Organizations." *American Journal of International Law* 113 (2): 221–71. https://doi.org/10.1017/ajil.2018.122.

Davies, Michael D. V. 2013. "Saouma, Edouard Victor." In *IO BIO: Biographical Dictionary of Secretaries-General of International Organizations,* edited by Bob Reinalda, Kent J. Kille, and Jaci Eisenberg. January 15. https://www.ru.nl/politicologie/io-bio/io-bio-biographical-dictionary-sgs-ios/.

Davis, Christina L. 2009. "Overlapping Institutions in Trade Policy." *Perspectives on Politics* 7 (1): 25–31. https://doi.org/10.1017/S1537592709090045.

Deep Ford, J. R., S. Koroma, Y. Yanoma, and H. Khaira. 2005. "'Identifying' Special Products: Developing Country Flexibility in the Doha Round." In *Commodity Market Review, 2005–2006,* edited by Food and Agriculture Organization, 5–31. Rome: Food and Agriculture Organization.

Deere Birkbeck, Carolyn, and Ron Marchant. 2011. "Implementation of the Technical Assistance Principles of the WIPO Development Agenda." *Journal of World Intellectual Property* 14 (2): 103–32. https://doi.org/10.1111/j.1747-1796.2010.00411.x.

de Gorter, Harry, Merlinda D. Ingco, and Ruiz Lilian. 2002. "Export Subsidies and WTO Trade Negotiations on Agriculture: Issues and Suggestions for New Rules." Background paper prepared for the World Bank. https://openknowledge.worldbank.org/handle/10986/5984.

Dekeyser, Koen, Lise Korsten, and Lorenzo Fioramonti. 2018. "Food Sovereignty: Shifting Debates on Democratic Food Governance." *Food Security* 10 (1): 223–33. https://doi.org/10.1007/s12571-017-0763-2.

Demeke, Mulat, Adriano Spinelli, Stefania Croce, Valentina Pernechele, Eugenia Stefanelli, Areej Jafari, Guendalina Pangrazio, Giovanni Carrasco, Barthelemy Lanos, and Camille Roux. 2014. *Food and Agriculture Policy Decisions: Trends, Emerging Issues and Policy Alignments since the 2007/08 Food Security Crisis.* Rome: Food and Agriculture Organization.

De Schutter, Olivier. 2008. *Background Note: Analysis of the World Food Crisis by the UN Special Rapporteur on the Right to Food.* Geneva: Office of the High Commissioner for Human Rights.

———. 2009a. *Background Document Prepared by the UN Special Rapporteur on the Right to Food, Mr. Olivier De Schutter, on His Mission to the World Trade Organization.* Geneva: Office of the High Commissioner for Human Rights.

———. 2009b. *International Trade in Agriculture and the Right to Food.* Occasional Paper No. 46. Geneva: Friedrich Ebert Stiftung. https://www.europarl.europa.eu/cmsdata/191691/20130715ATT69800EN-original.pdf.

————. 2009c. *Mission to the World Trade Organization*. Geneva: Human Rights Council.

————. 2009d. *Seed Policies and the Right to Food: Enhancing Agrobiodiversity and Encouraging Innovation*. New York: United Nations.

————. 2011. *The World Trade Organization and the Post-global Food Crisis Agenda: Putting Food Security First in the International Trade System*. Geneva: Office of the High Commissioner for Human Rights.

Desmarais, Annette A. 2007. *La Via Campesina: Globalization and the Power of Peasants*. London: Pluto Press.

Desta, Melaku Geboye. 2001. "Food Security and International Trade Law: An Appraisal of the World Trade Organization Approach." *Journal of World Trade* 35 (3): 449–68.

Deutsche Welle. 2004. "EU Offers to End Farm Export Aid." Last modified May 11. https://www.dw.com/en/eu-offers-to-end-farm-export-aid/a-1198434-0.

Diaz-Bonilla, Eugenio. 2014. *Agricultural Trade and Food Security: Some Thoughts about a Continuous Debate*. Geneva: International Centre for Trade and Sustainable Development and World Economic Forum.

Dijkstra, Hylke. 2015. "Shadow Bureaucracies and the Unilateral Control of International Secretariats: Insights from UN Peacekeeping." *Review of International Organizations* 10 (1): 23–41. https://doi.org/10.1007/s11558-014-9203-7.

————. 2017. "Collusion in International Organizations: How States Benefit from the Authority of Secretariats." *Global Governance: A Review of Multilateralism and International Organizations* 23 (4): 601–19. https://doi.org/10.1163/19426720-02304006.

Dingwerth, Klaus, and Clara Weinhardt. 2019. *The Language of World Trade Politics: Unpacking the Terms of Trade*. Abingdon: Routledge.

Dingwerth, Klaus, and Antonia Witt. 2019. "Legitimation Contests: A Theoretical Framework." Chap. 2 of *International Organizations under Pressure: Legitimating Global Governance in Challenging Times*. Oxford: Oxford University Press.

Diven, Polly J. 2001. "The Domestic Determinants of US Food Aid Policy." *Food Policy* 26 (5): 455–74. https://doi.org/10.1016/S0306-9192(01)00006-9.

Dommen, Caroline, and Lynne Finnegan. 2013. *New Framework for Trade and Investment in Agriculture: Draft Mapping of Alternative Proposals*. Geneva: Quaker United Nations Office.

Dudai, Ron. 2009. "Climate Change and Human Rights Practice: Observations on and around the Report of the Office of the High Commissioner for Human Rights on the Relationship between Climate Change and Human Rights." *Journal of Human Rights Practice* 1 (2): 294–307. https://doi.org/10.1093/jhuman/hup009.

Duncan, Jessica. 2015. *Global Food Security Governance: Civil Society Engagement in the Reformed Committee on World Food Security.* Abingdon: Routledge.

Eagleton-Pierce, Matthew D. 2013. *Symbolic Power in the World Trade Organization.* Oxford: Oxford University Press.

———. 2018. "Professionalizing Protest: Scientific Capital and Advocacy in Trade Politics." *International Political Sociology* 12 (3): 233–55. https://doi.org /10.1093/ips/oly011.

Ecker-Ehrhardt, Matthias. 2018. "Self-Legitimation in the Face of Politicization: Why International Organizations Centralized Public Communication." *Review of International Organizations* 13 (4): 519–46. https://doi.org/10 .1007/s11558-017-9287-y.

Eckersley, Robyn 2004. "The Big Chill: The WTO and Multilateral Environmental Agreements." *Global Environmental Politics* 4 (2): 24–50. https://doi .org/10.1162/152638004323074183.

Eckhard, Steffen, and Jörn Ege. 2016. "International Bureaucracies and Their Influence on Policy-Making: A Review of Empirical Evidence." *Journal of European Public Policy* 23 (7): 960–78. https://doi.org/10.1080/13501763.2016 .1162837.

Edelman, Marc, Tony Weis, Amita Baviskar, Saturnino M. Borras, Eric Holt-Giménez, Deniz Kandiyoti, and Wendy Wolford. 2014. "Introduction: Critical Perspectives on Food Sovereignty." *Journal of Peasant Studies* 41 (6): 911–31. https://doi.org/10.1080/03066150.2014.963568.

Ege, Jörn. 2020. "What International Bureaucrats (Really) Want: Administrative Preferences in International Organization Research." *Global Governance: A Review of Multilateralism and International Organizations* 26 (4): 577–600. https://doi.org/10.1163/19426720-02604003.

Ege, Jörn, Michael W. Bauer, and Nora Wagner. 2019. "Improving Generalizability in Transnational Bureaucratic Influence Research: A (Modest) Proposal." *International Studies Review* 22 (3): 551–75. https://doi.org/10.1093/isr/viz026.

Eggleston, Robert C. 1987. "Determinants of the Levels and Distribution of PL 480 Food Aid: 1955–1979." *World Development* 15 (6): 797–808. https://doi .org/10.1016/0305-750X(87)90061-1.

Eilstrup-Sangiovanni, Mette. 2020. "Death of International Organizations: The Organizational Ecology of Intergovernmental Organizations, 1815–2015." *Review of International Organizations* 15 (2): 339–70. https://doi.org/10 .1007/s11558-018-9340-5.

Elsig, Manfred. 2010. "The World Trade Organization at Work: Performance in a Member-Driven Milieu." *Review of International Organizations* 5 (3): 345–63.

———. 2011. "Principal-Agent Theory and the World Trade Organization: Complex Agency and 'Missing Delegation.'" *European Journal of International Relations* 17 (3): 495–517.

Elver, Hilal. 2016. "The Challenges and Developments of the Right to Food in the 21st Century: Reflections of the United Nations Special Rapporteur on the Right to Food." *UCLA Journal of International Law and Foreign Affairs* 20 (1): 1–44.

Emmerij, Louis, Robert Jolly, and Thomas G. Weiss. 2001. *Ahead of the Curve? UN Ideas and Global Challenges.* Bloomington: Indiana University Press.

EU (European Union). 2000. *European Union Proposal on Export Competition.* Geneva: World Trade Organization.

———. 2004. "WTO-DDA: EU Ready to Go the Extra Mile in Three Key Areas of the Talks." Press release, May 10. IP/04/622.

———. 2005. "Food Aid: EU Urges US Reform." Press release, December 13. EU Hong Kong office files.

Faaland, Jut, Diana Mclean, and Ole David Koht Norbye. 2000. "The World Food Programme (WFP) and International Food Aid." In *Food Aid and Human Security,* edited by Edward J. Clay and Olav Stokke, 221–55. London: Frank Cass.

Fakhri, Michael. 2015. "Food as a Matter of Global Governance." *Journal of International Law and International Relations* 11 (2): 68–83.

FAO (Food and Agriculture Organization). 1945. *Constitution of the United Nations Food and Agriculture Organization.* New York: FAO.

———. 1954. *Principles on Surplus Disposal Recommended (FAO Council Resolution No. 2/20).* Rome: FAO.

———. 1978. *The State of Food and Agriculture 1977.* Rome: FAO.

———. 1979. *Report of the Council of FAO: Seventy-Fifth Session.* Rome: FAO.

———. 1980. *The State of Food and Agriculture 1979.* Rome: FAO.

———. 1981. *The State of Food and Agriculture 1980.* Rome: FAO.

———. 1983. *The State of Food and Agriculture 1982.* Rome: FAO.

———. 1984. *The State of Food and Agriculture 1983.* Rome: FAO.

———. 1985a. *International Trade and World Food Security.* Rome: FAO.

———. 1985b. *Protectionism in Agricultural Trade: Review of Action Taken on Conference Resolution 2/79.* Rome: FAO.

———. 1985c. *The State of Food and Agriculture 1984.* Rome: FAO.

———. 1986a. *Food and Agriculture Organization: Statement by Mr. J. C. Vignaud. Representative, Office in Geneva.* Geneva: General Agreement on Tariffs and Trade.

———. 1986b. *Statement by the Director-General. Report of the Council of the FAO, Ninetieth Session, 17–28 November.* Rome: FAO.

———. 1987a. *FAO Conference. Twenty-Fourth Session. Verbatim Records of Meetings of Commission I.* Rome: FAO.

———. 1987b. *FAO Conference. Twenty-Fourth Session. Verbatim Records of Meetings of Commission II.* Rome: FAO.

———. 1987c. *FAO Conference. Twenty-Fourth Session. Verbatim Records of Meetings of the Conference III.* Rome: FAO.

———. 1987d. *Impact of World Food Security of Agricultural Policies in Industrialized Countries.* Rome: FAO.

———. 1987e. *Protectionism in Agricultural Trade: Review of Action Taken on Conference Resolution 2/79.* Rome: FAO.

———. 1987f. *Report of the FAO Conference: Twenty-Fourth Session.* Rome: FAO.

———. 1987g. *The State of Food and Agriculture 1986.* Rome: FAO.

———. 1988. *The State of Food and Agriculture 1987–1988.* Rome: FAO.

———. 1989. *Technical Assistance in the Context of the Uruguay Round: Statement by Mr. A. Purcell, Representative of the Food and Agriculture Organization.* Rome: FAO.

———. 1990. *The State of Food and Agriculture 1989.* Rome: FAO.

———. 1991a. *FAO Council Ninety-Ninth Session: Verbatim Report.* Rome: FAO.

———. 1991b. *The State of Food and Agriculture 1990.* Rome: FAO.

———. 1992. *The State of Food and Agriculture 1991.* Rome: FAO.

———. 1996. *Rome Declaration on World Food Security and World Food Summit Plan of Action.* Rome: FAO.

———. 1997. *FAO Technical Assistance and the Uruguay Round Agreements.* Rome: FAO.

———. 1999a. *Assessment of the Impact of the Uruguay Round on Agricultural Markets.* Rome: FAO.

———. 1999b. *The Food Situation in the Least Developed and Net Food-Importing Developing Countries.* Rome: FAO.

———. 2000a. *Agriculture, Trade and Food Security.* Vol. 1. *Issues and Options.* Rome: FAO.

———. 2000b. *Agriculture, Trade and Food Security.* Vol. 2. *Country Case Studies.* Rome: FAO.

———. 2001a. *Experience with the Implementation of the Uruguay Round Agreement on Agriculture.* Rome: FAO.

———. 2001b. *Towards Improving the Operational Effectiveness of the Marrakesh Decision on Measures Concerning the Possible Negative Effects of the Reform Programme on Least-Developed and Net Food-Importing Developing Countries.* Rome: FAO.

———. 2002a. *FAO Papers on Selected Issues Relating to the WTO Negotiations on Agriculture.* Rome: FAO.

———. 2002b. "Revolving Fund for the Purpose of Implementing the WTO Marrakesh Decision Relating to the Least-Developed and Net Food-Importing Developing Countries." In *FAO Papers on Selected Issues Relating to the WTO Negotiations on Agriculture,* edited by FAO, 150–68. Rome: FAO.

———. 2002c. "The WTO Negotiations on Agriculture: Post-Seattle Major Issues, Analytical Needs and Technical Assistance Requirements." In *FAO Papers on Selected Issues Relating to the WTO Negotiations on Agriculture*, edited by FAO, 255–80. Rome: FAO.

———. 2003. *Financing Normal Levels of Commercial Imports of Basic Foodstuffs in the Context of the Marrakesh Decision on Least-Developed and Net Food-Importing Developing Countries*. Rome: FAO.

———. 2004. *The State of Agricultural Commodity Markets: 2004*. Rome: FAO.

———. 2009a. *The State of Agricultural Commodity Markets: 2009*. Rome: FAO.

———. 2009b. *The State of Food Insecurity in the World 2009*. Rome: FAO.

———. 2020. *The State of Food Security and Nutrition in the World: Transforming Food Systems for Affordable and Healthy Diets*. Rome: FAO.

FAO (Food and Agriculture Organization), IFAD (International Fund for Agricultural Development), IMF (International Monetary Fund), OECD (Organisation for Economic Co-operation and Development), UNCTAD (United Nations Conference on Trade and Development), WFP (World Food Programme), World Bank, and WTO (World Trade Organization). 2011. *Interagency Report to the G20 on Food Price Volatility*. Rome: FAO.

Feichtner, Isabel. 2009. "The Waiver Power of the WTO: Opening the WTO for Political Debate on the Reconciliation of Competing Interests." *European Journal of International Law* 20 (3): 615–45. https://doi.org/10.1093/ejil/chp039.

Ferguson, Rhonda. 2018. *The Right to Food and the World Trade Organization's Rules on Agriculture: Conflicting, Compatible, or Complementary?* Leiden: Brill.

Finger, J. Michael, and Julio J. Nogués. 2001. "The Unbalanced Uruguay Round Outcome: The New Areas in Future WTO Negotiations." Policy Research Working Paper, World Bank, Washington, DC.

Finlayson, Jock A., and Mark W. Zacher. 1981. "The GATT and the Regulation of Trade Barriers: Regime Dynamics and Functions." *International Organization* 35 (4): 561–602.

Finnemore, Martha. 1993. "International Organizations as Teachers of Norms: The United Nations Educational, Scientific, and Cultural Organization and Science Policy." *International Organization* 47 (4): 565–97. https://doi.org/10.1017/S0020818300028101.

Foot, Rosemary. 2007. "The United Nations, Counter Terrorism, and Human Rights: Institutional Adaptation and Embedded Ideas." *Human Rights Quarterly* 29 (2): 489–514.

Forman, Lisa, and Gillian MacNaughton. 2015. "Moving Theory into Practice: Human Rights Impact Assessment of Intellectual Property Rights in Trade

Agreements." *Journal of Human Rights Practice* 7 (1): 109–38. https://doi.org/10.1093/jhuman/huv001.

Fouilleux, Eve, Nicolas Bricas, and Arlène Alpha. 2017. "'Feeding 9 Billion People': Global Food Security Debates and the Productionist Trap." *Journal of European Public Policy* 24 (11): 1658–77. https://doi.org/10.1080/13501763.2017.1334084.

Frey, Bruno S. 2008. "Outside and Inside Competition for International Organizations: From Analysis to Innovations." *Review of International Organizations* 3 (4): 335–50. https://doi.org/10.1007/s11558-008-9045-2.

Friedmann, Harriet. 1982. "The Political Economy of Food: The Rise and Fall of the Postwar International Food Order." *American Journal of Sociology* 88:248–86.

Friedmann, Harriet, and Philip McMichael. 1989. "Agriculture and the State System: The Rise and Decline of National Agricultures, 1870 to the Present." *Sociologia Ruralis* 29 (2): 93–117.

Friel, Sharon, Libby Hattersley, and Ruth Townsend. 2015. "Trade Policy and Public Health." *Annual Review of Public Health* 36 (1): 325–44. https://doi.org/10.1146/annurev-publhealth-031914-122739.

Fukuda-Parr, Sakiko, and Amy Orr. 2014. "The MDG Hunger Target and the Competing Frameworks of Food Security." *Journal of Human Development and Capabilities* 15 (2–3): 147–60. https://doi.org/10.1080/19452829.2014.896323.

Gaer, Felice D. 1995. "Reality Check: Human Rights Nongovernmental Organisations Confront Governments at the United Nations." *Third World Quarterly* 16 (3): 389–404.

Gaer, Felice D., and Christen L. Broecker. 2013. *The United Nations High Commissioner for Human Rights: Conscience for the World.* Leiden: Martinus Nijhoff.

Gallagher, Kevin P. 2007. "Understanding Developing Country Resistance to the Doha Round." *Review of International Political Economy* 15 (1): 62–85.

Garcia-Duran, Patricia, Miriam Casanova, and Leif Johan Eliasson. 2019. "International Institutions and Domestic Policy: Assessing the Influence of Multilateral Pressure on the European Union's Agricultural Policy." *Journal of European Integration* 41 (2): 131–46. https://doi.org/10.1080/07036337.2018.1553963.

GATT (General Agreement on Tariffs and Trade). 1986. *Ministerial Declaration on the Uruguay Round.* Geneva: GATT.

———. 1987a. *First Meeting of the Negotiating Group on Agriculture. Note by the Chairman.* Geneva: GATT.

———. 1987b. *Group of Negotiation on Goods. Fourth Meeting: 14 April 1987.* Geneva: GATT.

————. 1987c. *Group of Negotiation on Goods. Seventh Meeting: 26 June 1987.* Geneva: GATT.

————. 1987d. *Second Meeting of the Negotiating Group on Agriculture: Note by the Chairman.* Geneva: GATT.

————. 1987e. *Summary of Main Points Raised at the Fourth Meeting of the Negotiating Group on Agriculture, 26–77 October 1987.* Geneva: GATT.

————. 1987f. *Summary of Main Points Raised at the Third Meeting of the Negotiating Group on Agriculture, 6–7 July 1987: Note by the Secretariat.* Geneva: GATT.

————. 1987g. *Trade Negotiations Committee. Third Meeting: 3 July 1987.* Geneva: GATT.

————. 1988a. *Eighth Meeting of the Negotiating Group on Agriculture (Note by the Chairman).* Geneva: GATT.

————. 1988b. *Elaboration of US Agricultural Proposal with Respect to Food Security. Submitted by the United States, Negotiating Group on Agriculture.* Geneva: GATT.

————. 1988c. *Further Examination of Proposals Submitted: Statement by Jamaica at Eighth Meeting of Negotiating Group on Agriculture.* Geneva: GATT.

————. 1988d. *Negotiating Group on Agriculture: Communication from Jamaica.* Geneva: GATT.

————. 1988e. *Negotiating Group on Agriculture: Proposal by Egypt, Jamaica, Mexico and Peru.* Geneva: GATT.

————. 1988f. *Summary of Main Points Raised at the Eleventh Meeting of the Negotiating Group on Agriculture.* Geneva: GATT.

————. 1988g. *Summary of the Main Points Raised at the Eighth Meeting of the Negotiating Group on Agriculture.* Geneva: GATT.

————. 1988h. *Summary of the Main Points Raised at the Ninth Meeting of the Negotiating Group on Agriculture.* Geneva: GATT.

————. 1988i. *Trade Negotiations Committee Meeting at Ministerial Level.* Geneva: GATT.

————. 1989a. *Submission of the United States on Comprehensive Long-Term Agricultural Reform.* Geneva: GATT.

————. 1989b. *Summary of Main Points Raised at the Sixteenth Meeting of the Negotiating Group on Agriculture, 25–26 October 1989.* Geneva: GATT.

————. 1989c. *Trade Negotiations Committee: Eighth Meeting.* Geneva: GATT.

————. 1989d. *Ways to Take Account of the Negative Effects of the Agriculture Reform Process on Net Food-Importing Developing Countries: Proposal by Egypt, Jamaica, Mexico, Morocco and Peru.* Geneva: GATT.

————. 1990a. *Draft Act Embodying the Results of the Uruguay Round of Multilateral Trade Negotiations: Revision.* Geneva: GATT.

————. 1990b. *Framework Agreement on Agriculture Reform Programme. Draft Text by the Chairman.* Geneva: GATT.

———. 1990c. *Statements Made by Jamaica. Twenty-Third Session of the Negotiating Group on Agriculture.* Geneva: GATT.

———. 1990d. *Trade Negotiations Committee: Thirteenth Meeting (26 November 1990).* Geneva: GATT.

———. 1990e. "Working Paper Submitted by Egypt, Jamaica, Morocco and Peru: Uruguay Round Window for Net Food Importing Developing Countries." GATT Digital Library. https://exhibits.stanford.edu/gatt/catalog/rc439wm9496.

———. 1991. *Draft Final Act Embodying the Results of the Uruguay Round of Multilateral Trade Negotiations.* Geneva: GATT.

———. 1994a. *Agreement on Agriculture.* Geneva: GATT.

———. 1994b. *Decision on Measures Concerning the Possible Negative Effects of the Reform Programme on Least-Developed and Net Food-Importing Developing Countries.* Geneva: GATT.

Gehring, Thomas, and Benjamin Faude. 2014. "A Theory of Emerging Order within Institutional Complexes: How Competition among Regulatory International Institutions Leads to Institutional Adaptation and Division of Labor." *Review of International Organizations* 9 (4): 471–98. https://doi.org/10.1007/s11558-014-9197-1.

Gest, Nathaniel, and Alexandru Grigorescu. 2010. "Interactions among Intergovernmental Organizations in the Anti-corruption Realm." *Review of International Organizations* 5 (1): 53–72. https://doi.org/10.1007/s11558-009-9070-9.

Gill, Stephen. 2003. *Power and Resistance in the New World Order.* New York: Palgrave Macmillan.

Gillson, Ian, and Amir Fouad, eds. 2014. *Trade Policy and Food Security: Improving Access to Food in Developing Countries in the Wake of High World Prices.* Washington, DC: World Bank.

Goldin, Ian, and Odin Knudsen. 1990. "The Implications of Agricultural Trade Liberalization for Developing Countries." In *Agricultural Trade Liberalization: Implications for Developing Countries,* edited by Ian Goldin and Odin Knudsen, 475–83. Paris: Organisation for Economic Co-operation and Development.

Goldstein, Judith. 1988. "Ideas, Institutions, and American Trade Policy." *International Organization* 42 (1): 179–217.

———. 1993. *Ideas, Interests, and American Trade Policy.* Ithaca, NY: Cornell University Press.

Goldstein, Judith L., Miles Kahler, Robert O. Keohane, and Anne-Marie Slaughter, eds. 2001. *Legalization and World Politics.* Cambridge, MA: MIT Press.

Goldstein, Judith L., and Lisa L. Martin. 2000. "Legalization, Trade Liberalization, and Domestic Politics: A Cautionary Note." *International Organization* 54 (3): 603–32. https://doi.org/10.1162/002081800551226.

Gómez-Mera, Laura. 2016. "Regime Complexity and Global Governance: The Case of Trafficking in Persons." *European Journal of International Relations* 22 (3): 566–95. https://doi.org/10.1177/1354066115600226.

Gonzalez, Carmen G. 2002. "Institutionalizing Inequality: The WTO Agreement on Agriculture, Food Security, and Developing Countries." *Columbia Journal of Environmental Law* 27:433–89.

Grabel, Ilene. 2007. "Policy Coherence or Conformance? The New World Bank-International Monetary Fund-World Trade Organization Rhetoric on Trade and Investment in Developing Countries." *Review of Radical Political Economics* 39 (3): 335–41. https://doi.org/10.1177/0486613407305281.

Graddy-Lovelace, Garrett, and Adam Diamond. 2017. "From Supply Management to Agricultural Subsidies—and Back Again? The U.S. Farm Bill and Agrarian (In)viability." *Journal of Rural Studies* 50:70–83. https://doi.org/10.1016/j.jrurstud.2016.12.007.

Graeub, Benjamin E., M. Jahi Chappell, Hannah Wittman, Samuel Ledermann, Rachel Bezner Kerr, and Barbara Gemmill-Herren. 2016. "The State of Family Farms in the World." *World Development* 87:1–15. https://doi.org/10.1016/j.worlddev.2015.05.012.

Graham, Erin R. 2014. "International Organizations as Collective Agents: Fragmentation and the Limits of Principal Control at the World Health Organization." *European Journal of International Relations* 20 (2): 366–90. https://doi.org/10.1177/1354066113476116.

Graham, Erin R., and Alexander Thompson. 2015. "Efficient Orchestration? The Global Environment Facility in the Governance of Climate Adaptation." In *International Organizations as Orchestrators*, edited by Bernhard Zangl, Duncan Snidal, Kenneth W. Abbott, and Philipp Genschel, 114–38. Cambridge: Cambridge University Press.

Green, Jessica F., and Graeme Auld. 2017. "Unbundling the Regime Complex: The Effects of Private Authority." *Transnational Environmental Law* 6 (2): 259–84. https://doi.org/10.1017/S2047102516000121.

Greenfield, Jim, Maurizio de Nigris, and Panos Konandreas. 1996. "The Uruguay Round Agreement on Agriculture: Food Security Implications for Developing Countries." *Food Policy* 21 (4–5): 365–75.

Grigg, David. 1997. "The World's Hunger: A Review, 1930–1990." *Geography* 82 (3): 197–206. https://doi.org/10.2307/40572886.

Guha-Khasnobis, Basudeb, Shabd S. Acharya, and Benjamin Davis. 2007. *Food Security: Indicators, Measurement, and the Impact of Trade Openness.* Oxford: Oxford University Press.

Haas, Ernst B. 1990. *When Knowledge Is Power: Three Models of Change in International Organizations*. Berkeley: University of California Press.

Haas, Peter M. 1989. "Do Regimes Matter? Epistemic Communities and Mediterranean Pollution Control." *International Organization* 43 (3): 377–403.

Häberli, Christian. 2012. "The WTO and Food Security: What's Wrong with the Rules?" In *The Challenge of Food Security: International Policy and Regulatory Frameworks*, edited by Rosemary Rayfuse and Nicole Weisfelt. Cheltenham: Edward Elgar.

Hafner-Burton, Emilie M. 2008. "Sticks and Stones: Naming and Shaming the Human Rights Enforcement Problem." *International Organization* 62 (4): 689–716. https://doi.org/10.1017/S0020818308080247.

Haftel, Yoram Z., and Alexander Thompson. 2006. "The Independence of International Organizations." *Journal of Conflict Resolution* 50 (2): 253–75. https://doi.org/10.1177/0022002705285288.

Hall, Nina. 2015. "Money or Mandate? Why International Organizations Engage with the Climate Change Regime." *Global Environmental Politics* 15 (2): 79–97. https://doi.org/10.1162/GLEP_a_00299.

———. 2016. *Displacement, Development and Climate Change: International Organizations Moving beyond Their Mandates*. Abingdon: Routledge.

Hall, Nina, and Ngaire Woods. 2018. "Theorizing the Role of Executive Heads in International Organizations." *European Journal of International Relations* 24 (4): 865–86. https://doi.org/10.1177/1354066117741676.

Halliday, Terence C., Susan Block-Lieb, and Bruce G. Carruthers. 2010. "Rhetorical Legitimation: Global Scripts as Strategic Devices of International Organizations." *Socio-Economic Review* 8 (1): 77–112. https://doi.org/10.1093/ser/mwp024.

Hanegraaff, Marcel, Caelesta Braun, Dirk De Bièvre, and Jan Beyers. 2015. "The Domestic and Global Origins of Transnational Advocacy: Explaining Lobbying Presence during WTO Ministerial Conferences." *Comparative Political Studies* 48 (12): 1591–1621. https://doi.org/10.1177/0010414015591363.

Hannah, Erin. 2015. "Ratcheting Up Accountability? Embedded NGOs in the Multilateral Trade System." In *Expert Knowledge in Global Trade*, edited by Erin Hannah, James Scott, and Silke Trommer, 170–96. Abingdon: Routledge.

Hannah, Erin, Holly Ryan, and James Scott. 2017. "Power, Knowledge and Resistance: Between Co-optation and Revolution in Global Trade." *Review of International Political Economy* 24 (5): 741–75. https://doi.org/10.1080/09692290.2017.1324807.

Hannum, Hurst. 2006. "Human Rights in Conflict Resolution: The Role of the Office of the High Commissioner for Human Rights in UN Peacemaking and Peacebuilding." *Human Rights Quarterly* 28 (1): 1–85.

Hasenclever, Andreas, Peter Mayer, and Volker Rittberger. 1998. "Fair Burden-Sharing and the Robustness of International Regimes: The Case of Food Aid." Institute for Political Science Working Papers, University of Tübingen, Tübingen.

Hawkes, Shona, and Jagjit Kaur Plahe. 2013. "Worlds Apart: The WTO's Agreement on Agriculture and the Right to Food in Developing Countries." *International Political Science Review* 34 (1): 21–38. https://doi.org/10.1177/0192512112445238.

Hawkins, Darren G., David A. Lake, Daniel Nielson, and Michael J. Tierney. 2006. *Delegation and Agency in International Organizations.* Cambridge: Cambridge University Press.

Hawthorne, Helen. 2013. *Least Developed Countries and the WTO: Special Treatment in Trade.* London: Palgrave Macmillan.

Headey, Derek. 2011. "Rethinking the Global Food Crisis: The Role of Trade Shocks." *Food Policy* 36 (2): 136–46. http://dx.doi.org/10.1016/j.foodpol.2010.10.003.

Healy, Stephen, Richard Pearce, and Michael Stockbridge. 1998. *The Implications of the Uruguay Round Agreement on Agriculture for Developing Countries: A Training Manuel.* Rome: Food and Agriculture Organization.

Heldt, Eugénia C., and Henning Schmidtke. 2017. "Measuring the Empowerment of International Organizations: The Evolution of Financial and Staff Capabilities." *Global Policy* 8 (S5): 51–61. https://doi.org/10.1111/1758-5899.12449.

———. 2019. "Explaining Coherence in International Regime Complexes: How the World Bank Shapes the Field of Multilateral Development Finance." *Review of International Political Economy* 26 (6): 1160–86. https://doi.org/10.1080/09692290.2019.1631205.

Helfer, Laurence R. 1999. "Forum Shopping for Human Rights." *University of Pennsylvania Law Review* 148 (2): 285–400.

———. 2003. "Human Rights and Intellectual Property: Conflict or Coexistence." *Minnesota Intellectual Property Review* (1): [i]–62.

———. 2009. "Regime Shifting in the International Intellectual Property System." *Perspectives on Politics* 7 (1): 39–44.

Henning, C. Randall. 2017. *Tangled Governance: International Regime Complexity, the Troika, and the Euro Crisis.* Oxford: Oxford University Press.

Heri, Simone, and Christian Häberli. 2011. "Can the World Trade Organization Ensure That Food Aid Is Genuine?" *Developing World Review on Trade and Competition* 1 (1): 1–70.

Hertel, Shareen. 2015. "Hungry for Justice: Social Mobilization on the Right to Food in India." *Development and Change* 46 (1): 72–94. https://doi.org/10.1111/dech.12144.

Hertel, Thomas W. 1990. "The Impact of Trade Liberalization on Low-Income, Food-Deficit Countries." In *The GATT, Agriculture, and the Developing Countries*, edited by Nurul Islam and Alberto Valdés, 25–32. Washington, DC: International Food Policy Research Institute.

Hestermeyer, Holger. 2019. "International Human Rights Law and Dispute Settlement in the World Trade Organization." In *Human Rights Norms in "Other" International Courts*, edited by Martin Scheinin, 199–226. Cambridge: Cambridge University Press.

High Level Task Force on the Global Food Security Crisis. 2008. *The Comprehensive Framework for Action*. Geneva: United Nations.

Ho, P. Sai-wing. 2008. "Arguing for Policy Space to Promote Development: Prebisch, Myrdal, and Singer." *Journal of Economic Issues* 42 (2): 509–16.

Hoda, Anwarul. 2005. *Special Products: Options for Negotiating Modalities*. Geneva: International Centre for Trade and Sustainable Development.

Hoekman, Bernard M., and Michael M. Kostecki. 2001. *The Political Economy of the World Trading System: The WTO and Beyond*. Oxford: Oxford University Press.

Hoekman, Bernard M., Constantine Michalopoulos, and L. Alan Winter. 2004. "Special and Differential Treatment of Developing Countries in the WTO: Moving Forward after Cancún." *World Economy* 27 (4): 481–506. https://doi.org/10.1111/j.0378-5920.2004.00610.x.

Hofmann, Stephanie C. 2009. "Overlapping Institutions in the Realm of International Security: The Case of NATO and ESDP." *Perspectives on Politics* 7 (1): 45–52. https://doi.org/10.1017/S1537592709090070.

———. 2019. "The Politics of Overlapping Organizations: Hostage-Taking, Forum-Shopping and Brokering." *Journal of European Public Policy* 26 (6): 883–905. https://doi.org/10.1080/13501763.2018.1512644.

Holzscheiter, Anna. 2017. "Coping with Institutional Fragmentation? Competition and Convergence between Boundary Organizations in the Global Response to Polio." *Review of Policy Research* 34 (6): 767–89. https://doi.org/10.1111/ropr.12256.

Hopewell, Kristen. 2013. "New Protagonists in Global Economic Governance: Brazilian Agribusiness at the WTO." *New Political Economy* 18 (4): 603–23.

———. 2015a. "Different Paths to Power: The Rise of Brazil, India and China at the World Trade Organization." *Review of International Political Economy* 22 (2): 311–38. https://doi.org/10.1080/09692290.2014.927387.

———. 2015b. "Multilateral Trade Governance as Social Field: Global Civil Society and the WTO." *Review of International Political Economy* 22 (6): 1128–58. https://doi.org/10.1080/09692290.2015.1066696.

———. 2016. *Breaking the WTO: How Emerging Powers Disrupted the Neoliberal Project*. Stanford, CA: Stanford University Press.

———. 2017. "Invisible Barricades: Civil Society and the Discourse of the WTO." *Globalizations* 14 (1): 51–65. https://doi.org/10.1080/14747731.2016.1162984.

———. 2019. "US-China Conflict in Global Trade Governance: The New Politics of Agricultural Subsidies at the WTO." *Review of International Political Economy* 26 (2): 207–31. https://doi.org/10.1080/09692290.2018.1560352.

———. 2020. *Clash of Powers: US-China Rivalry in Global Trade Governance.* Cambridge: Cambridge University Press.

Hopkins, Raymond F. 1992. "Reform in the International Food Aid Regime: The Role of Consensual Knowledge." *International Organization* 46 (1): 225–64. https://doi.org/10.1017/S0020818300001491.

Hopkins, Raymond F., and Donald J. Puchala. 1978. "Perspectives on the International Relations of Food." *International Organization* 32 (3): 581–616. https://doi.org/10.1017/S0020818300031878.

Hufbauer, Gary, and Cathleen Cimino. 2013. "What Future for the WTO?" *International Trade Journal* 27 (5): 394–410. https://doi.org/10.1080/08853908.2013.836068.

Hughes, Steve, and Rorden Wilkinson. 1998. "International Labour Standards and World Trade: No Role for the World Trade Organization?" *New Political Economy* 3 (3): 375–89. https://doi.org/10.1080/13563469808406366.

HRC (Human Rights Council). 2009. *Resolution 10/12. The Right to Food.* Geneva: United Nations.

Hunt, Paul. 2017. "Configuring the UN Human Rights System in the 'Era of Implementation': Mainland and Archipelago." *Human Rights Quarterly* 39 (3): 489–538.

Hurd, Ian. 1999. "Legitimacy and Authority in International Politics." *International Organization* 53 (2): 379–408. https://doi.org/10.1162/002081899550913.

———. 2002. "Legitimacy, Power, and the Symbolic Life of the UN Security Council." *Global Governance: A Review of Multilateralism and International Organizations* 8 (1): 35–51.

ICTSD (International Centre for Trade and Sustainable Development). 2004. "Ag Committee: Members Question US Aid Program." *Bridges Weekly*, March 31.

———. 2005a. "Time Running Out for Ag Compromise; Groser Delivers Downbeat Assessment." *Bridges Weekly* 9 (27).

———. 2005b. "WTO Agriculture Negotiations Progress on Technical Issues." *Bridges Weekly* 8 (40).

———. 2007. "Agriculture: 'Degrees' of Progress, While Broad Divisions Persist." *Bridges Weekly* 11 (35).

———. 2009. "The Right to Food—A Trade Issue?" *Bridges Weekly* 13 (25).

———. 2011. "Troubled State of Doha Talks Causing WTO 'Paralysis,' Says Lamy; Focus for December Ministerial Shifts." *Bridges Weekly* 15 (28).

———. 2012. "Developing Countries Table Food Security Proposal at WTO." *Bridges Weekly*, November 14.

———. 2013. "'Peace Clause' Controversy Pushes Bali Deal into Eleventh Hour." *Bridges Weekly*, December 5.

IFAD (International Fund for Agricultural Development) and UNEP (United Nations Environment Programme). 2013. *Smallholders, Food Security, and the Environment*. Rome: IFAD.

IPCC (Intergovernmental Panel on Climate Change). 2019. *Special Report on Climate Change, Desertification, Land Degradation, Sustainable Land Management, Food Security, and Greenhouse Gas Fluxes in Terrestrial Ecosystems*. Geneva: IPCC.

Ismail, Faizel. 2009. "An Assessment of the WTO Doha Round July–December 2008 Collapse." *World Trade Review* 8 (4): 579–605.

———. 2012. "Narratives and Myths in the WTO Doha Round: The Way Forward?" *Economic and Political Weekly* 47 (31): 55–60.

Ito, Shinya. 2020. "Re-evaluating a Conflict between WTO Law and the Right to Food: The Case of Public Food Stockholding." *Manchester Journal of International Economic Law* 17 (3).

Jachertz, Ruth. 2014. "'To Keep Food Out of Politics': The UN Food and Agriculture Organization, 1945–1965." In *International Organizations and Development, 1945–1990*, edited by Marc Frey, Sönke Kunkel, and Corinna R. Unger, 75–100. London: Palgrave Macmillan UK.

Jachertz, Ruth, and Alexander Nützenadel. 2011. "Coping with Hunger? Visions of a Global Food System, 1930–1960." *Journal of Global History* 6 (1): 99–119. https://doi.org/10.1017/S1740022811000064.

Jinnah, Sikina. 2014. *Post-treaty Politics: Secretariat Influence in Global Environmental Governance*. Cambridge, MA: MIT Press.

Joachim, Jutta. 2003. "Framing Issues and Seizing Opportunities: The UN, NGOs, and Women's Rights." *International Studies Quarterly* 47 (2): 247–74. https://doi.org/10.1111/1468-2478.4702005.

Joachim, Jutta, Bob Reinalda, and Bertjan Verbeek. 2007. *International Organizations and Implementation: Enforcers, Managers, Authorities?* Abingdon: Routledge.

Johns, Leslie. 2007. "A Servant of Two Masters: Communication and the Selection of International Bureaucrats." *International Organization* 61 (2): 245–75. https://doi.org/10.1017/S0020818307070099.

Johnson, Hope. 2018. *International Agricultural Law and Policy*. Cheltenham: Edward Elgar.

Johnson, Tana. 2014. *Organizational Progeny: Why Governments Are Losing Control over the Proliferating Structures of Global Governance*. Oxford: Oxford University Press.

Johnson, Tana, and Johannes Urpelainen. 2012. "A Strategic Theory of Regime Integration and Separation." *International Organization* 66 (4): 645–77. https://doi.org/10.1017/S0020818312000264.

Jones, Emily, Carolyn Deere-Birkbeck, and Ngaire Woods. 2010. *Manoeuvring at the Margins: Constraints Faced by Small States in International Trade Negotiations.* London: Commonwealth Secretariat.

Joseph, Sarah. 2011. *Blame It on the WTO? A Human Rights Critique.* Oxford: Oxford University Press.

Josling, Timothy E. 2005. "The WTO Agricultural Negotiations: Progress and Prospects." *Choices* 20 (2): 131–36.

Josling, Timothy E., Stefan Tangermann, and K. T. Warley. 1996. *Agriculture in the GATT.* Basingstoke: Palgrave Macmillan.

Jurkovich, Michelle. 2020. *Feeding the Hungry: Advocacy and Blame in the Global Fight against Hunger.* Ithaca, NY: Cornell University Press.

Kanade, Mihir. 2017. *The Multilateral Trading System and Human Rights: A Governance Space Theory on Linkages.* New Dehli: Routledge.

Kapoor, Ilan. 2004. "Deliberative Democracy and the WTO." *Review of International Political Economy* 11 (3): 522–41.

Karapinar, Baris. 2012. "Defining the Legal Boundaries of Export Restrictions: A Case Law Analysis." *Journal of International Economic Law* 15 (2): 443–79. https://doi.org/10.1093/jiel/jgs021.

Keck, Margaret E., and Katherine Sikkink. 1998. *Activists beyond Borders: Advocacy Networks in International Politics.* Ithaca, NY: Cornell University Press.

Kent, George. 2005. *Freedom from Want: The Human Right to Adequate Food.* Washington, DC: Georgetown University Press.

Kentikelenis, Alexander E., and Leonard Seabrooke. 2017. "The Politics of World Polity: Script-Writing in International Organizations." *American Sociological Review* 82 (5): 1065–92. https://doi.org/10.1177/0003122417728241.

Keohane, Robert O., and David G. Victor. 2011. "The Regime Complex for Climate Change." *Perspectives on Politics* 9 (1): 7–23. https://doi.org/10.1017/S1537592710004068.

Khor, Martin. 2005. "More Finger Pointing, Less Negotiation, as Ministerial Gets under Way." Third World Network, December 15. https://www.twn.my/title2/twninfo325.htm.

Kille, Kent J., and Roger M. Scully. 2003. "Executive Heads and the Role of Intergovernmental Organizations: Expansionist Leadership in the United Nations and the European Union." *Political Psychology* 24 (1): 175–98. https://doi.org/10.1111/0162-895x.00321.

Kirkpatrick, Colin. 1985. "The IMF's Food Financing Facility: Much Ado about Nothing." *Food Policy* 10 (4): 303–5. https://doi.org/10.1016/0306-9192(85)90021-1.

Kirton, John J., Joseph P. Daniels, and Andreas Freytag. 2019. *Guiding Global Order: G8 Governance in the Twenty-First Century.* Abingdon: Routledge.

Kneteman, Christie. 2009. "Tied Food Aid: Export Subsidy in the Guise of Charity." *Third World Quarterly* 30 (6): 1215–25.

Knill, Christoph, Louisa Bayerlein, Jan Enkler, and Stephan Grohs. 2018. "Bureaucratic Influence and Administrative Styles in International Organizations." *Review of International Organizations* 14 (1): 83–106. https://doi.org/10.1007/s11558-018-9303-x.

Knox, John H. 2009. "Linking Human Rights and Climate Change at the United Nations." *Harvard Environmental Law Review* 33 (2): 477–98.

Kodras, Janet E. 1993. "Shifting Global Strategies of US Foreign Food Aid, 1955–1990." *Political Geography* 12 (3): 232–46. https://doi.org/10.1016/0962-6298(93)90055-C.

Konandreas, Panos. 2007. "WTO Negotiations on Agriculture: A Compromise on Food Aid Is Possible." In *WTO Rules for Agriculture Compatible with Development*, edited by Jamie Morrison and Alexander Sarris, 313–32. Rome: Food and Agriculture Organization.

Konandreas, Panos, and George Mermigkas. 2014. "WTO Domestic Support Disciplines: Options for Alleviating Constraints to Stockholding in Developing Countries in the Follow-up to Bali." FAO Commodity and Trade Policy Research Working Paper 45, Food and Agriculture Organization, Geneva. https://www.fao.org/fileadmin/templates/est/meetings/stocks/Konandreas-Mermigkas_16Feb2014.pdf.

Koremenos, Barbara, Charles Lipson, and Duncan Snidal. 2001. "The Rational Design of International Institutions." *International Organization* 55 (4): 761–99. https://doi.org/10.1162/002081801317193592.

Krämer-Hoppe, Rike, ed. 2020. *Positive Integration: EU and WTO Approaches towards the "Trade and" Debate.* Cham: Springer.

Kranke, Matthias. 2020. "Exclusive Expertise: The Boundary Work of International Organizations." *Review of International Political Economy*, prepublished online August 27. https://doi.org/10.1080/09692290.2020.1784774.

Krasner, Stephen D. 1976. "State Power and the Structure of International Trade." *World Politics* 28 (3): 317–47. https://doi.org/10.2307/2009974.

———. 1982. "Structural Causes and Regime Consequences: Regimes as Intervening Variables." *International Organization* 36 (2): 185–205.

Kreuder-Sonnen, Christian, and Michael Zürn. 2020. "After Fragmentation: Norm Collisions, Interface Conflicts, and Conflict Management." *Global Constitutionalism* 9 (2): 241–67. https://doi.org/10.1017/S2045381719000315.

Kripke, Gawain. 2009. "The Uses of Crisis: Progress on Implementing US Local/Regional Procurement of Food Aid." In *The Global Food Crisis: Gov-

ernance Challenges and Opportunities, edited by Jennifer Clapp and Mark J. Cohen, 113–26. Waterloo, Ontario: Wilfrid Laurier University Press.

Krisch, Nico, Francesco Corradini, and Lucy Lu Reimers. 2020. "Order at the Margins: The Legal Construction of Interface Conflicts over Time." *Global Constitutionalism* 9 (2): 343–63. https://doi.org/10.1017/S2045381719000327.

Krueger, Anne O. 1998. *The WTO as an International Organization*. Chicago: University of Chicago Press.

Kustermans, Jorg, and Rikkert Horemans. 2021. "Four Conceptions of Authority in International Relations." *International Organization*, prepublished online April 28. https://doi.org/10.1017/S0020818321000230.

Lake, David A. 1989. "Export, Die, or Subsidize: The International Political Economy of American Agriculture, 1875–1940." *Comparative Studies in Society and History* 31 (1): 81–105. https://doi.org/10.1017/S0010417500001567X.

———. 2010. "Rightful Rules: Authority, Order, and the Foundations of Global Governance." *International Studies Quarterly* 54 (3): 587–613. https://doi.org/10.1111/j.1468-2478.2010.00601.x.

Lall, Ranjit. 2017. "Beyond Institutional Design: Explaining the Performance of International Organizations." *International Organization* 71 (2): 245–80. https://doi.org/10.1017/S0020818317000066.

Lang, Andrew. 2006. "Re-thinking Trade and Human Rights." *Tulane Journal of International and Comparative Law* (2): 335–414.

———. 2011. *World Trade Law after Neoliberalism*. Oxford: Oxford University Press.

Lang, Tim, and David Barling. 2012. "Food Security and Food Sustainability: Reformulating the Debate." *Geographical Journal* 178 (4): 313–26. https://doi.org/10.1111/j.1475-4959.2012.00480.x.

Langille, Joanna. 2020. "The Trade–Labour Relationship in the Light of the WTO Appellate Body's Embrace of Pluralism." *International Labour Review* 159 (4): 569–89. https://doi.org/10.1111/ilr.12184.

Leary, Virginia A. 1997. "The WTO and the Social Clause: Post-Singapore Kaleidoscope." *European Journal of International Law* (1): 118–22.

Lebovic, James H., and Erik Voeten. 2006. "The Politics of Shame: The Condemnation of Country Human Rights Practices in the UNCHR." *International Studies Quarterly* 50 (4): 861–88. https://doi.org/10.1111/j.1468–2478.2006.00429.x.

Lentz, Erin. 2014. "The Future of Food Assistance: Opportunities and Challenges." *Pennsylvania State Journal of Law and International Affairs* 3 (2): 84–98.

Lesser, Taryn. 2010. "The Role of United Nations Special Procedures in Protecting the Human Rights of Migrants." *Refugee Survey Quarterly* 28 (4): 139–64. https://doi.org/10.1093/rsq/hdq007.

Limon, Marc, and Hilary Power. 2014. *United Nations Special Procedures Mechanism: Origins, Evolution and Reform.* Versoix: Universal Rights Groups.

Lipson, Michael. 2017. "Organization Theory and Cooperation and Conflict among International Organizations." In *Palgrave Handbook of Interorganizational Relations in World Politics*, edited by Joachim A. Koops and Rafael Biermann, 67–96. London: Palgrave Macmillan UK.

Littoz-Monnet, Annabelle. 2017a. "Expert Knowledge as a Strategic Resource: International Bureaucrats and the Shaping of Bioethical Standards." *International Studies Quarterly* 61 (3): 584–95. https://doi.org/10.1093/isq/sqx016.

———. 2017b. "Production and Uses of Expertise by International Bureaucracies." In *The Politics of Expertise in International Organizations: How International Bureaucracies Produce and Mobilize Knowledge*, edited by Annabelle Littoz-Monnet, 1–18. Abingdon: Routledge.

Luck, Edward C. 2003. "Blue Ribbon Power: Independent Commissions and UN Reform." *International Studies Perspectives* 1 (1): 89–104. https://doi.org/10.1111/1528-3577.00007.

Lütz, Susanne, Sven Hilgers, and Sebastian Schneider. 2019. "Accountants, Europeanists and Monetary Guardians: Bureaucratic Cultures and Conflicts in IMF-EU Lending Programs." *Review of International Political Economy* 26 (6): 1187–1210. https://doi.org/10.1080/09692290.2019.1632916.

Mably, Paul. 2009. "Centralized Production: The Group of 33." In *The Politics of Trade*, edited by Diana Tussie, 239–71. Leiden: Martinus Nijhoff.

MacNaughton, Gillian, and Mariah McGill. 2018. "The Office of the UN High Commissioner for Human Rights: Mapping the Evolution of the Right to Health." In *Human Rights in Global Health: Rights-Based Governance for a Globalizing World*, edited by Benjamin M. Meier and Lawrence O. Gostin, 463–86. Oxford: Oxford University Press.

Madokoro, Daisuke. 2019. "International Commissions as Norm Entrepreneurs: Creating the Normative Idea of the Responsibility to Protect." *Review of International Studies* 45 (1): 100–119. https://doi.org/10.1017/S0260210518000219.

Mallard, Grégoire. 2014. "Crafting the Nuclear Regime Complex (1950–1975): Dynamics of Harmonization of Opaque Treaty Rules." *European Journal of International Law* 25 (2): 445–72. https://doi.org/10.1093/ejil/chu028.

Mandleson, Peter, and Mariann Fisher Boel. 2005. "Advertisement from UN Agencies." Letter to *Financial Times*, December 14, 14.

Manitra, A. R., Massimo Iafrate, and Marianna Paschali. 2011. *Why Has Africa Become a Net Food Importer: Explaining African Agricultural and Food Trade Deficits.* Rome: Food and Agriculture Organization.

Marceau, G. 2002. "WTO Dispute Settlement and Human Rights." *European Journal of International Law* 13 (4): 753–814.

Margulis, Matias. 2012. "Global Food Security Governance: The Committee for World Food Security, Comprehensive Framework for Action and the G8/G20." In *The Challenge of Food Security*, edited by Rosemary Rayfuse and Nicole Weisfelt, 231–54. Cheltenham: Edward Elgar.

———. 2013. "The Regime Complex for Food Security: Implications for the Global Hunger Challenge." *Global Governance: A Review of Multilateralism and International Organizations* 19 (1): 53–67.

———. 2014. "Trading Out of the Global Food Crisis? The World Trade Organization and the Geopolitics of Food Security." *Geopolitics* 19 (2): 322–50. https://doi.org/10.1080/14650045.2014.920233.

———. 2017. "The Forgotten History of Food Security in Multilateral Trade Negotiations." *World Trade Review* 16 (1): 25–57. https://doi.org/10.1017/S1474745616000410.

———. 2018. "Negotiating from the Margins: How the UN Shapes the Rules of the WTO." *Review of International Political Economy* 25 (3): 364–91. https://doi.org/10.1080/09692290.2018.1447982.

Marin-Bosch, Miguel. 1987. "How Nations Vote in the General Assembly of the United Nations." *International Organization* 41 (4): 705–24.

Martin, Lisa L. 2006. "Distribution, Information, and Delegation to International Organizations: The Case of IMF Conditionality." In *Delegation and Agency in International Organizations*, edited by Darren G. Hawkins, David A. Lake, Daniel Nielson, and Michael J. Tierney, 140–64. Cambridge: Cambridge University Press.

Martin, Lisa L., and Beth A. Simmons. 1998. "Theories and Empirical Studies of International Institutions." *International Organization* 52 (4): 729–57.

Mary, Sébastien. 2019. "Hungry for Free Trade? Food Trade and Extreme Hunger in Developing Countries." *Food Security* 11 (2): 461–77. https://doi.org/10.1007/s12571-019-00908-z.

Mathiason, John. 2007. *Invisible Governance*. Bloomfield, CT: Kumarian Press.

Matthews, Alan. 2005. "The Road from Doha to Hong Kong in the WTO Agricultural Negotiations: A Developing Country Perspective." *European Review of Agricultural Economics* 32 (4): 561–74. https://doi.org/10.1093/erae/jbi031.

———. 2014. "Trade Rules, Food Security and the Multilateral Trade Negotiations." *European Review of Agricultural Economics* 41 (3): 511 35. https://doi.org/10.1093/erae/jbu017.

Maxwell, Simon. 1990. "Food Security in Developing Countries: Issues and Options for the 1990s." *IDS Bulletin* 21 (3): 2–13. https://doi.org/10.1111/j.1759-5436.1990.mp21003002.x.

———. 1996. "Food Security: A Post-modern Perspective." *Food Policy* 21 (2): 155–70. https://doi.org/10.1016/0306-9192(95)00074-7.

McArthur, John W. 2014. "The Origins of the Millennium Development Goals." *SAIS Review of International Affairs* 34 (2): 5–24.

McKeon, N. 2009. *The United Nations and Civil Society: Legitimating Global Governance—Whose Voice?* New York: Zed Books.

McMichael, Philip. 1993. "World Food System Restructuring under a GATT Regime." *Political Geography* 12 (3): 198–214.

———, ed. 1994. *The Global Restructuring of Agro-Food Systems.* Ithaca, NY: Cornell University Press.

———. 1996. "Globalization: Myths and Realities." *Rural Sociology* 61 (1): 25–55.

———. 2014. "Historicizing Food Sovereignty." *Journal of Peasant Studies* 41 (6): 933–57.

McNeill, Desmond. 2007. "'Human Development': The Power of the Idea." *Journal of Human Development* 8 (1): 5–22. https://doi.org/10.1080/1464 9880601101366.

Mechlem, Kerstin. 2004. "Food Security and the Right to Food in the Discourse of the United Nations." *European Law Journal* 10 (5): 631–48.

Mekay, Emad. 2005. "US, EU Spar over Food Aid, Subsidies Sidelined." Inter Press Service, December 14. http://www.ipsnews.net/2005/12/wto-special -us-eu-spar-over-food-aid-subsidies-sidelined/.

Meunier, Sophie. 1998. "Divided but United: European Trade Policy Integration and EC-US Agricultural Negotiations in the Uraguay Round." In *The European Union in the World Community*, edited by Carolyn Rhodes, 193–212. Boulder, CO: Lynee Rienner Press.

Milsom, Penelope, Richard Smith, Phillip Baker, and Helen Walls. 2020. "Corporate Power and the International Trade Regime Preventing Progressive Policy Action on Non-communicable Diseases: A Realist Review." *Health Policy and Planning*, prepublished online December 4. https://doi.org/10 .1093/heapol/czaa148.

Momani, Bessma, and Mark Hibben. 2015. "Cooperation or Clashes on 19th Street? Theorizing and Assessing IMF and World Bank Collaboration." *Journal of International Organization Studies* 6 (2): 27–43.

Montemayor, Raul. 2014. *Public Stockholding for Food Security Purposes: Scenarios and Options for a Permanent Solution.* Issue Paper No. 51, ICTSD Programme on Agricultural Trade and Sustainable Development. Geneva: International Centre for Trade and Sustainable Development. https://www.files.ethz.ch /isn/182744/Public%20Stockholding%20for%20Food%20Security%20Pur poses%20Scenarios%20and%20Options.pdf.

Moon, Gillian. 2013. "Trading in Good Faith? Importing States' Economic Human Rights Obligations into the WTO's Doha Round Negotiations." *Human Rights Law Review* 13 (2): 245–85.

MOPAN (Multilateral Organisation Performance Assessment Network). 2018. *World Food Programme (WFP): 2017–18 Performance Assessment.* Paris: MOPAN.

Morawa, Alexander H. E. 2003. "'Vulnerability' as a Concept in International Human Rights Law." *Journal of International Relations and Development* 10:139–55.

Morin, Jean-Frédéric, and Amandine Orsini. 2014. "Policy Coherency and Regime Complexes: The Case of Genetic Resources." *Review of International Studies* 40 (2): 303–24. https://doi.org/10.1017/S0260210513000168.

Morris, James T. 2005. "We Are Solely Concerned for Needs of Poor and Hungry." Letter to *Financial Times,* December 23.

Morse, Julia C., and Robert O. Keohane. 2014. "Contested Multilateralism." *Review of International Organizations* 9 (4): 385–412. https://doi.org/10.1007/s11558-014-9188-2.

Murdoch, Zuzana, Hussein Kassim, Sara Connolly, and Benny Geys. 2018. "Do International Institutions Matter? Socialization and International Bureaucrats." *European Journal of International Relations* 25 (3): 852–77. https://doi.org/10.1177/1354066118809156.

Murphy, Craig N. 1983. "What the Third World Wants: An Interpretation of the Development and Meaning of the New International Economic Order Ideology." *International Studies Quarterly* 27 (1): 55–76.

Murphy, Hannah. 2010. *The Making of International Trade Policy: NGOs, Agenda-Setting and the WTO.* Cheltenham: Edward Elgar.

Murphy, Hannah, and Aynsley Kellow. 2013. "Forum Shopping in Global Governance: Understanding States, Business and NGOs in Multiple Arenas." *Global Policy* 4 (2): 139–49. https://doi.org/10.1111/j.1758-5899.2012.00195.x.

Murphy, Sophia. 2005. *Food Aid: What Role for the WTO?* Minneapolis: Institute for Agriculture and Trade Policy.

———. 2015. "Food Security and International Trade: Risk, Trust and Rules." *Canadian Food Studies / La Revue Canadienne des Études sur l'Alimentation* 2 (2): 88–96.

Murray-Evans, Peg. 2020. "Rising Powers in Complex Regimes: South African Norm Shopping in the Governance of Cross-border Investment." *New Political Economy* 25 (5):773–90. https://doi.org/10.1080/13563467.2019.1584172.

Muzaka, Valbona. 2011. "Linkages, Contests and Overlaps in the Global Intellectual Property Rights Regime." *European Journal of International Relations* 17 (4): 755–76. https://doi.org/10.1177/1354066110373560.

Nakuja, Tekuni. 2018. "Do WTO Commitments Restrict the Policy Space of Countries Wishing to Provide Food Security through Stockholding Programs?" *Journal of World Trade* 52 (6): 967–93.

Naples-Mitchell, Joanna. 2011. "Perspectives of UN Special Rapporteurs on Their Role: Inherent Tensions and Unique Contributions to Human Rights." *International Journal of Human Rights* 15 (2): 232–48. https://doi.org/10 .1080/13642987.2011.537468.

Narlikar, Amrita. 2003. *International Trade and Developing Countries: Bargaining Coalitions in the GATT and WTO.* Abingdon: Routledge.

Narlikar, Amrita, and Diana Tussie. 2004. "The G20 at the Cancun Ministerial: Developing Countries and Their Evolving Coalitions in the WTO." *World Economy* 27 (7): 947–66.

———. 2016. "Breakthrough at Bali? Explanations, Aftermath, Implications." *International Negotiation* 21 (2): 209–32. https://doi.org/10.1163/15718069 -12341331.

Narlikar, Amrita, and Rorden Wilkinson. 2004. "Collapse at the WTO: A Cancun Post-mortem." *Third World Quarterly* 25 (3): 447–60.

Newell, Peter, Olivia Taylor, and Charles Touni. 2018. "Governing Food and Agriculture in a Warming World." *Global Environmental Politics* 18 (2): 53–71. https://doi.org/10.1162/glep_a_00456.

Newfarmer, Richard, Hans Timmer, Aristomene Varoudakis, Aaditya Mattoo, Carsten Fink, Keith Maskus, and Dominique Van der Mensbrugghe. 2002. *Global Economic Prospects and the Developing Countries 2002: Making Trade Work for the World's Poor.* Washington, DC: World Bank.

Ng, Francis, and M. Ataman Aksoy. 2008. "Who Are The Net Food Importing Countries?" Working Paper 4457, World Bank, Washington, DC.

Nielson, Daniel L., and Michael J. Tierney. 2003. "Delegation to International Organizations: Agency Theory and World Bank Environmental Reform." *International Organization* 57 (2): 241–76. https://doi.org/10.1017/S0020818 303572010.

Nielson, Daniel L., Michael J. Tierney, and Catherine E. Weaver. 2006. "Bridging the Rationalist-Constructivist Divide: Re-engineering the Culture of the World Bank." *Journal of International Relations and Development* 9 (2): 107–39.

Nifosi, Ingrid. 2005. *The UN Special Procedures in the Field of Human Rights.* Antwerpen: Intersentia.

Nifosi-Sutton, Ingrid. 2017. *The Protection of Vulnerable Groups under International Human Rights Law.* Abingdon: Routledge.

Nolan, Aoife, Rosa Freedman, and Thérèse Murphy. 2017. *The United Nations Special Procedures System.* Leiden: Brill.

Öberg, Marko Divac. 2005. "The Legal Effects of Resolutions of the UN Security Council and General Assembly in the Jurisprudence of the ICJ." *European Journal of International Law* 16 (5): 879–906. https://doi.org/10.1093 /ejil/chi151.

Oberthür, Sebastian, and Thomas Gehring. 2006. "Institutional Interaction in Global Environmental Governance: The Case of the Cartagena Protocol and the World Trade Organization." *Global Environmental Politics* 6 (2): 1–31. https://doi.org/10.1162/glep.2006.6.2.1.

O'Brien, John B. 2000. "F. L. McDougall and the Origins of the FAO." *Australian Journal of Politics and History* 46 (2): 164–74. https://doi.org/10.1111/1467-8497.00091.

O'Brien, Robert, Anne Marie Goetz, Jan Aart Scholte, and Marc Williams. 2000. *Contesting Global Governance: Multilateral Economic Institutions and Global Social Movements.* Cambridge: Cambridge University Press.

Ocampo, José Antonio. 2018. "Global Economic and Social Governance and the United Nations System." In *Just Security in an Undergoverned World*, edied by William Durch, Joris Larik, and Richard Ponzio, 265–89. Oxford: Oxford University Press.

Odell, John S. 2009. "Breaking Deadlocks in International Institutional Negotiations: The WTO, Seattle, and Doha." *International Studies Quarterly* 53 (2): 273–99. https://doi.org/10.1111/j.1468-2478.2009.00534.x.

Oestreich, Joel E. 2007. *Power and Principle: Human Rights Programming in International Organizations.* Washington, DC: Georgetown University Press.

———. 2012. *International Organizations as Self-Directed Actors: A Framework for Analysis.* New York: Routledge.

OHCHR (Office of the High Commissioner for Human Rights). 2000. *The Right to Food: Report of the High Commissioner for Human Rights Submitted in Accordance with Commission Resolution 1999/24.* Geneva: OHCHR.

———. 2002a. *Globalization and Its Impact on the Full Enjoyment of Human Rights: Report of the High Commissioner for Human Rights Submitted in Accordance with Commission on Human Rights Resolution 2001/32.* Geneva: OHCHR.

———. 2002b. *The Right to Food: Achievements and Challenges.* Geneva: OHCHR.

———. 2003. *Human Rights and Trade, Submission to the 5th WTO Ministerial Conference, Cancun, Mexico, 10–14 September 2003.* Geneva: OHCHR.

———. 2004. *Analytical Study of the High Commissioner for Human Rights on the Fundamental Principle of Non-discrimination in the Context of Globalization.* Geneva: OHCHR.

———. 2005. *Human Rights and the World Trade Agreements: Using General Exception Clauses to Protect Human Rights.* Geneva: OHCHR.

———. 2008. *Manual of Operations of the Special Procedures of the Human Rights Council.* Geneva: OHCHR.

———. 2011. "Food Security Hostage to Trade in WTO Negotiations—UN Right to Food Expert." OHCHR. Last modified November 16. https://news

archive.ohchr.org/en/NewsEvents/Pages/DisplayNews.aspx?NewsID=1160
8&LangID=E.

Orford, Anne. 2015. "Food Security, Free Trade, and the Battle for the State."
Journal of International Law and International Relations 11 (2): 1–67.

Orsini, Amandine. 2013. "Multi-forum Non-state Actors: Navigating the Regime
Complexes for Forestry and Genetic Resources." *Global Environmental Politics* 13 (3): 34–55. https://doi.org/10.1162/GLEP_a_00182.

Orsini, Amandine, and Claire Godet. 2018. "Food Security and Biofuels Regulations: The Emulsifying Effect of International Regime Complexes." *Journal
of Contemporary European Research* 14 (1): 4–22.

Orsini, Amandine, Philippe Le Prestre, Peter M. Haas, Malte Brosig, Philipp
Pattberg, Oscar Widerberg, Laura Gomez-Mera, Jean-Frédéric Morin, Neil
E. Harrison, Robert Geyer, and David Chandler. 2019. "Forum: Complex
Systems and International Governance." *International Studies Review* 22 (4):
1008–38. https://doi.org/10.1093/isr/viz005.

Orsini, Amandine, Jean-Frédéric Morin, and Oran Young. 2013. "Regime Complexes: A Buzz, a Boom, or a Boost for Global Governance?" *Global Governance: A Review of Multilateralism and International Organizations* 19 (1):
27–39.

Ostry, Sylvia. 2002. "The Uruguay Round North-South Grand Bargain: Implications for Future Negotiations." In *The Political Economy of International
Trade Law: Essay in Honour of Robert E. Hudec,* edited by Daniel L. M. Ken-
nedy and James D. Southwick, 285–300. Cambridge: Cambridge University
Press.

Our World Is Not for Sale. 2011. "Statement of Our World Is Not for Sale on the
de Schutter-WTO Debate." December 17. https://ourworldisnotforsale.net/
0/it/article/statement-our-world-not-sale-owinfs-schutter-wto-debate.html.

Oxfam. 2005a. *Africa and the Doha Round: Fighting to Keep Development Alive.*
Briefing Paper 80. Oxford: Oxfam.

———. 2005b. *Kicking Down the Door: How Upcoming WTO Talks Threaten
Farmers in Poor Countries.* Oxford: Oxfam.

Paarlberg, Robert. 1997. "Agricultural Policy Reform and the Uruguay Round:
Synergistic Linkage in a Two-Level Game?" *International Organization* 51
(3): 413–44. https://doi.org/10.1162/002081897550410.

Paasch, Armin, ed. 2007. *Trade Policies and Hunger.* Geneva: Ecumenical Advocacy Alliance.

Pantzerhielm, Laura, Anna Holzscheiter, and Thurid Bahr. 2019. "Governing
Effectively in a Complex World? How Metagovernance Norms and Changing
Repertoires of Knowledge Shape International Organization Discourses on
Institutional Order in Global Health." *Cambridge Review of International
Affairs* 32:1–26. https://doi.org/10.1080/09557571.2019.1678112.

Park, Susan. 2005. "Norm Diffusion within International Organizations: A Case Study of the World Bank." *Journal of International Relations and Development* 8 (2): 111–41. https://doi.org/10.1057/palgrave.jird.1800051.

Parotte, J. H. 1983. "The Food Aid Convention: Its History and Scope." *IDS Bulletin* 14 (2): 10–15.

Pauwelyn, Joost. 2003. *Conflict of Norms in Public International Law: How WTO Law Relates to Other Rules of International Law.* Cambridge: Cambridge University Press.

———. 2018. "Interplay between the WTO Treaty and Other International Legal Instruments and Tribunals: Evolution after 20 Years of WTO Jurisprudence." In *Proceedings of the Québec City Conference on the WTO at 20,* edited by C.-E. Côté, V. Guèvremont, and R. Ouellet. Quebec City: Presses de l'Université de Laval. https://dx.doi.org/10.2139/ssrn.2731144.

Pegram, Tom. 2014. "Global Human Rights Governance and Orchestration: National Human Rights Institutions as Intermediaries." *European Journal of International Relations* 21 (3): 595–620. https://doi.org/10.1177/13540661 14548079.

Perkins, John H. 1997. *Geopolitics and the Green Revolution: Wheat, Genes, and the Cold War.* New York: Oxford University Press.

Pernet, Corinne A., and Amalia Ribi Forclaz. 2019. "Revisiting the Food and Agriculture Organization (FAO): International Histories of Agriculture, Nutrition,and Development." *International History Review* 41 (2): 345–50. https://doi.org/10.1080/07075332.2018.1460386.

Peters, Ralf. 2008. *Roadblock to Reform: The Persistence of Agricultural Export Subsidies.* Policy Studies in International Trade and Commodities. Geneva: United Nations Conference on Trade and Development.

Petersmann, Ernst-Ulrich. 2004. "The 'Human Rights Approach' Advocated by the UN High Commissioner for Human Rights and by the International Labour Organization: Is It Relevant for WTO and Policy?" *Journal of International Economic Law* 7 (3): 605–27. https://doi.org/10.1093/jiel/7.3.605.

Phillips, Lynne, and Suzan Ilcan. 2003. "'A World Free from Hunger': Global Imagination and Governance in the Age of Scientific Management." *Sociologia Ruralis* 43 (4): 434–53.

Phillips, Ralph W. 1981. *FAO: Its Origins, Formations and Evolution, 1945–1981.* Rome: Food and Agriculture Organization.

Picciotto, Salomone. 2007. "The WTO as a Node of Global Governance: Economic Regulation and Human Rights Discourses." *Law, Social Justice and Global Development Journal* (1). https://warwick.ac.uk/fac/soc/law/elj/lgd /2007_1/picciotto.

Piccone, Ted. 2012. *Catalysts for Change: How the U.N.'s Independent Experts Promote Human Rights.* Washington, DC: Brookings Institution Press.

Pinheiro, Paulo Sergio. 2011. "Being a Special Rapporteur: A Delicate Balancing Act." *International Journal of Human Rights* 15 (2): 162–71. https://doi.org/10.1080/13642987.2011.537464.

Pollack, Mark A. 1997. "Delegation, Agency, and Agenda Setting in the European Community." *International Organization* 51 (1): 99–134. https://doi.org/10.1162/002081897550311.

Pratt, Tyler. 2018. "Deference and Hierarchy in International Regime Complexes." *International Organization* 72 (3): 561–90.

Prowse, Susan. 2002. "The Role of International and National Agencies in Trade-Related Capacity Building." *World Economy* 25 (9): 1235–61.

Puchala, Donald J., and Raymond F. Hopkins. 1978. "Toward Innovation in the Global Food Regime." *International Organization* 32 (3): 855–68. https://doi.org/10.1017/S0020818300031969.

Quark, Amy A. 2013. *Global Rivalries: Standards Wars and the Transnational Cotton Trade.* Chicago: University of Chicago Press.

Rabitz, Florian. 2014. "Explaining Institutional Change in International Patent Politics." *Third World Quarterly* 35 (9): 1582–97. https://doi.org/10.1080/01436597.2014.970860.

Rae, Isabella, Julian Thomas, and Margret Vidar. 2007. "The Right to Food as a Fundamental Human Right: FAO's Experience." In *Food Insecurity, Vulnerability and Human Rights Failure,* edited by Basudeb Guha-Khasnobis, Shabd S. Acharya, and Benjamin Davis, 266–85. London: Palgrave Macmillan UK.

Raghavan, Chakravarthi. 2000a. "After Seattle, World Trade System Faces Uncertain Future." *Review of International Political Economy* 7 (3): 495–504. https://doi.org/10.1080/09692290050174060.

———. 2000b. "WTO Concerned over Human Rights Appraisal Report." *South-North Development Monitor,* August 27.

Rahman, Atiqur, and John Westley. 2001. "The Challenge of Ending Rural Poverty." *Development Policy Review* 19 (4): 553–62. https://doi.org/10.1111/1467-7679.00152.

Raja, Kanaga 2013. "Minister Sharma Explains India's Position on Food Security." *South-North Development Monitor,* December 6. https://www.twn.my/title2/resurgence/2014/281-282/cover05.htm.

Rajagopal, Balakrishnan. 2005. "The Role of Law in Counter-hegemonic Globalization and Global Legal Pluralism: Lessons from the Narmada Valley Struggle in India." *Leiden Journal of International Law* 18 (3): 345–87. https://doi.org/doi:10.1017/S0922156505002797.

Ramcharan, Bertrand G. 2004. *A UN High Commissioner in Defence of Human Rights: No License to Kill or Torture.* Leiden: Brill Nijhoff.

Ratner, Steven R. 2015. *The Thin Justice of International Law: A Moral Reckoning of the Law of Nations.* Oxford: Oxford University Press.

Raustalia, Kal, and David G. Victor. 2004. "The Regime Complex for Plant Ge- netic Resources." *International Organization* 58 (2): 277–309.

Reinalda, Bob, and Bertjan Verbeek. 1998. *Autonomous Policy Making by Interna- tional Organisations.* Abingdon: Routledge.

———. 2004. *Decision Making within International Organisations.* Abingdon: Routledge.

Rhoads, Emily Paddon. 2016. *Taking Sides in Peacekeeping: Impartiality and the Future of the United Nations.* Oxford: Oxford University Press.

Rietkerk, Aaron D. 2016. "'The Constructive Use of Abundance': The UN World Food Programme and the Evolution of the International Food-Aid System during the Post-war Decades." *International History Review* 38 (4): 788–813. https://doi.org/10.1080/07075332.2015.1038844.

Risse, Thomas. 1999. "International Norms and Domestic Change: Arguing and Communicative Behavior in the Human Rights Area." *Politics and Society* 27 (4): 529–59.

———. 2000. "'Let's Argue!': Communicative Action in World Politics." *Inter- national Organization* 54 (1): 1–39.

Risse, Thomas, Stephen C. Ropp, and Kathryn Sikkink, eds. 1999. *The Power of Human Rights: International Norms and Domestic Change.* Cambridge: Cambridge University Press.

Rodrik, Dani. 2018. "What Do Trade Agreements Really Do?" *Journal of Eco- nomic Perspectives* 32 (2): 73–90. https://doi.org/10.1257/jep.32.2.73.

Rosenau, James N. 2004. "Globalization and Governance: Bleak Prospects for Sustainability." In *Challenges of Globalization: New Trends in International Politics and Society,* edited by Alfred Pfaller and Marika Lerch, 131–54. Abing- don: Routledge.

Ross, Sandy. 2011. *The World Food Programme in Global Politics.* Boulder, CO: First Forum Press.

Rosset, Peter M. 2006. *Food Is Different.* Halifax, Nova Scotia: Fernwood.

Ruggie, John Gerard. 1982. "International Regimes, Transactions, and Change: Embedded Liberalism in the Postwar Economic Order." *International Orga- nization* 36 (2): 379–415. https://doi.org/10.1017/S0020818300018993.

———. 2003. "The United Nations and Globalization: Patterns and Limits of Institutional Adaptation." *Global Governance: A Review of Multilateralism and International Organizations* 9 (3): 301–21.

Ryu, Jeheung, and Randall W. Stone. 2018. "Plaintiffs by Proxy: A Firm-Level Approach to WTO Dispute Resolution." *Review of International Organiza- tions* 13 (2): 273–308. https://doi.org/10.1007/s11558-018-9304-9.

Sagafi-Nejad, Tagi, and John H. Dunning. 2008. *The UN and Transnational Corporations: From Code of Conduct to Global Compact.* Bloomington: Indi- ana University Press.

Sage, Colin. 2014. "Food Security, Food Sovereignty and the Special Rapporteur: Shaping Food Policy Discourse through Realising the Right to Food." *Dialogues in Human Geography* 4 (2): 195–99. https://doi.org/10.1177/2043820614537156.

Sarfaty, Galit A. 2009. "Why Culture Matters in International Institutions: The Marginality of Human Rights at the World Bank." *American Journal of International Law* 103 (4): 647–83. https://doi.org/10.1017/S0002930000159810.

Schapper, Andrea. 2020. "From the Local to the Global: Learning about the Adverse Human Rights Effects of Climate Policies." *Environmental Politics* 29 (4): 628–48. https://doi.org/10.1080/09644016.2020.1743423.

Schindler, Sebastian. 2014. "The Morality of Bureaucratic Politics: Allegations of 'Spoiling' in a UN Inter-agency War." *Journal of International Organizations Studies* 5 (1): 59–70.

Schmidt, Vivien A. 2008. "Discursive Institutionalism: The Explanatory Power of Ideas and Discourse." *Annual Review of Political Science* 11 (1): 303–26. https://doi.org/10.1146/annurev.polisci.11.060606.135342.

Schroeder, Michael. 2014. "Executive Leadership in the Study of International Organization: A Framework for Analysis." *International Studies Review* 16 (3): 339–61. https://doi.org/10.1111/misr.12147.

Schultz, Theodore W. 1960. "Value of U.S. Farm Surpluses to Underdeveloped Countries." *Journal of Farm Economics* 42 (5): 1019–30.

Schwab, Susan C. 2011. "After Doha: Why the Negotiations Are Doomed and What We Should Do about It." *Foreign Affairs* 90 (3): 104–17.

Scott, James. 2008. "The Use and Misuse of Trade Negotiation Simulations." *Journal of World Trade* 42 (1): 87–103.

———. 2017. "The Future of Agricultural Trade Governance in the World Trade Organization." *International Affairs* 93 (5): 1167–84. https://doi.org/10.1093/ia/iix157.

Scott, James, and Sophie Harman. 2013. "Beyond TRIPS: Why the WTO's Doha Round Is Unhealthy." *Third World Quarterly* 34 (8): 1361–76. https://doi.org/10.1080/01436597.2013.831539.

Seiderman, Ian. 2019. "The UN High Commissioner for Human Rights in the Age of Global Backlash." *Netherlands Quarterly of Human Rights* 37 (1): 5–13. https://doi.org/10.1177/0924051918822854.

Sell, Susan K. 2001. "TRIPS and the Access to Medicines Campaign." *Wisconsin International Law Journal* 20 (3): 481–522.

———. 2003. *Private Power, Public Law: The Globalization of Intellectual Property Rights*. Cambridge: Cambridge University Press.

Sell, Susan K., and Aseem Prakash. 2004. "Using Ideas Strategically: The Contest between Business and NGO Networks in Intellectual Property Rights."

International Studies Quarterly 48 (1): 143–75. https://doi.org/10.1111/j.00 20-8833.2004.00295.x.

Shadlen, Kenneth C. 2004. "Patents and Pills, Power and Procedure: The North-South Politics of Public Health in the WTO." *Studies in Comparative International Development* 39 (3): 76–108. https://doi.org/10.1007/bf02686283.

Shaffer, Gregory. 2009. "Power, Governance and the WTO: A Comparative Institutional Approach." In *Power in Global Governance*, edited by Michael Barnett and Raymond Duvall, 130–60. Cambridge: Cambridge University Press.

Shaffer, Gregory, Manfred Elsig, and Sergio Puig. 2017. "The Law and Politics of WTO Dispute Settlement." In *Research Handbook on the Politics of International Law*, edited by Wayne Sandholtz and Christopher A. Whytock, 269–306. Cheltenham: Edward Elgar.

Sharma, Anand. 2013. "Address by Shri Anand Sharma Union Minister of Commerce and Industry at the Plenary Session of the 9th Ministerial Conference of the WTO." December 4. https://pib.gov.in/newsite/PrintRelease.aspx?rel id=101013.

Sharman, Jason C. 2009. "The Bark Is the Bite: International Organizations and Blacklisting." *Review of International Political Economy* 16 (4): 573–96. https://doi.org/10.1080/09692290802403502.

Shaw, D. John. 2007. *World Food Security: A History since 1945*. London: Palgrave Macmillan.

———. 2011. *The World's Largest Humanitarian Agency: The Transformation of the UN World Food Programme and of Food Aid*. Basingstoke: Palgrave Macmillan.

Shaw, D. John, and Edward J. Clay. 1998. "Global Hunger and Food Security after the World Food Summit." *Canadian Journal of Development Studies / Revue Canadienne d'Études du Développement* 19 (4): 55–76. https://doi.org/10.1080/02255189.1998.9669778.

Shaw, D. John, and Hans W. Singer. 1996. "A Future Food Aid Regime: Implications of Final Act of the Uruguay Round." *Food Policy* 21 (4–5): 447–60.

Sikkink, Kathryn. 1993. "Human Rights, Principled Issue-Networks, and Sovereignty in Latin America." *International Organization* 47 (3): 411–41.

Siles-Brügge, Gabriel. 2014. *Constructing European Union Trade Policy: A Global Idea of Europe*. Houndmills, Basingstoke, Hampshire: Palgrave Macmillan.

Simmons, Beth A. 2000. "International Law and State Behavior: Commitment and Compliance in International Monetary Affairs." *American Political Science Review* 94 (4): 819–35. doi:10.2307/2586210.

Sinclair, Guy Fiti. 2017. *To Reform the World: International Organizations and the Making of Modern States*. Oxford: Oxford University Press.

Singer, Hans W. 1994. "Two Views of Food Aid." In *Market Forces and World*

Development, edited by Renee Prendergast and Frances Stewart, 207–11. London: Palgrave Macmillan UK.

Singh, J. P. 2017. *Sweet Talk: Paternalism and Collective Action in North-South Trade Relations.* Stanford, CA: Stanford University Press.

Singh, J. P., and Surupa Gupta. 2016. "Agriculture and Its Discontents: Coalitional Politics at the WTO with Special Reference to India's Food Security Interests." *International Negotiation* 21 (2): 295–326. https://doi.org/10.1163/15718069-12341334.

Skogstad, Grace Darlene. 2008. *Internationalization and Canadian Agriculture: Policy and Governing Paradigms.* Toronto: University of Toronto Press.

Smeets, Maarten. 2013. "Trade Capacity Building in the WTO: Main Achievements since Doha and Key Challenges." *Journal of World Trade* 47 (5): 1047–90.

Smith, Fiona. 2000. "'Multifunctionality' and 'Non-trade Concerns' in the Agriculture Negotiations." *Journal of International Economic Law* 3 (4): 707–13. https://doi.org/10.1093/jiel/3.4.707.

Smith, Jackie. 2001. "Globalizing Resistance: The Battle of Seattle and the Future of Social Movements." *Mobilization: An International Quarterly* 6 (1): 1–19.

———. 2005. "Globalization and Transnational Social Movement Organizations." In *Social Movements and Organization Theory*, edited by Gerald F. Davis, Doug McAdam, W. Richard Scott, and Mayer N. Zald, 226–48. Cambridge: Cambridge University Press.

Smith, Lisa C., Amani E. El Obeid, and Helen H. Jensen. 2000. "The Geography and Causes of Food Insecurity in Developing Countries." *Agricultural Economics* 22 (2): 199–215.

Smith, Rhona K. M. 2011. "The Possibilities of an Independent Special Rapporteur Scheme." *International Journal of Human Rights* 15 (2): 172–86. https://doi.org/10.1080/13642987.2011.537465.

Sneyd, Adam. 2011. *Governing Cotton: Globalization and Poverty in Africa.* New York: Palgrave Macmillan.

———. 2015. "The Poverty of 'Poverty Reduction': The Case of African Cotton." *Third World Quarterly* 36 (1): 55–74. https://doi.org/10.1080/01436597.2015.976017.

Sneyd, Lauren Q., Alexander Legwegoh, and Evan D. G. Fraser. 2013. "Food Riots: Media Perspectives on the Causes of Food Protest in Africa." *Food Security* 5 (4): 485–97.

Soper, Rachel. 2020. "From Protecting Peasant Livelihoods to Essentializing Peasant Agriculture: Problematic Trends in Food Sovereignty Discourse." *Journal of Peasant Studies* 47 (2): 265–85. https://doi.org/10.1080/03066150.2018.1543274.

Squatrito, Theresa, Magnus Lundgren, and Thomas Sommerer. 2019. "Shaming by International Organizations: Mapping Condemnatory Speech Acts across 27 International Organizations, 1980–2015." *Cooperation and Conflict* 54 (3): 356–77. https://doi.org/10.1177/0010836719832339.

Srinivasan, T. N. 2007. "The Dispute Settlement Mechanism of the WTO: A Brief History and an Evaluation from Economic, Contractarian and Legal Perspectives." *World Economy* 30 (7): 1033–68. https://doi.org/10.1111/j.1467-9701.2007.01011.x.

Staples, Amy L. S. 2003. "To Win the Peace: The Food and Agriculture Organization, Sir John Boyd Orr, and the World Food Board Proposals." *Peace and Change* 28 (4): 495–523.

———. 2006. *The Birth of Development: How the World Bank, Food and Agriculture Organization, and World Health Organization Changed the World, 1945–1965.* Kent, OH: Kent State University Press.

Steffek, Jens. 2003. "The Legitimation of International Governance: A Discourse Approach." *European Journal of International Relations* 9 (2): 249–75. https://doi.org/10.1177/1354066103009002004.

———. 2015. "The Output Legitimacy of International Organizations and the Global Public Interest." *International Theory* 7 (2): 263–93. https://doi.org/10.1017/S1752971915000044.

Steffek, Jens. 2012. "Awkward Partners: NGOs and Social Movements at the WTO." In *The Oxford Handbook on the World Trade Organization*, edited by Amrita Narlikar, Martin Daunton, and Robert M. Stern, 301–19. Oxford: Oxford University Press.

Steinberg, Richard H. 2002. "In the Shadow of Law or Power? Consensus-Based Bargaining and Outcomes in the GATT/WTO." *International Organization* 56 (2): 339–74.

Stewart-Brown, Ronald. 2009. "So Near and Yet So Far in Geneva." *Economic Affairs* 29 (1): 58–63. https://doi.org/10.1111/j.1468-0270.2009.01869.x.

Stoler, Andrew L. 2010. "The Evolution of Subsidies Disciplines in GATT and the WTO." *Journal of World Trade* 44 (4): 797–808.

Strange, Michael. 2013. *Writing Global Trade Governance: Discourse and the WTO.* Abingdon: Routledge.

Sub-Commission on the Promotion and Protection of Human Rights. 2002. *Human Rights, Trade and Investment: Sub-Commission on Human Rights Resolution 2002/11.* Geneva: OHCHR.

Subedi, Surya P. 2011. "Protection of Human Rights through the Mechanism of UN Special Rapporteurs." *Human Rights Quarterly* 33 (1): 201–28.

———. 2016. "The UN Human Rights Special Rapporteurs and the Impact of Their Work: Some Reflections of the UN Special Rapporteur for Cambodia." *Asian Journal of International Law* 6 (1): 1–14. https://doi.org/10.1017 /S2044251315000132.

———. 2017. *The Effectiveness of the UN Human Rights System: Reform and the Judicialisation of Human Rights*. Abingdon: Routledge.

Symons, Jonathan. 2011. "The Legitimation of International Organisations: Examining the Identity of the Communities That Grant Legitimacy." *Review of International Studies* 37 (5): 2557–83. https://doi.org/10.1017/S026021051 000166X.

Talbot, Ross B. 1979. "The European Community's Food Aid Programme: An Integration of Ideology, Strategy, Technology and Surpluses." *Food Policy* 4 (4): 269–84.

———. 1982. "The Four World Food Organizations: Influence of the Group of 77." *Food Policy* 7 (3): 207–21. https://doi.org/10.1016/0306-9192(82)90058-6.

Talbot, Ross B., and H. Wayne Moyer. 1987. "Who Governs the Rome Food Agencies?" *Food Policy* 12 (4): 349–64. https://doi.org/10.1016/0306-9192(87) 90007-8.

Tallberg, Jonas, and Michael Zürn. 2019. "The Legitimacy and Legitimation of International Organizations: Introduction and Framework." *Review of International Organizations* 14 (4): 581–606. https://doi.org/10.1007/s11558-018 -9330-7.

Taylor, Ian, and Karen Smith. 2007. *United Nations Conference on Trade and Development (UNCTAD)*. New York: Routledge.

Terman, Rochelle, and Erik Voeten. 2018. "The Relational Politics of Shame: Evidence from the Universal Periodic Review." *Review of International Organizations* 13 (1): 1–23. https://doi.org/10.1007/s11558-016-9264-x.

Therien, Jean-Philippe. 1999. "Beyond the North-South Divide: The Two Tales of World Poverty." *Third World Quarterly* 20 (4): 723–42. https://doi.org/10 .1080/01436599913523.

Thérien, Jean-Philippe, and Vincent Pouliot. 2006. "The Global Compact: Shifting the Politics of International Development?" *Global Governance: A Review of Multilateralism and International Organizations* 12 (1): 55–76.

Thies, Cameron G. 2001. "A Historical Institutionalist Approach to the Uruguay Round Agricultural Negotiations." *Comparative Political Studies* 34 (4): 400–428. https://doi.org/10.1177/0010414001034004003.

Thompson, Alexander. 2006. "Coercion through IOs: The Security Council and the Logic of Information Transmission." *International Organization* 60 (1): 1–34. https://doi.org/10.1017/S0020818306060012.

Torero, Maximo. 2012. "Food Prices: Riding the Rollercoaster." In *2012 Global Food Policy Report*, edited by International Food Policy Research Institute, 15–24. Washington, DC: International Food Policy Research Institute.

Toye, John. 2014. "Assessing the G77: 50 Years after UNCTAD and 40 Years after the NIEO." *Third World Quarterly* 35 (10): 1759–74.

Toye, John, and Richard Toye. 2004. *The UN and Global Political Economy: Trade, Finance and Development, United Nations Intellectual History Project.* Bloomington: Indiana University Press.

Trebilcock, Michael J., and Robert Howse. 2005. *The Regulation of International Trade.* 3rd ed. Abingdon: Routledge.

Trebilcock, Michael J., and Kristen Pue. 2015. "The Puzzle of Agricultural Exceptionalism in International Trade Policy." *Journal of International Economic Law* 18 (2): 233–60. https://doi.org/10.1093/jiel/jgv022.

UN (United Nations). 2002. *Commission on Human Rights: Report on the Fifty-Eighth Session. Supplement 3.* New York: UN.

———. 2020. "Revenue by Entity." UN System Chief Executives Board. Accessed July 29, 2020. https://unsceb.org/fs-revenue-agency.

UN (United Nations) Conference on Food and Agriculture. 1943. *Text of the Final Act.* Washington, DC: Department of State.

UNGA (United Nations General Assembly). 1994. *Resolution Adopted by the United Nations General Assembly A/RES/48/141.* Edited by United Nations General Assembly. New York: United Nations.

UN (United Nations) News Centre. 2005a. "Exclude Humanitarian Food Aid from Trade Talks, UN Expert Advises." Last modified July 19. https://news .un.org/en/story/2005/07/145642-exclude-humanitarian-food-aid-trade -talks-un-expert-advises.

———. 2005b. "UN Agency Calls for 'Food-First Policy' after Global Aid Plummets by a Third in 2004." May 4. https://news.un.org/en/story/2005/05/136782-un -agency-calls-food-first-policy-after-global-aid-plummets-third-2004.

———. 2005c. "UN Agency Heads Call on World Trade Negotiators to Protect In-Kind Food Aid." December 8. https://news.un.org/en/story/2005/12/ 162962-un-agency-heads-call-world-trade-negotiators-protect-kind-food-aid.

———. 2005d. "UN Urges Trade Forum to Support Food Aid in Talks on Agricultural Reform." Last modified May 9. https://news.un.org/en/story/2005 /05/137302-un-urges-trade-forum-support-food-aid-talks-agricultural-reform.

US Department of State. 2005. "Briefing by USAID Administrator Natsios and Deputy U.S. Trade Representative Bhatia." December 14. https://2001-2009 .state.gov/e/eeb/rls/rm/2005/58044.htm.

Uvin, Peter. 1992. "Regime, Surplus, and Self-Interest: The International Politics of Food Aid." *International Studies Quarterly* 36 (3): 293–312.

———. 1994. *The International Organization of Hunger.* London: Kegan Paul International.

———. 2007. "From the Right to Development to the Rights-Based Approach:

How 'Human Rights' Entered Development." *Development in Practice* 17 (4–5): 597–606. https://doi.org/10.1080/09614520701469617.

Valdés, Alberto, and W. Foster. 2003. "Special Safeguards for Developing Country Agriculture: A Proposal for WTO Negotiations." *World Trade Review* 2 (1): 5–31.

Valdés, Alberto, and Joachim Zietz. 1987. "Export Subsidies and Minimum Access Guarantees in Agricultural Trade: A Developing Country Perspective." *World Development* 15 (5): 673–83. https://doi.org/10.1016/0305-750X(87)90010-6.

VanGrasstek, Craig. 2013. *The History and Future of the World Trade Organization.* Geneva: World Trade Organization.

Vetterlein, Antje. 2012. "Seeing Like the World Bank on Poverty." *New Political Economy* 17 (1): 35–58. https://doi.org/10.1080/13563467.2011.569023.

von Billerbeck, Sarah. 2019. "'Mirror, Mirror on the Wall': Self-Legitimation by International Organizations." *International Studies Quarterly* 64 (1): 207–19. https://doi.org/10.1093/isq/sqz089.

Wade, Robert H. 2003. "What Strategies Are Viable for Developing Countries Today? The World Trade Organization and the Shrinking of 'Development Space.'" *Review of International Political Economy* 10 (4): 621–44.

Walch, Karen S. 2003. "Feminist Ideas on Cooperation and Self-Interest for International Relations." In *Partial Truths and the Politics of Community*, edited by Mary Ann Tétreault and Robin L. Teske, 161–79. Columbia: University of South Carolina Press.

Watkins, Kevin. 1991. "Agriculture and Food Security in the GATT Uruguay Round." *Review of African Political Economy* 50:38–50.

Watkins, Kevin, and Joachim Von Braun. 2003. *Time to Stop Dumping on the World's Poor.* Washington, DC: International Food Policy Research Institute.

Weaver, Catherine. 2007. "The World's Bank and the Bank's World." *Global Governance: A Review of Multilateralism and International Organizations* 13 (4): 493–512.

———. 2008. *Hypocrisy Trap: The World Bank and the Poverty of Reform.* Princeton, NJ: Princeton University Press.

Weaver, Catherine, and Stephen C. Nelson. 2016. "Organizational Culture." In *The Oxford Handbook of International Organizations*, edited by Jacob Katz Cogan, Ian Hurd, and Ian Johnstone, 920–39. Oxford: Oxford University Press.

Weinlich, Silke. 2014. *The UN Secretariat's Influence on the Evolution of Peacekeeping.* London: Palgrave Macmillan.

Weiss, Thomas G. 2009. "Moving beyond North-South Theatre." *Third World Quarterly* 30 (2): 271–84.

Weiss, Thomas G., and Robert S. Jordan. 1976. "Bureaucratic Politics and the World Food Conference: The International Policy Process." *World Politics* 28 (3): 422–39.

Weissbrodt, David, Penny Parker, Laura Gerber, Muria Kruger, and Joe W. Chip Pitts III. 2003. "A Review of the Fifty-Fourth Session of the United Nations Sub-Commission on the Promotion and Protection of Human Rights." *Netherlands Quarterly of Human Rights* 21 (2): 291–342.

Weissbrodt, David, and Kell Schoff. 2003. "Human Rights Approach to Intellectual Property Protection: The Genesis and Application of Sub-Commission Resolution 2000/7." *Minnesota Intellectual Property Review* 5 (1): 1–46.

Weissbrodt, David, Bret Thiele, Mayra Gomez, and Muria Kruger. 2002. "A Review of the Fifty-Third Session of the United Nations Sub-Commission on the Promotion and Protection of Human Rights." *Netherlands Quarterly of Human Rights* 20 (2): 231–61.

Well, Mareike, Barbara Saerbeck, Helge Jörgens, and Nina Kolleck. 2020. "Between Mandate and Motivation: Bureaucratic Behavior in Global Climate Governance." *Global Governance: A Review of Multilateralism and International Organizations* 26 (1): 99–120. https://doi.org/10.1163/19426720-02601006.

WFP (World Food Programme). 1995. *Annual Report of the Executive Director.* Rome: WFP.

———. 1996. *Mission Statement.* Rome: WFP.

———. 1997. *Policies on the Use of WFP Food Aid in Relief and Development Activities: Monetization.* Rome: WFP.

———. 2004. *Consolidated Framework on WFP Policies.* Rome: WFP.

———. 2005a. *Statement by the Deputy Executive Director of the WFP.* Rome: WFP.

———. 2005b. *Statement by the Executive Director of the WFP.* Rome: WFP.

———. 2005c. *Summary of the Work of the Annual Session of the Executive Board, 2005.* Rome: WFP.

———. 2005d. "WFP Seeks WTO Agreement on Humanitarian Food Aid." Press release, December 16.

———. 2005e. "Will WTO's Trade Negotiators Take the Food Out of Their Mouths?" *Financial Times,* December 12, 15.

———. 2013. *Food Aid Flows 2012.* Rome: WFP.

———. 2017. *World Food Programme and Agriculture Export Restrictions: Presentation by Gordana Jerger, Director, WFP Geneva Office.* Geneva: WFP.

———. 2020a. *Evaluation of the WFP People Strategy (2014–2017).* Rome: WFP.

———. 2020b. "Funding and Donors." WFP. Accessed July 29. https://www.wfp.org/funding-and-donors.

———. 2020c. "Overview." WFP. Accessed July 29. https://www.wfp.org/overview.

———. 2020d. *Strategic Evaluation of Funding WFP's Work: Evaluation Report.* Rome: WFP.

WikiLeaks. 2011. "WFP Asks Support of Secretary General Annan to Remove Jean Ziegler, UN Special Repporteur on the Right to Food (02ROME5540)." Wikileaks publication of cable dated November 14, 2002. https://www.scoop .co.nz/stories/WL0211/S00209/cablegate-wfpasks-support-of-secretary-gen eral-annan-to.htm.

Wilkinson, Michael D. 1996. "Lobbying for Fair Trade: Northern NGDOs, the European Community and the GATT Uruguay Round." *Third World Quarterly* 17 (2): 251–67.

Wilkinson, Rorden. 1999. "Labour and Trade-Related Regulation: Beyond the Trade-Labour Standards Debate?" *British Journal of Politics and International Relations* 1 (2): 165–91. https://doi.org/10.1111/1467-856x.00009.

———. 2012. "Of Butchery and Bicycles: The WTO and the 'Death' of the Doha Development Agenda." *Political Quarterly* 83 (2): 395–401.

———. 2015. "Changing Power Relations in the WTO—Why the India–U.S. Trade Agreement Should Make Us Worry More, Rather than Less, about Global Trade Governance." *Geoforum* 61:13–16. https://doi.org/10.1016/j .geoforum.2015.02.007.

Wilkinson, Rorden, Erin N. Hannah, and James Scott. 2014. "The WTO in Bali: What MC9 Means for the Doha Development Agenda and Why It Matters." *Third World Quarterly* 35 (6): 1032–50. https://doi.org/10.1080/01436597.20 14.907726.

———. 2016. "The WTO in Nairobi: The Demise of the Doha Development Agenda and the Future of the Multilateral Trading System." *Global Policy* 7 (2): 247–55. https://doi.org/10.1111/1758-5899.12339.

Wilson, Craig Alan. 1980. "Rehearsal for a United Nations: The Hot Springs Conference." *Diplomatic History* 4 (3): 263–82. https://doi.org/10.1111/j.14 67-7709.1980.tb00348.x.

Winders, Bill. 2004. "Sliding toward the Free Market: Shifting Political Coalitions and U.S. Agricultural Policy, 1945–1975." *Rural Sociology* 69 (4): 467–89. https://doi.org/10.1526/0036011042722750.

———. 2009. *The Politics of Food Supply: US Agricultural Policy in the World Economy.* New Haven, CT: Yale University Press.

Winters, Alan L. 1989. *How Developing Countries Might Influence the Talks on Agriculture in the GATT's Uruguay Round.* Washington, DC: World Bank.

Wise, Timothy A., and Sophia Murphy. 2012. *Resolving the Food Crisis: Assessing Global Policy Reforms since 2007.* Medford, MA: Institute for Agriculture and Trade Policy and Global Development and Environment Institute.

Wolfe, Robert. 1998. *Farm Wars: The Political Economy of Agriculture and the International Trade Regime.* Basingstoke: Macmillan.

———. 2004. "Crossing the River by Feeling the Stones: Where the WTO Is

Going after Seattle, Doha and Cancun." *Review of International Political Economy* 11 (3): 574–96. https://doi.org/10.1080/0969229042000252909.

———. 2009. "The Special Safeguard Fiasco in the WTO: The Perils of Inadequate Analysis and Negotiation." *World Trade Review* 8 (4): 517–44. https://doi.org/:10.1017/S1474745609990048.

Woll, Cornelia. 2008. *Firm Interests: How Governments Shape Business Lobbying on Global Trade.* Ithaca, NY: Cornell University Press.

Woods, Ngaire. 2006. *The Globalizers: The IMF, the World Bank, and Their Borrowers.* Ithaca, NY: Cornell University Press.

Woodward, R. 2009. *The Organisation for Economic Co-operation and Development (OECD).* Abingdon: Routledge.

Woolcock, Stephen. 2011. "The Scope for Asymmetry in the World Trade Organisation." In *Asymmetric Trade Negotiations*, edited by Sanoussi Bilal, Diana Tussie and Philippe De Lombaerde, 27–44. Farnham: Ashgate.

World Bank. 1986. *World Development Report.* Washington, DC: World Bank.

Wright, Brian, and Carlo Cafiero. 2011. "Grain Reserves and Food Security in the Middle East and North Africa." *Food Security* 3 (1): 61–76. https://doi.org/10.1007/s12571-010-0094-z.

WTO (World Trade Organization). 1995a. *Committee on Agriculture: Summary Report of the Meeting Held on 8 June.* Geneva: WTO.

———. 1995b. *Committee on Agriculture: Summary Report of the Meeting Held on 28–29 September.* Geneva: WTO.

———. 1996. *Committee on Agriculture: Summary Report of the Meeting Held on 28–29 March.* Geneva: WTO.

———. 1997a. *Annual Monitoring Exercise in Respect of the Follow-up to the Ministerial Decision on Measures Concerning the Possible Negative Effects of the Reform Programme on Least-Developed and Net Food-Importing Developing Countries.* Geneva: WTO.

———. 1997b. *Follow-up to Paragraph 18(i) of the Committee's Report for the Singapore Ministerial Conference on the Marrakesh Ministerial Decision.* Geneva: WTO.

———. 1998a. *Annual Monitoring Exercise in Respect of the Follow-up to the Ministerial Decision on Measures Concerning the Possible Negative Effects of the Reform Programme on Least-Developed and Net Food-Importing Developing Countries.* Geneva: WTO.

———. 1998b. *Committee on Agriculture: Summary Report of the Meeting Held on 17–18 November.* Geneva: WTO.

———. 1998c. *Statement Circulated by Mr. Jacques Diouf, FAO Director-General (as an Observer).* Geneva: WTO.

———. 1999a. *Committee on Agriculture: Summary Report of the Meeting Held on 29–30 September.* Geneva: WTO.

———. 1999b. *Statement by the Observer from the Food and Agriculture Organization Presented to the 25–26 March 1999 Meeting of the Committee on Agriculture (Part ii, Agenda Item a(ii))*. Geneva: WTO.

———. 2000a. *Committee on Agriculture: Summary Report on the Meeting of the Special Session Held on 28–29 September*. Geneva: WTO.

———. 2000b. *Committee on Agriculture: Summary Report on the Meeting of the Special Session Held on 29–30 June 2000*. Geneva: WTO.

———. 2000c. *European Communities Proposal: Export Competition*. Geneva: WTO.

———. 2000d. *General Council: Decision of 15 December 2000*. Geneva: WTO.

———. 2000e. *General Council: Minutes of Meeting Held in the Centre William Rappard on 7 and 8 February 2000*. Geneva: WTO.

———. 2001a. *Committee on Agriculture: Implementation-Related Issues: Report to the General Council by the Vice-Chairman*. Geneva: WTO.

———. 2001b. *Committee on Agriculture: Summary Report on the Meeting of the Special Session Held on 6 December*. Geneva: WTO.

———. 2001c. *Detailed Terms of Reference for the Inter-Agency Panel on Financing Normal Levels of Commercial Imports of Basic Foodstuffs within the Framework of the Marrakesh Ministerial Decision on Measures Concerning the Possible Negative Effects of the Reform Programme on Least-Developed and Net Food-Importing Developing Countries*. Geneva: WTO.

———. 2001d. *Doha Ministerial Declaration*. Geneva: WTO.

———. 2001e. *Examination of Possible Means of Improving the Effectiveness of the Implementation of the Decision on Measures Concerning the Possible Negative Effects of the Reform Programme on Least-Developed and Net Food-Importing Developing Countries. Report by the Vice-Chairman, Minister Yoichi Suzuki, to the General Council*. April 25. Geneva: WTO.

———. 2001f. *Examination of Possible Means of Improving the Effectiveness of the Implementation of the Decision on Measures Concerning the Possible Negative Effects of the Reform Programme on Least-Developed and Net Food-Importing Developing Countries: Report by the Vice-Chairman, Minister Yoichi Suzuki, to the General Council*. July 6. Geneva: WTO.

———. 2001g. *General Council: Minutes of Meeting of Special Session Held 15 December 2000*. Geneva: WTO.

———. 2001h. *Implementation-Related Issues and Concerns: Decision of 14 November 2001*. Geneva: WTO.

———. 2001i. *Proposal by Burkina Faso on the Negotiation on Agriculture*. Geneva: WTO.

———. 2001j. *Proposal to Implement the Marrakesh Ministerial Decision in Favour of LDCs and NFIDCs*. Geneva: WTO.

———. 2001k. *WTO African Group: Joint Proposal on the Negotiations on Agriculture*. Geneva: WTO.

————. 2002. *Report of the Inter-Agency Panel.* Geneva: WTO.

————. 2004a. *Decision Adopted by the General Council on 1 August 2004.* Geneva: WTO.

————. 2004b. *WTO Agriculture Negotiations: The Issues, and Where We Are Now.* Geneva: WTO.

————. 2005a. "Agriculture: 'Modalities' Would Boost Entire Round." WTO. https://www.wto.org/english/thewto_e/minist_e/min05_e/brief_e/brief03_e.htm.

————. 2005b. *Agriculture Negotiations: Status Report II Looking Forward to the Hong Kong Ministerial.* Geneva: WTO.

————. 2005c. *Agriculture Negotiations: Status Report Key Issues to Be Addressed by 31 July 2005.* Geneva: WTO.

————. 2005d. *Doha Work Programme: Ministerial Declaration Adopted on 18 December 2005.* Geneva: WTO.

————. 2005e. *Negotiations on Agriculture: Report by the Chairman, H. E. Crawford Falconer, to the TNC.* Geneva: WTO.

————. 2005f. *Proposed Modality for Special Products.* Geneva: WTO.

————. 2005g. *Revised Draft Ministerial Text (December 1, 2005).* Geneva: WTO.

————. 2005h. *Thirtieth and Thirty-First (Suspended) Special Session of the Committee on Agriculture.* Geneva: WTO.

————. 2007a. *Cairns Group Proposal on Food Aid.* Geneva: WTO.

————. 2007b. *Communications from the Chairman of the Committee on Agriculture, Special Session.* Geneva: WTO.

————. 2007c. *Relationship with Codex, IPPC and OIE.* Geneva: WTO.

————. 2008a. *Lamy Says Food Crisis Adds Urgency to Concluding the Round.* Geneva: WTO.

————. 2008b. *Report to the Trade Negotiations Committee by the Chairman of the Special Session of the Committee on Agriculture, Ambassador Crawford Falconer.* Geneva: WTO.

————. 2008c. *Revised Draft Modalities for Agriculture.* Fourth version. December 6. TN/AG/W/4/Rev.4. Geneva: WTO.

————. 2009a. "Information Session: Dr. Olivier De Schutter, UN Special Rapporteur on Human Rights 2 July 2009." Unpublished transcript in author's possession.

————. 2009b. "UN Rapporteur and WTO Delegates Debate the Right to Food." July 2. https://www.wto.org/English/news_e/news09_e/ag_02jul09_e.htm.

————. 2011a. "Agriculture Committee Continues to Discuss Export Restraints." Last modified March 21, 2011, accessed April 23, 2020. https://www.wto.org/english/news_e/news11_e/ag_com_31mar11_e.htm.

———. 2011b. *Eighth Ministerial Conference: Chairman's Concluding Statement.* Geneva: WTO.

———. 2011c. *Food Export Barriers and Humanitarian Food Aid by the WFP (World Food Programme): Communication from the European Union.* Geneva: WTO.

———. 2011d. "Lamy Rebuts UN Food Rapporteur's Claim That WTO Talks Hold Food Rights 'Hostage.'" December 14. https://www.wto.org/english/news_e/news11_e/agcom_14dec11_e.htm#comments.

———. 2011e. "Restricted Exports, Breached Limits and Cotton Aired in Farm Committee." Last modified June 23. https://www.wto.org/english/news_e/news11_e/agcom_23jun11_e.htm.

———. 2011f. "Stabilization Policies Could Destabilize Food Prices, Farm Committee Hears." Last modified November 17. https://www.wto.org/english/news_e/news11_e/agcom_17nov11_e.htm.

———. 2011g. *The WTO Response to the Impact of the Food Crisis on LDCs and NFIDCs: Communication from the NFIDCs, African and Arab Groups.* Geneva: WTO.

———. 2011h. *The WTO Response to the Impact of the Food Crisis on LDCs and NFIDCs: Communication from the NFIDCs, African and Arab Groups. Revision.* Geneva: WTO.

———. 2013a. *Export Competition: Ministerial Declaration of 7 December 2013.* Geneva: WTO.

———. 2013b. "Farm Produce Stockholding Worries Members Who Fear Impact on Trade and Incomes." September 26. https://www.wto.org/english/news_e/news13_e/agcom_26sep13_e.htm.

———. 2013c. *Public Stockholding for Food Security Purposes: Ministerial Decision of 7 December 2013.* Geneva: WTO.

———. 2015a. "DG Azevêdo's Address to the MC10 Closing Ceremony." December 19. https://www.wto.org/english/news_e/spra_e/spra108_e.htm.

———. 2015b. "Export Competition: Ministerial Decision of 19 December 2015." In *Ministerial Conference, Tenth Session, Nairobi, 15–19 December 2015,* 17–26. Geneva: Centre William Rappard. https://www.wto.org/english/thewto_e/minist_e/mc10_e/nairobipackage_e.pdf.

———. 2019a. *Committee on Agriculture: Summary Report of Meeting Committee on Agriculture Held on 26–27 November 2018.* Geneva: WTO.

———. 2019b. "Information Session on International Food Aid." June 26. https://www.wto.org/english/tratop_e/agric_e/inf_sess_foodaid_26jun19_e.htm.

———. 2021. "WTO in Brief." Accessed June 20. https://www.wto.org/english/thewto_e/whatis_e/inbrief_e/inbr_e.htm.

Wyles, John. 1993. "Compensation: The Consolation Prize." *CERES: FAO Review on Agriculture and Development* 141:28–31.

Xu, Yi-Chong, and Patrick Weller. 2008. "'To Be, but Not to Be Seen': Exploring the Impact of International Civil Servants." *Public Administration* 86 (1): 35–51. https://doi.org/10.1111/j.1467-9299.2007.00706.x.

———. 2018. *The Working World of International Organizations: Authority, Capacity, Legitimacy.* Oxford: Oxford University Press.

Yang, Hai. 2021. "Contesting Legitimacy of Global Governance Institutions: The Case of the World Health Organization during the Coronavirus Pandemic." *International Studies Review* 23 (4): 1813–34. https://doi.org/10.1093/isr/viab047.

Young, Helen. 2007. "Looking beyond Food Aid to Livelihoods, Protection and Partnerships: Strategies for WFP in the Darfur States." *Disasters* 31 (s1): S40–S56. https://doi.org/10.1111/j.1467-7717.2007.00348.x.

Young, Linda M., Philip C. Abbott, and Susan E. Leetmaa. 2001. *Export Competition: Issues and Options in the Agricultural Negotiations.* St. Paul, MN: International Agricultural Trade Research Consortium.

Zarakol, Ayşe. 2014. "What Made the Modern World Hang Together: Socialisation or Stigmatisation?" *International Theory* 6 (2): 311–32. https://doi.org/10.1017/S1752971914000141.

Zaum, Dominik, ed. 2013. *Legitimating International Organizations.* Oxford: Oxford University Press.

Zelli, Fariborz, Aarti Gupta, and Harro van Asselt. 2013. "Institutional Interactions at the Crossroads of Trade and Environment: The Dominance of Liberal Environmentalism?" *Global Governance: A Review of Multilateralism and International Organizations* 19 (1): 105–18.

Zelli, Fariborz, Ina Möller, and Harro van Asselt. 2017. "Institutional Complexity and Private Authority in Global Climate Governance: The Cases of Climate Engineering, REDD+ and Short-Lived Climate Pollutants." *Environmental Politics* 26 (4): 669–93. https://doi.org/10.1080/09644016.2017.1319020.

Zhang, Ruosi. 2004. "Food Security: Food Trade Regime and Food Aid Regime." *Journal of International Economic Law* 7 (3): 565–84. https://doi.org/10.1093/jiel/7.3.565.

Zhao, Jingjing. 2020. "The Role of International Organizations in Preventing Conflicts between the SPS Agreement and the Cartagena Protocol on Biosafety." *Review of European, Comparative and International Environmental Law* 29 (2): 271–81. https://doi.org/10.1111/reel.12326.

Ziegler, Jean. 2001a. *Preliminary Report of the Special Rapporteur of the Commission on Human Rights on the Right to Food, Jean Ziegler.* New York: United Nations.

———. 2001b. *Report by the Special Rapporteur on the Right to Food.* Geneva: Commission on Human Rights.

———. 2002. *Report by the Special Rapporteur on the Right to Food.* Geneva: Commission on Human Rights.

———. 2004. *Report Submitted by the Special Rapporteur on the Right to Food.* Geneva: Commission on Human Rights.

———. 2005. *Report of the Special Rapporteur on the Right to Food.* Geneva: Commission on Human Rights.

Ziegler, Jean, Christophe Golay, Claire Mahon, and Sally-Anne Way. 2011. *The Fight for the Right to Food: Lessons Learned.* Basingstoke: Palgrave Macmillan.

Zürn, Michael. 2018. *A Theory of Global Governance: Authority, Legitimacy, and Contestation.* Oxford: Oxford University Press.

Zürn, Michael, Martin Binder, and Matthias Ecker-Ehrhardt. 2012. "International Authority and Its Politicization." *International Theory* 4 (1): 69–106. https://doi.org/10.1017/S1752971912000012.

Index

Action Aid, 109, 204n61
African Group, 88
agenda setting: Doha Round and, 85–90, 93, 103–5, 137, 140, 156–57; FAO and, 71–76, 93; intervention by IOs, 13–14, 43–44, 45; mobilizing states and, 61, 62, 93; public shaming and, 116; UN actors' influence and, 176; Uruguay Round and, 71–76
Agreement on Agriculture (AoA): agricultural subsidies and, 102, 135–36, 167–68, 173, 196–97nn2–3; asymmetries in, 154, 155; creation of, 61; flexibility in, 136, 140, 144–45; food aid and, 100, 101–2, 117; food export bans and, 165; food prices and, 82–83, 167; food security and, 57–58, 194ch2n3; Marrakesh Decision and, 86; OHCHR and, 146; public food stockholding and, 167, 168,

172, 173; right to food and, 153; SRRTF and, 150; SSM and, 155; Uruguay Round and, 56–57, 79; WTO and, 1–2, 18
Agreement on Trade-Related Intellectual Property Rights (TRIPS), 125–26, 145
agricultural dumping, 4, 57, 109
agricultural research, 50
agricultural subsidies: AoA and, 102, 167–68, 173; barriers to trade and, 197n4; definition of, 196–97n3; developed versus developing countries and, 65–66, 154, 168; elimination of, 70, 78, 100, 102–3, 105, 111–12, 115, 119, 140, 196n2; EU and, 103–4, 105, 163; food aid and, 19, 99–100, 102–4, 109, 111–12; food security and, 135, 136, 157; NFIDCs and, 72; public food stockholding and, 165, 167–68, 171–75; surplus food stocks and,

257

Special Rapporteur on the Right to
Food (SRRTF): backlash against
and criticism of, 10–11, 157–64,
169–70, 185, 189; challenges to
powerful states by, 184; establishment of, 51, 149; impact of interventions by, 45, 171–75; impetus
for intervention by, 32–33, 58; lack
of formal authority of, 13, 151,
161–62, 176, 178, 181, 188; mandate of, 11, 15, 34, 35, 120n1, 148,
149, 160, 161, 188, 200–201n3;
NGOs and, 201n12; Our World Is
Not for Sale and, 170; public food
stockholding and, 15, 148, 167–69,
173–74, 181; public shaming of
WTO and, 114; reports of, 153–61,
165–67, 169, 201nn16–17, 201n36;
research methods and, 16–17; as
self-directed actor, 31–32, 148;
SSM and, 155–56, 159, 162–63;
support for WTO mandate and, 28,
182; taking sides and, 19–20, 147,
151–58, 167–68, 175, 181; types of
authority exercised by, 183–84. See
also De Schutter, Olivier; Ziegler,
Jean
Special Safeguard Mechanism (SSM),
155–57, 159, 162–63, 167, 175
Sri Lanka, 196n28
SRRTF (Special Rapporteur on
the Right to Food). See Special
Rapporteur on the Right to Food
(SRRTF)
SSM (Special Safeguard Mechanism).
See Special Safeguard Mechanism
(SSM)
St. Lucia, 196n28
starvation. See malnutrition and
starvation

Sub-Commission on the Promotion
and Protection of Human Rights,
138, 199n23
surplus food stocks: agricultural subsidies and, 83–84, 99–100; FAO
Principles on Surplus Disposal
and, 99, 100; food aid and, 83, 96,
98–100, 102, 104; food prices and,
83, 84, 96; public food stockholding and, 148; reasons for surpluses
and, 196n1
Sustainable Development Goals
(SDGs), 53
Switzerland, 59, 196n2
Syria, 124, 148

taking sides: goal of, 42; IOs' intervention strategies and, 182;
SRRTF and, 16, 19–20, 147, 151,
156, 167–68, 175, 181; UN actors'
political strategies and, 176
Tanzania, 163
tariffs: AoA flexibilities and, 136;
conversion of agricultural barriers
into, 56; cost of, 70; developed
versus developing countries and,
154–55; IMF-mandated cuts and,
72; processed versus unprocessed
commodities and, 155; SDT and,
143; Special Products and, 144;
Uruguay Round and, 81, 155
terms-of-trade thesis, 8
Thailand, 59, 89, 117, 179n5, 200n26
Third World Network, 144, 204n61
Third Worldism, 64
trade regimes: agricultural trade
liberalization and, 1–2, 55; at and
beyond the border, 4, 56; dominance by powerful states and,
2; food insecurity and, 1, 2–3,

CPSIA information can be obtained
at www.ICGtesting.com
Printed in the USA
JSHW070716051222
34275JS00002B/2